ITALY IN TRANSITION

ITALY
IN
TRANSITION

Conflict and Consensus

Edited by
Peter Lange
and
Sidney Tarrow

FRANK CASS

First published 1980 in Great Britain by
FRANK CASS AND COMPANY LIMITED
Gainsborough House, Gainsborough Road,
London, E11 1RS, England

and in the United States of America by
FRANK CASS AND COMPANY LIMITED
c/o Biblio Distribution Centre
81 Adams Drive, P.O. Box 327, Totowa, N.J. 07511

British Library Cataloguing in Publication Data

Italy in transition.
 1. Italy — Politics and government — 1945–
I. Lange, Peter II. Tarrow, Sidney George
320.9'45'092   JN5451

ISBN 0–7146–3147–7

This group of studies first appeared in a Special Issue
on 'Italy in Transition: Conflict and Consensus' of *West
European Politics,* Vol. 2, No. 3, published by Frank
Cass & Co. Ltd.

Printed in Great Britain by
The Bourne Press, Bournemouth

Contents

Preface   Peter Lange   1

Changes in Italian Electoral Behaviour: The Relationships
  Between Parties and Voters   **Arturo Parisi and**
                                            Gianfranco Pasquino   6

Muddling Through: Economics and Politics in
  Italy 1969–1979   **Michele Salvati**   31

Labour Unions, Industrial Action, and Politics   **Marino Regini**   49

Organised Business and Italian Politics: Confindustria and the
  Christian Democrats in the Postwar Period   **Alberto Marinelli**   67

Italian Christian Democracy: A Party for all Seasons?
                                            Gianfranco Pasquino   88

Crisis and Consent, Change and Compromise: Dilemmas of
  Italian Communism in the 1970s   **Peter Lange**   110

The Italian Socialist Party under Craxi: Surviving
  but not Reviving   **David Hine**   133

The Available State: Problems of Reform   **Giuseppe Di Palma**   149

Italy: Crisis, Crises or Transition?   **Sidney Tarrow**   166

Preface

Peter Lange

Italy has passed through a decade of great and constant change which has often perplexed journalists, policy makers and scholars alike. Her once 'miraculous' economy has foundered, and then, rather than sinking, partially righted itself. Her trade unions have assumed the most militant and innovative posture among those of the advanced industrial democracies, and then adopted a strikingly moderate, if still innovative, platform. Her industrialists have seemed bereft of the will which once made them entrepreneurial paragons in Europe, and then have recomposed themselves and once more sought to assert the validity of their role and prerogatives. Her State institutions have appeared inalterably compromised and corrupt, and yet have not only survived but have also been the seat of several potentially noteworthy participatory innovations.

Similar perplexities are apparent in politics, more narrowly understood. The Christian Democratic Party, seemingly in disarray and decay, has resisted and reasserted its political leadership. The Communist Party, apparently positioned for a breakthrough, has suffered a setback, and not so much due to its militancy and revolutionary image as to its moderation and perceived alacrity to compromise. The Socialist Party, about to be squeezed into powerlessness by polarisation around the two great parties, has retained its role of arbiter of national political coalitions. The even smaller laical parties of the centre have hung on as well. And electoral behaviour, once renowned for its stability, and then supposedly transformed, has retained many of its old continuities. Perhaps the greatest victim of the Italian crisis of the 1970s has been the power of prediction.

The apparent inscrutability of Italian developments has been reflected in academic and journalistic analysis in Italy's northern and western neighbours. The country's crisis has often been treated with a combination of confusion and desperation. Her internal problems seem too overwhelming, her politics and social structure too complex, her economy too chaotic to be fathomed by the assumedly more orderly and direct concepts and language used to describe the other advanced industrial democracies. The result has been, on the one hand, a tendency to treat Italy with a language all its own: witness the use of '*trasformismo*' to describe Italian practices often seen in other countries but there described as consociationalism or 'log rolling', or the application of the term 'clientelism' to practices which often look suspiciously like constituency or 'pork-barrel' politics. This is not to suggest that there are not peculiar features to these and other Italian political processes, but only that the application of terms drawn directly from the Italian context has tended to stress the uniqueness of the Italian case beyond reasonable conceptual rigour. Historicism has provided a convenient, if uncomfortable, refuge.

The other reflection of the confusion provoked by Italian developments has been the frequent search for metaphors and paradoxical catch-phrases which might capture through indirection what is otherwise beyond intelligent reach. Thus, in the last decade, we have seen the Italian economy referred to as a potential 'Bangladesh' of the West and the Italian political system as a 'Republic without Government'. Leaving aside the pejorative undertone of such descriptions, their strained nature expresses the incapacity to come to terms with the reality of the Italian experience and to make it comprehensible within a more useful comparative framework. They tend also, like the afore-mentioned historicism, to set Italy apart, to put it once again where it has traditionally been: outside the group of cases which inform much of comparative political theory building.

It is our firm conviction, lying behind the preparation of this volume, that if confusion and perplexity have been widespread, and historicism and indirection the understandable responses, the roots of these lie less in the realities of the postwar Italian political economy than in this isolation of Italy within the field of comparative politics. Isolation (the exceptions to which are sufficiently noteworthy to raise even greater doubts about its validity) has had three major effects. Firstly, it has tended to make knowledge of Italian developments primarily accessible and of interest to Italian specialists alone. The absence of Italy in most undergraduate and even graduate curricula in the social sciences, its relatively rare appearance in comparative textbooks, its only occasional inclusion in broad comparative research projects has meant that the start-up costs of dealing with Italy have been extremely high, thereby encouraging either further neglect or superficial analysis of the Italian case. Secondly, it has meant that Italy has been treated as an anomaly in the development of social science theory. The number of theories, models and 'confirmed' hypotheses to which Italy represents an 'exception' are legion. Finally, it has also tended to encourage Italianists to stick with 'their' country, to fail fundamentally to engage the more general body of work in comparative studies.

This self-breeding isolation is at the root of the perception of 'dilemmas' in the Italian experience of the 1970s. It arises less from the uniqueness of the developments than from the failure of those developments to meet expectations built on poor factual bases and theories which never factored in the Italian experience in the past. As Tarrow's essay and others in this volume clearly show, analyses of Italian economic, and social and political life not only often posed incorrect hypotheses, but even asked the wrong questions.

It would have been presumptuous to attempt through this volume to redress this situation. No single set of essays could accomplish the task and certainly not one which had, of necessity, to devote the bulk of its attention to the details of the Italian case. Nonetheless, we did set ourselves the goals of providing data and analyses which would make the Italian case more accessible, penetrable and tractable for comparativists, avoiding the treatment of Italy as a case unto itself, with its own unique problems and its own peculiar language. Italy *is* one of the advanced industrial democracies and, as the essays demonstrate many of the problems which have marked the Italian crisis have appeared in other of these democracies. There is then, much which is common or general in the Italian case. To the extent—and the essays, taken together, show that it is considerable—that there is also something particular, it would seem to lie in the *mix* of problems and crises and in some of the responses to them. Here too, however, as several of the authors indicate, the historical conditions which lie behind this mix and these responses are themselves a product of earlier patterns of dealing with problems and processes common to the same set of nations. Italy is peculiar like the others are peculiar, no more and no less. It is in presenting the Italian case alongside the others, therefore, that the most fascinating and fruitful analytical endeavours lie.

There are two more substantive themes which we, as editors, had in mind in preparing this volume and which appear repeatedly throughout the essays. The first is the web-like character of the Italian crisis: the tight entanglement of economic, social and political strands, analytically separable only with great care. The Italian crisis—or crises—of the 1970s cannot be analysed by confining one's attention solely to civil society or the State, or to the economy, social structure and social relations or the political system. The crisis is manifested in each of these and its roots are intertwined, overlapping disciplinary boundaries and confounding single-factor explanations.

The collection reflects this. It is not confined to traditional political science topics but includes as well examination of other actors and arenas which have played a critical role in the '70s. Thus, alongside essays on the electoral system, the institutions of State and the most important political parties, there are also ones on the economy, the trade unions and the employers' association. Furthermore, the individual essays are striking for the degree to which they too stretch beyond traditional disciplinary lines to seek explanations. Those on the economy and the producer groups make continual reference to the character of the State, the strategies of the parties and the balances and dynamics of power in the party system. Those on the more traditional political topics refer repeatedly to developments in society, in the economy and in the strategies of the interest associations. There are nodes and seams in this web. The authors make clear that one can identify critical junctures and partial discontinuities, that there are points when the explanatory weight falls heavily on particular variables. Nonetheless, the character of the crisis as one which invests and has its roots in all of the major arenas of society, stands out clearly.

The pervasive character of the crisis might suggest that an underlying theme of the collection is that Italy is indeed the 'sick man' of Europe, suffering from a possibly terminal systemic disease. Such an impression would be out of place. There is no question that the Italian system is suffering from varieties of maladies. The extent to which these are more severe and less susceptible to cure than in the other advanced industrial democracies will have to await systematic comparative analysis. Nonetheless, the essays trace several themes which make the outlook for Italy appear less bleak—or, to put it positively, more optimistic—than might appear and is often stated to be the case.

These themes are treated at length in Tarrow's conclusion. They are, however, worthwhile briefly stating here. Firstly, a number of authors point out that Italy's problems are often ones of growth rather than degeneration. This appears to be the case not only in terms of economic growth and the changes, advantages and problems it brings. It is also so in terms of the expansion of democratic and participatory institutions, the growing integration of the working class into economic and political decision-making, the secularisation of society and the democratic maturation of some of the major political forces. In all these senses, Italy has, in the 1970s, been coming to terms with many of the historically rooted limits of its democratic order, a process which could only be expected to be tension-laden and difficult.

Secondly, the essays suggest that the difficulties may at times be incapacitating but not terminal. It is striking, in fact, to what degree doomsday predictions have rapidly been proven incorrect. Despite the depth and pervasiveness of the crisis, the Italian economy is doing better, Italian society is more composed, Italian voters are more calculating and their preferences more judicious, and Italian political actors are more able to achieve the compromises and consent necessary to defend the institutions than was foreseen by many even a few years ago. This is not to say that the crisis has passed, that the underlying problems have been eliminated. It simply indicates that the capacity of the major social and political actors in the Italian system to deal with the most potentially dangerous and debilitating aspects of the crisis within a democratic framework has been sorely underestimated.

Thirdly, several of the articles make it evident that resolutions to the underlying features of the crisis may require more change rather than less. It is striking, in fact, to what extent continuities of behaviour by the major political and social actors pervade the period covered by the authors. Several of them show the extent to which significant changes in relationships of power and in social and political values have been adjusted to by only marginal changes in analysis and strategy. This lag sometimes appears to have hindered rather than facilitated addressing the underlying structural aspects of the crisis. Continuities have tended to allow the diffusion and management of the worst tensions and manifestations of crisis, but at the expense of changes which might permit something more than the crucial but insecure democratic and economic survival.

Finally, and this is the most optimistic and therefore hazarded theme in the essays, it appears that a more systematic and thoroughgoing resolution to the crisis may yet be possible without drastic cures, within the democratic framework and with the resources and social and political actors already on the scene. Balancing the worst features of crisis, there are also changes and innovations indicating new skills and capacities, unexpected sources of fundamental stability and emerging factors of dynamism. What this suggests is that Italy today is still in transition. The crisis of the last decade and the responses to it have seemingly made catastrophe more remote. Whether they have also created the possibility of a new democratic stability built around a strong economy, expanded democratic opportunities and revitalized and restructured political and social institutions remains to be seen. These essays make clear why such an outcome will be difficult to attain. They also demonstrate the extent to which it remains a real possibility.

In the preparation of this manuscript we wish to thank the authors for their efforts to adhere to our general guidelines. Their task has not been easy, especially in the face of the constantly changing Italian domestic situation.

The fact that they have been able to include even a rapid glance at the June, 1979 elections in the analyses is testament to their diligence and foresight. We also wish to thank Jane Szurek and Emily Chatfield for their excellent typing under considerable pressure, Paul Mattick for the translation of Michele Salvati's article and Paul Levenson for his general help. They made the job of completing the details of manuscript preparation both easier and more enjoyable.

Changes in Italian Electoral Behaviour: The Relationships between Parties and Voters

Arturo Parisi* and Gianfranco Pasquino †

Traditionally characterised by a consistently very high turnout rate and by a fundamental stability in the distribution of electoral preferences, in the last five years the Italian electoral scene has suddenly and manifestly experienced deep changes and might hold even more changes for the future. In order not to overemphasise the stability of the first period and the volatility of the contemporary period, however, it is necessary to look at the overall picture of Italian elections from the Constituent Assembly in 1946 to the national elections of 1979. This can be done satisfactorily with reference to the major political groupings as well as by identifying significant political and electoral thresholds. A note of caution is needed. While the party system has not changed in its fundamental components, some parties have gone through splits, mergers, and coalition arrangements which make the analysis slightly complicated, particularly for purposes of comparisons of the strength of the different groupings. This said, however, it is possible, without excessively oversimplifying the picture, to identify three major groupings: the right, the centre and the left. Table 1 presents their evolution through the thirty-three year period.[1]

TABLE 1

DISTRIBUTION OF VOTES BY POLITICAL AREAS IN PERCENT
(HOUSE OF DEPUTIES)

	1945	1948	1953	1958	1963	1968	1972	1976	1979
Right[1]	5·3	4·8	12·7	9·6	6·9	5·8	8·7	6·1	5·9
Centre[2]	46·3	62·4	49·7	52·3	53·2	52·3[a]	51·1	47·0	47·6
	(11·1)	(13·9)	(8·8)	(10·1)	(14·9)	(13·2)	(12·4)	(8·3)	(9·3)
Left[3]	42·0	31·0	35·4	37·6	39·3	41·0[a]	40·1	46·6	45·9

Percentages do not add up to 100 because very minor groups and local parties have not been counted.

1. Uomo Qualunque, MSI, Monarchist Parties, MSI-DN.
2. PLI, DC, PRI, PSDI, Südtiroler Volkspartei (the figures in parentheses refer to the total for minor parties only).
3. PCI, PSI, plus, in 1958: Comunita'; in 1968 and 1972: PSIUP; in 1972: Manifesto and Movimento Politico dei lavoratori; in 1976: Democrazia Proletaria and Partito Radicale; in 1979: Partito Radicale, Nuova Sinistra Unita and Partito di Unita Proletaria.
[a]PSDI among the centre parties: estimated 4·9 per cent; PSI among leftist parties: estimated 9·6 per cent.

*Associate Professor of Sociology, University of Bologna.
†Professor of Political Science, University of Bologna.

One can identify one fundamental threshold in 1948, when the DC defeated the Popular Front, and a trend of progressive growth of the left which breaks through its all-time high point of 1946 only in 1976. An additional interesting element is supplied by the Table with regard to the 1953 elections, when a law providing for a seat bonus to the party or the coalition polling 50·1 per cent of the votes (and being thus allotted 2/3 of the seats)—the so-called *legge truffa*, or swindle law—was defeated by the electorate thanks to some PLI and PSDI splinter groups (and minor parties polled, also because of defections to the right, their second lowest percentage. While that percentage was the product of conjunctural factors, though, their all-time low point of 1976 was only slightly improved in 1979).[2]

Table 1, though identifying the decline of the rightist and centrist areas, conceals another significant process that can be defined as polarisation, that is, the concentration of votes on the two major parties: the DC and the PCI. This process is shown in Table 2. In addition to the elements visible in the Table, it might be interesting to note that while in 1946 the DC constituted 76 per cent of the total strength of the centrist forces, its percentage was 74 in 1976, but the PCI, which constituted only 45 per cent of the combined left percentage in 1946, in the meantime climbed to an impressive 73 per cent. Thus, it would appear correct to underline that indeed a process of polarisation has taken place—again only slightly reversed in 1979.

TABLE 2

POLARISATION OF THE ITALIAN ELECTORATE:
CONCENTRATION OF VOTES AND SEATS ON THE DC AND PCI

	1948	1953	1958	1963	1968	1972	1976	1979
Votes per cent	79·5[1]	66·7	65·1	63·6	66·0	66·0	73·1	68·7
Seats per cent	85·0[2]	68·8	69·3	67·6	70·3	70·8	77·9	73·5

1. This is the combined percentage DC+Popular Front. A reasonable estimate of the distribution of the votes would give the PCI 18·6 per cent and the PSI 12·4 per cent. Then the combined DC+PCI percentage would be 67·1.
2. On the basis of the allocation of seats in the House of Deputies, that is PCI: 133 and PSI: 50, the combined DC+PCI percentage would be 76·2.

Since reference is often made to recent profound changes in electoral results, it is appropriate to recall that at least until 1953, the party system was not yet structured and consequently the electorate appeared to be floating and rather volatile, understandably so. To give a few examples, between 1946 and 1948, the right lost 0·5 per cent, the centre gained 16·1 per cent and the left lost 11·0 per cent, for an overall total of 27·6 per cent changes. And between 1948 and 1953, the right gained 7·9 per cent, the centre lost 12·7 per cent and the left gained 4·4 per cent, for an overall total of 25·0 per cent change. From then on, one can say that the party system became established and between the 1958 and the 1972 elections, electoral stability and partisan continuity characterised the Italian political system. This is the period which has prompted scholars and observers to stress the alleged immobility of the Italian electorate, and it is with reference to this period that many predictions were made to the effect that very little change could be expected from electoral consultations and trends.[3]

Not even the 1976 elections, to be sure, produced as massive a shift as those of 1948 and 1953: the overall combined amount of change was only 13·2 per cent (right −2·6; centre −4·1; left +6·5). Of course, what is of more importance than the sheer amount of changes is, in this particular case, the direction of changes—that is, the dramatic increase of votes for the PCI (which, alone, accounts for 7·2 per cent, more than making up for the losses of the Socialists) as well as the sharp decline of the PSDI and PLI (together they lost almost half their electorate: down from 9 per cent to 4·7 per cent).

Table 3 shows that, while electoral shifts took place in the period 1958–1972, the mean was only 5·22 per cent and no clearcut trend could be detected in the balance of power among the various groups. Once more, the only visible change was due to the slow, gradual, but not irresistible increase of the PCI (22·7; 25·3; 27; 27·2) and, to some extent, by the progressive fragmentation of the non-Communist Socialist area.

TABLE 3

CHANGES IN THE DISTRIBUTION OF POLITICAL PREFERENCES
ACCORDING TO THE MAJOR AREAS

	1946–48	1948–53	1953–58	1958–63	1963–68	1968–72	1972–76	1976–79
Right	−0·5	+7·9	−3·1	−2·7	−1·1	+1·9	- 2·6	−0·2
Centre	+16·1	−12·7	+1·5	+0·9	−0·9	−1·2	·1	+0·8
Left	−11·0	+4·4	+2·2	+1·7	+1·7	−0·9	·5	+0·2
TOTAL	27·6	25·0	6·8	5·3	3·7	4·0	13·2	2·0

Finally, two additional elements have to be mentioned with reference to the results of the 1976 elections and the evolution of the two major parties. Obviously, the Communist party increased its percentage in all regions but, what is more important, its 1976 vote became more evenly distributed in the different geographic zones of the country than at any time before. From what we know of the nature of the Communist vote, solidly rooted in political traditions and channeled through organisational networks, the changes documented in Table 4 are particularly impressive. They entailed many difficult problems for the party in the establishment of flexible ties with its new voters (this point is further elaborated below). The inability to solve these problems lies at the roots of the sharp electoral setback of 1979 (significantly sharper in the South).

TABLE 4

CHANGES IN THE GEOGRAPHICAL DISTRIBUTION
OF THE COMMUNIST VOTE (IN PER CENT)

	1979	1976	1975	1972	1972–79	1976–79	1972–76
North	30·5	33·5	32·4	26·4	+4·1	−3·0	+7·1
Centre	37·8	41·3	39·5	34·4	+3·4	−3·5	+6·9
South	25·5	31·4	26·6	20·8	+4·7	−5·9	+9·6
ITALY	30·4	34·4	32·0	27·2	+3·2	−4·0	+7·2

1972, 1976, and 1979 = parliamentary elections
1975 = regional elections

As to the Christian Democrats, in 1976 they held on to their 1972 percentage, but their recovery was made at a high cost for their allies which were almost devoured. In 1979 minor centrist parties regained some of what they lost in 1976 and the DC suffered a limited but significant loss in the light of its expectations of crossing the 40 per cent threshold. Moreover, in 1976 the quality of the DC vote changed in many important respects:

> . . . besides being interclassist, the Christian Democratic vote appears to be a decisively peripheric vote, originating from the poorest strata, the most isolated, and consequently the most uninformed of the country, from those who live far from the processes of industrialisation and urbanisation. The absorption of a proportion of social-democratic and liberal votes, which come from a typically urban and northern electorate, and of floating anti-communist votes, they too predominantly coming from the urban bourgeoisie, has not substantially altered the sociological configuration of the DC vote.[4]

These elements have not been altered by the 1979 results.

Two questions emerge from this presentation of the quantitative and qualitative changes of the 1972–1979 period. The first one has to do with what appears to be a sharp break with the apparent continuity of Italian voting behaviour during the 1958–1972 period. In particular, what factors account for the big leap forward of the PCI and then for its unprecedented setback? The second question refers to the recovery of the DC.

Any analysis of the 1972–1979 period must start from the appreciation of the fact that there were six major electoral consultations: three parliamentary elections (1972, 1976, and 1979); three national referenda on the controversial law allowing divorce (May 1974), on the public financing of political parties and on a law on public order (June 1978); and local (municipal, provincial, and regional) elections affecting almost the entire national territory (June 1975). The most visible and dramatic outcome of the 1974–75 period was the defeat of the DC. In the referendum, the MSI–DC coalition favouring the repeal of the law polled 40·9 per cent, that is 6·5 per cent less than the combined percentage polled by the two parties in 1972.[5] Some commentators interpreted this result as the intimation of the demise of the Catholic subculture. In 1975, the DC percentage dropped to 35·6 per cent, the lowest since 1946 (35·2 per cent) and the party was ominously approached by the PCI which experienced its greatest gain ever (+5·2) to reach 32·4.[6]

The results of the referendum could be explained partially with reference to the dissent of progressive Catholics. The results of the local elections could be explained again only partially with reference to the lowering of the voting age. The new law gave the vote to the 18–21 age group, a disproportionate number of whom cast their first vote for the left (this trend was not new, though it had been hidden by the fragmentation of the leftist non-Communist area).[7] An additional reason for the electoral losses of the DC was to be found, according to some observers, in the breakdown of the patronage system built by the party. This system had become excessively cumbersome, increasingly inefficient and no longer capable of providing services and distributing benefits.

The outflow of dissenting Catholics, the decline in the share of the youth votes, and the reduced effectiveness of patronage activities, all seemed to conjure up a sudden demise of the Christian Democratic Party as the dominant power in the Italian political system. Conversely, they seemed to suggest the ascent to power of a leftist coalition led by the PCI as the party polling the relative majority of votes.

The 1976 results sharply arrested the downturn quantitative trend for the DC—without, however, preventing several qualitative transformations. On the other hand, the favourable trend for the PCI especially, and for the left as a whole, was confirmed but not enhanced in 1976 and then slightly reversed in 1979. For these reasons the electoral evolution which took place in the 1972–1979 period is worthy of detailed attention because it has also signalled important qualitative changes in the content of Italian voting behaviour. It is time to turn to an exploration of two different explanations.

1. THE ROOTS OF ELECTORAL CONTINUITY

In analysing electoral behaviour, continuity as much as change needs to be accounted for and explained. It is true that many authors, focusing their attention on the 1958–1972 period, have overemphasised continuity and stability, while changes in the distribution of preferences and shifts certainly took place, even if they were not easily noticeable. It is also true that today we might run the risk of overstressing change and discontinuities. Still, the important and permanent phenomenon of partisan allegiance and electoral continuity with particular reference to the two major parties requires some explanation.

Generally, this explanation has been offered in terms of traditional political and organisational networks. In Italy, some scholars have specifically pointed at a fundamental continuity between partisan preferences in the early republican period and party roots in the pre-fascist era.[8] Other scholars have stressed that the major influence in shaping partisan behaviour is exerted by the family. 'The family clearly outranked the group of friends and co-workers as a perceived source of influence', and have stressed that 'the two social contexts that in terms of heterogeneity and frequency of interaction are potentially more significant as vehicles of change are also the least effective as sources of influence', and, finally, that the 'configuration of characteristics of the primary groups would suggest that they operate more frequently as reinforcers of partisan preferences than as agents of shifts in partisan orientations'.[9]

Political preferences acquired within the families are then reinforced by affiliation or interaction with partisan organisations in a conducive environment, that is in communities where that political tradition is widespread. There is enough supporting evidence for the assertion that 'affiliations with left-wing organisations combined with a strong Socialist tradition . . . produce a higher proportion of Communist and Socialist voters than when one of these two favourable conditions is missing.' On the other hand, in addition to family influence and community homogeneity, the major variable in producing and explaining a Christian Democratic vote is to be found in the rate of Church attendance (which is, to some extent, a mediating factor in promoting affiliation with Catholic and Christian Democratic collateral organisations).

In sum,

the partisan preferences emerging at the beginning of the postwar period took roots in the primary groups and were transmitted to the younger generations. Linkages of specific segments of the population with non-overlapping organisational structures facilitated the reinforcement and the passing on of these partisan attachments. Minority subcultures relied on politically homogeneous primary groups and organisational affiliations to survive even under the negative impact of hostile community traditions.[10]

Stability and continuity can thus be satisfactorily explained fundamentally with reference to the socialising capacity of the family and to the strength and pervasiveness of subcultural organisations. Shifts of votes and discontinuities may require either the identification of modifications of these two major factors or the emergence of changes in the composition of the electorate or an altogether different interpretation. An attempt will be made in the following pages to pursue both alternatives and formulate a slightly new theoretical framework.

As to the first point, the decline of the socialising capacity of Italian families seems a likely occurrence produced or perhaps accelerated because of and in the aftermath of the events of 1968. While there is no reason to believe that this trend should have negatively affected the sharing of similar values within single families, it has certainly had an impact on the possibility of transmitting political values. The fact that there has been a shift leftwards by the young does not necessarily indicate that leftist families have been able to maintain an influence over their offspring, but the process of socialisation through peer groups works in the same direction as that of leftist families (while other processes, such as the emergence of dissident Catholics, in the aftermath of the Vatican Council, have opened the way to new influences). Thus, the overall shift appears particularly pronounced and visible. Sani himself has collected and analysed substantial and convincing evidence of this shift and its implications for centre-right parties, particularly negatively affected by the two-pronged process, as well as for the Socialist Party.

On the whole, perhaps the most important element to be retained is that the percentage of the youth vote acquired by the left (starting probably as far back as 1968, accentuated in 1972, and even more so in 1975 and 1976) is such that it no longer guarantees the reproduction of the prevailing distribution of political preferences, but gives a seemingly growing advantage to the parties of the left, above all to the PCI. Also, there is some evidence that among young female voters the left is at last redressing its long-term imbalance and is, for the first time, acquiring as many female as male voters[11] (an equalising trend which is, in all likelihood, an important by-product of the 1968 movement as well as of the feminist movement).

Having identified one source of vote shifts in a decline of the effectiveness of socialisation by families, we have also highlighted one group of voters as most likely to have produced a change in actual electoral outcomes: the young. Pursuing this theme we will encounter a second related element: the changing composition of the electorate. Before tackling that, however, let us look at the second major variable used in the past to explain continuities in electoral behaviour: organisational affiliation.

Not surprisingly, major changes have taken place in this area too, affecting particularly the Catholic Church satellite organisations. Since the organisational strength and the political appeal of Catholic associations is highly dependent on religious attitudes and practices, it is easy to understand why an overall membership decline has taken place for these organisations, accompanying the process of secularisation. Moreover, in the aftermath of the Vatican Council there has also been a fragmentation of the Catholic world and an increase in the distance between groups locating themselves on the left and on the right. Therefore, political mediation of different demands and interpretations became virtually impossible. Finally, on the one hand, the ability of Catholic associations to channel their members' votes in support of the DC has declined along with their willingness to do so and, on the other hand, even the parish priests' commitment to the DC and their willingness to make political appeals have been rather lukewarm in the 1970s.[12]

To complete the picture, one should add that even once-powerful organisations such as the Small Farmers Association (*Coldiretti*) and the DC-affiliated trade union (CISL) are today of less importance (though by no means unimportant) in mobilising support for the Christian Democrats. The former because socio-economic transformations have produced a decline in membership (the ceiling was reached in the early '60s with 3 million members) and because the predicament of the agricultural sector had been widely imputed to the poor performance of the relationship between *Coldiretti* and the Ministry of Agriculture (the head of the Ministry being appointed only after having secured *Coldiretti's* approval): The latter taking independent positions because of sharp differences among its different branches and thus becoming unreliable instruments to turn out the Christian Democratic vote.

In contrast with this situation, satellite organisations of the left, the sharecroppers federation, a recently created Italian Confederation of Farmers (including Socialists and Communists) and the major trade union CGIL, especially strong among industrial workers, and the powerful League of Co-operatives, largely created and subsequently staffed by Communist militants, have not gone through a similar decline in membership or in terms of their political commitment. The intensity of the commitment may have somewhat mellowed, but its direction has not changed, and while a more flexible relationship between, for instance, the CGIL and the PCI, has been achieved and a more independent policy followed, the electoral connection is still at work and in a consistent and effective way. If a problem is likely to arise, it will be the product of the sharp competition recently launched by the Socialists within the trade union and the co-operative movement. For the time being, however, while this competition might affect the balance of power of the two parties, it does not imply a loss of organisational strength or of electoral support.

It has been noted that an important source of electoral shifts can be found in the changing composition of the electorate. Indeed, Giacomo Sani has convincingly shown that this was the case in the last elections (1975 and 1976). On the basis of census data and survey evidence, which has repeatedly and convincingly ascertained that older voters tended (tend) to be more conservative than younger ones (that is, supporters of the centre-right parties), and combining an evaluation of the outflow of old voters and the accelerated inflow of young voters into the electorate (due to the lowering of the voting age to 18 years old just prior to the 1975 regional elections), Sani has been able to give a maximum and a minimum estimate of the shifts due to the generational turnover. 'In all likelihood, the turnover of the electorate has brought to the PCI, the PSI, and other lists of the left one and a half million voters more than those obtained by the other group of parties.'[13] Building on generational turnover expectations, on the distribution of political preference and party identifications as revealed by mass surveys, it appeared that, even discounting defections, there might be, as Sani put it, an electoral leftist hegemony in the making.

Of course, there is no way of underestimating the importance in actual and potential terms of these findings and of the light they throw even on recent electoral changes. However, there is something mechanistic in these explanations which does not seem to capture some additional elements of novelty in Italian electoral behaviour and some problems emerging in the relationships between parties and voters. To these elements and problems we now address our attention.

2. QUALITATIVE CHANGES IN ELECTORAL BEHAVIOUR

The studies previously analysed have produced important and useful material and interpretations. They are especially good for understanding quantitative changes in the distribution of electoral preferences. Indeed, they have provided the indispensable source for a comprehensive account of Italian electoral evolution. We believe, however, that it is necessary today to go beyond this type of approach in order to look as well at qualitative transformations in the behaviour of the Italian electorate. We hope that an analysis of these transformations, although not yet fully grounded on a satisfactory amount of evidence, can lead toward a fruitful reorientation of electoral studies.

Briefly, it is our contention that there are additional aspects which need to be identified and isolated in order to allow us to understand what has changed in Italian voting behaviour as well as to make reasonable predictions on what might be changing. These aspects do not concern so much a growing inclination to electoral mobility (even though they do have an impact on it) and not simply the relationships which bind some social groups to some political parties. They refer more significantly to the content of the relationship,[14] than to the actors involved (individual voters, groups and parties).

In our view, the emerging issue on the research agenda (as well as a very relevant problem for party leaders and organisers) concerns not only who votes and for whom, but also who votes and for what. The *what* of the equation is then defined not so much in terms of the formal characteristics of the relationship which binds the 'elector' and the 'elected'. It is our starting assumption that in the recent past, perhaps the change of major relevance destined to have the most important impact on future electoral consultations is exactly the modification of the structure of Italian electoral behaviour considered in terms of its content. On the basis of this modification, we believe that more attention should be devoted both to the persistence and to the probable increase of a perceptible electoral mobility and, albeit to a more limited extent, to the direction of this mobility.

In order to give more analytical precision to our hypothesis and to submit it to empirical tests, it might be useful to identify and isolate within the multiplicity of electoral behaviours three ideal-types. It is likely that these types (and their subtypes) may also be found in existence in other countries, but here they will be defined with prevailing reference to the Italian situation, and no attempt will be made to provide generalisations. For each of the three types we shall give more details as to:

(a) the content and the purpose of the electoral option which we consider to be its distinctive feature,
(b) the social basis from which it is predominantly expressed,
(c) the channels of communication and the structure of the organisational network which bind the elector to the elected, and
(d) the consequences that derive from each type of vote with respect to the stability through time of the options available to the voter.

i. The Vote of Opinion

Our analysis starts by taking into consideration the vote of opinion because increasingly Italian media and political commentators have devoted so much attention to this type of vote, viewing it as the epitome of 'modern' electoral behaviour.[15]

As to its content, this type of vote is, above all, the expression of a choice which accepts as its range of variation and field of action the programmatic definitions proposed by the competing parties. The evaluation of these programmatic definitions is the end result of an analysis which takes into account both the contingent and structural parameters of the political arena and the subjective characteristics of the individual parties. The purpose of this evaluation is an assessment of each single alternative on the basis of interest satisfaction. For this type of vote, the distinctive element is not the nature of the interest pursued, which remains in the last instance individual, but the fact that satisfaction of this interest is not tied to electoral behaviour based on a direct personal relationship between the elector and the elected. It derives rather from the type of political action which the vote will presumably make possible. The connection between the expression of the vote and the achievement of the interest is the product of the fact that the individually pursued benefit is always conceptualised as a part of a collective good, whether it refers to a precise group or social class, or whether it is generically attached to the whole system.

Passing to the identification of the social base within which this type of vote seems to be prevailing, it is clear that it presupposes as a rule a high degree of integration into the political system, a substantial adherence to, and trust in, the method and the procedures which regulate the choice, a good control (or presumption of control) over the terms which define the range within which the choice can take place. These characteristics can be detected, first of all, amongst those groups which belong to the 'central' area of the socio-political system, and especially, amongst the middle classes, and partially, also amongst some sectors of the industrial proletariat.

For this type of vote, the *organisational and communication structures* which relate the elector to the elected are necessarily complex, diffuse, and articulated. In a society such as Italy, the most important of these structures is the mass media—the daily and weekly press and the State Radio–TV broadcasting agency. These are the channels through which the voter (this specific type of voter) obtains access to political information. He is supplied with most of the elements which define his scope of choice and the boundaries within which he will proceed to the evaluation leading to his vote. Of course, this does not exclude the possibility that, in practice, vote orientations will be very diversified, since they are less dependent on the way they are shaped and come into being than on the collective frames of reference (groups, class, . . .) which are deemed to mediate one's own individual interests. Nevertheless, the way vote orientations are shaped might have an influence on the width of the scope of choice.

While it is true that the range of choice is essentially defined by these affiliations and collective references, it is also true that its definition is widely exposed to the influences of the communication channels. And this exposure is more important as, on the one hand, the voter has not made up his mind about the collective references which ought to mediate his own individual interest and, on the other hand, as the correspondence between the interests of the reference group and available electoral choices is more uncertain. Both consequences are due to the existence of several options as well as to the relative inadequacy of the different options. This situation is likely to arise especially for some middle strata. Now well-established in the central areas of the social system (urbanised and enjoying job security), they might find their political evaluations disturbed by organisational or cultural reference frameworks surviving from periods in which their position in the social system was different in terms of class and of centrality.

The relevant consequences of this way of shaping the electoral evaluation are: a high degree of uncertainty, wide susceptibility to political circumstances (that is, to their changing definitions), instability and variability through time, specificity, that is its dependence on the type of electoral consultation (national, regional, municipal, referendum, . . .).

ii. The Vote of Appartenenza[16]

If the vote of opinion is the one most often singled out in order to explain change, the vote of *appartenenza*, our second type, is as a rule given privileged attention when phenomena of continuity are analysed or, better, emphasised. The content of this type of vote differs from the previous one because it is the testimony of being socially embedded more than the expression of choice. Those who cast this type of vote consider their act as the affirmation of subjective identification with a political force which is seen as having an organic liaison with the social group to which the voters belong, rather than a simple institutional representation. Thus, *appartenenza* is the sum of social embeddedness and party identification. The expression of *appartenenza* is manifested by the exclusion of any assessment of the programmatic positions of the parties. This stand does not preclude the possibility of a judgment concerning the correspondence between individual interests and collective interests. But, this judgment does not derive from a previous stage which would somehow shape the vote in a precisely determined way. Rather, it is part of a global and more complex assessment in which the vote is but one type of behaviour—among many—that stresses again the sense, the feeling of *appartenenza* (belonging). In this case, the vote is endowed with limited autonomy, specificity, and salience, in the sense that while voting in conformity with one's *appartenenza* is not a particularly distinctive act, voting in a way incongruent with it would be a very serious break.

The social base which expresses this type of vote is represented consequently by those subcultural areas produced by the encounter between subordinate or marginal social groups and organised collective movements which have accepted, in a strategy of adaptation to the system or in a logic of retrenchment, some form of participation in the institutional context. With reference to the socio-political system as a whole, the vote of *appartenenza* posits itself as the expression of conflictual integration, sharply differentiated from the vote of opinion which is the expression of high integration in the system and of full acceptance of its institutional structure. The best examples of conflictually integrated groups can be found within the agricultural and industrial proletariat in the Socialist-Communist area of *appartenenza* and among the small, independent farmers in the area of Catholic *appartenenza*.

With these considerations in mind, it is easy to understand that the *organisational structure and the communication channels* behind this type of vote are not specifically related to any electoral event nor can one isolate and single out within it special structures and channels. Rather, the subcultural fabric has to be identified with the entire system which provides the framework for the relationships and the communications of the subcultural area of *appartenenza,* which set into motion as a whole (even though leaving some room for sectoral peculiarities) in the event of electoral contests. Thus it includes occupational associations, recreational groups, trade union branches, and, of course, religious organisations. The contents with respect to which this mobilisation is launched are also unspecified. It should be stressed that such mobilisation is not intended to supply this type of electorate with information necessary to allow the expression of the vote on the basis of a choice but rather to reconfirm the symbols of *appartenenza*, diversity, and conflictuality: the existence of goals well beyond the reach of the ballot.

In contrast with the vote of opinion, therefore, the vote of *appartenenza* is characterised by a strong partisan commitment of the voter, limited exposure to political conjunctural events, continuity through time and lack of specificity, that is, little discrimination among types of electoral consultation.

iii. *The Vote of Exchange*[17]

Always given some attention by the students of electoral behaviour in Italy, the vote of exchange has often been considered little more than a residual type useful in explaining continuities or changes unaccounted for by the vote of opinion and the vote of *appartenenza*. This type of vote requires, in our opinion, specific attention and a separate category because it possesses peculiar elements.

The content of the vote of exchange is neither the simple expression of a programmatic choice nor the reaffirmation of social embeddedness. Rather, it is the attempt to secure a contribution in an exchange relationship which is premised upon a specific electoral behaviour. Again, the relationship takes place between an elector and elected. It is very important to note, however, that in this case the elected is always an individual or an easily recognisable group because only such an actor can respond directly to this kind of expectation and request and offer basically individualistic incentives and sanctions.

The vote is exchanged, as a trade-off, for the satisfaction of a need or the achievement or reinforcement of an interest of the voter. In contrast with the vote of opinion, the relationship established between the electoral act and the achievement of the interest is immediate and personalised. The distinguishing characteristic of this type of vote is precisely the existence of this relationship of 'immediacy'. No matter whether the exchange takes place before or after the vote, the candidate is expected to provide rewards to the voter himself, to his close relatives, or to the primary group.

It follows that the social base which is more likely to resort to this type of vote is to be found above all in those social areas substantially outside or on the periphery of the dominant political system. In fact, this type of vote expresses at the same time the refusal and the impossibility to take a pro- grammatic stand, in a personal and specific way (as does the vote of opinion) or in an aggregate and global way (as in the vote of *appartenenza*), with respect to the merit of the choice at stake. It is the translation into terms of one's own social relations system and within one's daily life of an event such as an election which is totally alien as a problem of 'choice' among alter- natives. When, for reasons related to organisational problems, this type of vote is unable to find expression in an exchange relationship, it transforms itself into a 'vote against'. It thus becomes a vote of protest—either cast in favour of a party or as a blank or void ballot—or even taking the form of abstention (however limited it may be in Italy, with some interesting trends emerging for the referenda).

It is not difficult to identify the urban and rural lumpenproletariat as the breeding ground for the vote of exchange. However, one should not under- estimate, particularly but not only in the South, the diffusion of this type of vote among other social strata as well: above all among small farmers and the rural petty bourgeoisie, as well as among considerable proportions of recently urbanised petty bourgeoisie which, culturally and structurally, maintain some ties with its social and geographic background.

With reference to this aspect, it might be appropriate to note that the family plays quite a different role among lumpenproletariat sectors from that among petty bourgeois groups. In the first case, the mediating structure between the two actors in the exchange relationship is immediately clientelistic; in the second, the *parentela* structure commands a considerable influence. Therefore, even if both subtypes are part of the vote of exchange, these specific variations which imply some concrete practical differentiations, should be taken into account. More specifically, the *parentela* variant shows some overlapping with the vote of *appartenenza*, since it gives birth to alliances and exchange processes which are not merely confined to electoral periods.

Passing to a consideration of the *channels of communication* and the *organisational structures*, it must be stressed that these are highly specific to each election, provisional and largely unstructured—apart from the *parentela* variant. In fact, we are dealing with structures that, even when they can take advantage of some pre-existing networks, are created *ad hoc*, with reference to a specific electoral consultation. They are rapidly disbanded thereafter.

Obviously, these arrangements have an impact on the lack of coherence and stability of electoral orientations through time. The vote of exchange is directly and closely tied with the conspicuousness and the reliability of the corresponding performance. It is highly discontinuous. It shows a high degree of specificity. That is to say, it varies according to the nature of the election, because in different electoral consultations the number and the characteristics of the actors and the quantity of resources supplied by them are bound to vary. That said, however, the factor which perhaps conditions in a decisive way the stability/volatility of this type of vote is the state of the economy. The performance of the economic system quite obviously determines both the quantity of pressing individual needs which require satisfaction, and the availability to different political actors of resources adequate to satisfy the needs of the 'exchange' voters immediately and individually.

VOTE RELATIONSHIPS AND ELECTORAL CONSENSUS

It is our contention that the three types of vote identified and analysed above according to their major distinctive characteristics can be effectively used to understand the changes which have taken place in Italian electoral behaviour in the last decade and hopefully also to forecast some of the important problems to be faced by the major parties in their relationship with the voters. Before coming to this, however, we would like to stress that without definitely ruling out the existence of mixed types, we do believe that in most cases one dimension is sufficient satisfactorily to define and explain the specific relationship established between the electors and the elected. One concrete example may suffice. There is a marked difference between the behaviour of a voter who votes for a party only in order to support a specific candidate in an exchange relationship from the behaviour of one who votes for a party in order to express or to reconfirm the relationship of *appartenenza* which ties him to the group represented by the party. This is true even if, in so doing, but subordinately to this reconfirmation which can be taken for granted, the latter expresses through the vote of preference also an exchange relationship with a specific candidate or an opinion concerning the policies formulated by that candidate or by the faction the candidate represents within the party.

One additional point needs to be stressed: the sharp conceptual distinctiveness and practical autonomy of the three types of vote with reference both, on the one hand, to the class structure, and, on the other, to the party structure. In other words, 'for what' one votes is a conceptually distinct and relatively independent question both from 'who votes' and from 'for whom' one votes. With reference to who votes, we have pointed out above the existence of some association between the various types of relationships and some social groups. We must now stress that, though this association is not random and derives in fact from the very definition of the different types, it is not to be taken for granted or applied in a mechanistic way. Indeed, most of the variations and the variants of electoral behaviour and, in any case, of the difficulty of resorting to social class as the only or the decisive predictive variable of electoral behaviour stem exactly from the lack of overlap. In each class and social group different types of vote co-exist, whether they are channeled to the same party or addressed to different parties. This is due to the always present lack of fit between structure and superstructure which leads some patterns of political (and electoral) behaviour to anticipate or to survive some structural modifications of social groups as well as of the social status of individuals.

There are many anomalous (from a social class perspective) types of electoral behaviour. Among the most striking ones, one can find the persistence of the vote of *appartenenza* among some sectors of the Catholic subculture. Groups that, even though they have substantially modified their social status, keep intact their ties of identification and embeddedness, culturally and organisationally, with the Catholic world, and base the patterns and the direction of their electoral behaviour upon them.

When it comes to the analysis of the relationship between electoral behaviour and political parties, our previous note of caution is then meant to stress that the three types of vote are simultaneously present in all parties. Of course, this is not to deny that one type may be predominant in some parties and another almost irrelevant. However, there is no doubt that all three types are present within the mass parties or, more precisely, that it is very unlikely that a party will be able to acquire the features of a mass party without succeeding in drawing electoral support from all three types of vote. No doubt this is quite clear in the case of the DC, for which party the Catholic vote of *appartenenza* has obviously never been sufficient to explain its mass following. But the need to appeal to all three types of vote cannot certainly be ruled out for the PSI and for the PCI which have always relied (albeit obviously to a different extent and with different modes) in addition to the vote of *appartenenza* and that of opinion (in its two components: support for policies and protest against the government) also on the vote of exchange. At least this has occurred where and to the extent that control of resources by the two parties of the left made it possible.

It is very important to keep this point in mind in order fully to understand the organisational strategies implemented for the acquisition of electoral consent. From this consideration, in fact, it follows that whatever the political line which aims at acquiring a majority of the votes, it can do so only by tackling the problem of the simultaneous resort to multipronged strategies, while defining its scope of action in such a way as to encompass many classes. It is clear that, to the extent that the vote of *appartenenza* plays a relevant role for the continuity of the whole system, it ends up by having a decisive weight. This is the case, if for no other reason than because of its characteristics of stability through time and of organic relationship it has established between voters and the parties well beyond the time and space limits of single electoral contests. It is also clear that in order to acquire new voters and to expand the constituencies from which its own electorate is drawn, a party cannot rely solely nor even primarily on recruitment within the subcultural area of *appartenenza*.

INTERPRETATIONS

On the basis of these definitions it is now possible to formulate some hypotheses to be tested with more precision. We are now in a better position to clarify what we mean when we maintain that in the years of the 'electoral earthquake', what has changed is not only the direction of the vote ('for whom': polarisation and leftward shift of the electorate) and not even only the vote orientation of the different social groups ('who'), but also and more specifically and significantly, the very structure of the relationships between electors and elected which finds its expression through the vote.

Analytically, our hypothesis can be better articulated by stating that this change in the structure of the vote presents the following components:

(a) a reduction in the weight of the vote of *appartenenza* both with respect to its relevance for the electorate as a whole and for each political area,

(b) a consequent related expansion of the area of the vote of opinion,

(c) a modification of the vote of exchange which, though remaining substantially stable in its overall dimension, has undergone a change in orientation by expanding the area of parties involved.

The shrinking of the vote of *appartenenza* can be singled out as the engine which has set in motion the electoral changes in question. It has certainly found its epicentre in the crisis of the Catholic subculture. As is well known, this subculture constitutes the central core of that socio-cultural and organisational system whose dominant political expression the DC was and still is. This is not the place to dwell in detail on the nature, origin, and consequences of this crisis.[18] Suffice it to say that its roots and premises can be traced farther back than the referendum on divorce and even the post-Vatican Council reforms. Rather, the Council has accelerated and made more visible a process whose stages were, first, the breakdown of the fabric of social relations centred on the agricultural world, then, the crisis of the organisational structure which had partially delayed (and partially 'radicalised') the consequences on the cultural level of the objective crisis of the foundations and the most important reference points of the 'Catholic world'.

The crisis of the Catholic subculture (in the rank-order: structural, cultural, and organisational) was finally dramatised by the quasi-hegemony acquired by leftist ideas and ideals in the post-1968 period. Nevertheless, if a cultural explanation is satisfactory for the post-1968 youth generation (mass education and growing exposure to the mass media), the weakening of other sectors of the Catholic subculture was accelerated by the emergence of a class appeal. This is particularly true for some advanced working class strata and for that proportion of the female vote that the strength of the Church organisational appeal had been able to draw away from the prevailing political orientations of the social groups to which they belonged (conflicting *appartenenza*).

While it is difficult to hold doubts about the crisis and the reduction of the size of the vote of *appartenenza* in the Catholic area and as a consequence of the Christian Democratic electorate, one should not underestimate the elements of crisis in other groups of *appartenenza* as well. The same processes of transformation, which have broken and made volatile those relationships constituting the socio-cultural fabric of the fundamental background of the Catholic vote of *appartenenza*, have in our opinion, created a crisis and problems for leftist subcultural alignments as well. They have weakened the intensity and the exclusiveness of the relationships internal to the subcultures, especially mellowing the positions of conflict and estrangement which counterposed them to the socio-political system in its entirety.

This said, in order to avoid the risk of a misunderstanding, it is necessary to remind the reader that, in our reasoning, the type of vote is quite a different thing from the political orientation of the vote. This means that a modification of the relationship which ties the elector to the elected is not automatically followed by a modification of the vote orientation: the two phenomena are relatively independent of one another. For instance, a voter might modify the type of relationship that ties his vote to the DC and keep on voting for the DC and, vice-versa, he might shift to another party without modifying his type of relationship. Incidentally, this is the major reason why the profound crisis of the Catholic *appartenenza* has not been accompanied by as great a crisis of the Christian Democratic vote.

Similarly, a legitimate question would be to ask whether the growth of the vote for the left and in particular for the PCI has been accompanied by a corresponding growth of the vote of *appartenenza*. Our answer is essentially negative. We believe that, on the one hand, the old area of the vote of *appartenenza* of the left has modified its ties of *appartenenza*, making them more flexible (or even loose), and, on the other, that the new left-oriented vote has not inserted itself into the texture of relationships which constitutes the milieu of *appartenenza* That is to say that the Catholic worker who began voting for the PCI in 1975 or 1976 has not substantially, because of that action, become a member of that sharply delimited system which, in the fifties constituted the Communist world. If his vote for the PCI has indeed meant his joining the complex web of relationships of the Communist subculture, this could happen exactly because that system had in the meantime gone through a remarkable process of secularisation. No doubt, the Catholic worker himself had contributed to the reduction of the rigidity of the constitutive type of internal relationship of the Communist world.

The case of the youth vote is perhaps different, since it is at least partially the expression of a reality which borders on that of a subculture. As a matter of fact, one must not forget that one of the most important characteristics of the youth vote is not so much the fact that it is expressed by some age groups having undergone a leftward socialisation experience, but especially the fact that it is expressed in a stage of belonging to a fabric of relationships which posit themselves as distinct, being conflictual vis-à-vis the dominant ones. Of course, it is a peculiar subculture, especially for its transient quality and also because it is not tied to one single party or to a political area, although it is predominantly left-oriented. Both features deprive the youth vote of most of its stability—a major component of the vote of *appartenenza*—making it instead floating in its orientation and changeable through time.

Summing up the argument so far, it can be hypothesised that a shrinking of the vote of *appartenenza* for the Catholic area has been accompanied by the stability, at best, of the same type of vote for the leftist area. Since this area has experienced an electoral expansion, the overall vote of *appartenenza* for the left is today of less relative importance than in the past, as is the case for the electorate at large.

As to the other types of vote, there is no need to put the emphasis on the expansion of the vote of opinion. As a result of the weakening and sometimes dissolution of subcultural relationships and the growing integration of the socio-political system, the growth of the vote of opinion has modified the relationships between voters and parties, though not necessarily the direction of the vote. This type of vote implies for all parties and especially for the DC a modification in the quality of electoral consent more than in its quantity.

The factors to be analysed concerning the vote of exchange are more numerous and complex. First of all, there is the question whether its dimension has changed or not. We would surmise that the increasing cultural integration which has produced the crisis of the vote of *appartenenza* has, at the same time, reduced the space for the vote of exchange or, at least, has contained its possible expansion in a time of socio-economic difficulties. Rather than the size, the inner structure of the vote of exchange has certainly undergone major transformations. On the one hand, the baricentre of the social area of the vote of exchange has increasingly shifted from the rural to the urban lumpen-proletariat, especially in the South and in the Centre, even affecting some Northern pockets. On the other, the relative weight of the clientelistic vote has certainly become heavier than the *parentela* vote. Moreover, the weakening of the kinship ties and rural socio-cultural relationships previously at the roots of the resort to this type of vote by the petty bourgeoisie of rural origins is probably producing a shrinking of the *parentela* variant.

The most important modification, however, is represented by the diffusion among many parties of this type of vote. More specifically, the fact that the left and especially the PCI have gained control of many local administrations (particularly in the South) and of the public agencies dependent on them has created the prerequisites for a consistent shift of the vote of exchange toward the left. This is due to the very simple fact that the political orientation of this type of vote is closely related to the control, on the part of the elected, over the resources which might represent the necessary condition for the compensation to be offered in exchange for the vote. Furthermore, we must make clear that sole control over the resources is not enough to determine the electoral orientation of this vote in favour of who exercises such control. What is certain is that the demand for performance and the supply of votes cannot be addressed except to those who have the power to implement the requested activities. This does not mean that the bargain will be struck. In order to do that, it is indispensable that the political counterpart be favourably inclined or be willing to do it in terms of a sheer exchange relationship. It may also occur that even if and when available, the political counterpart does not possess adequate structures to strike the bargain or to guarantee its concrete fulfilment. As to the intentions, the elected might reject the exchange not so much for moralistic reasons, but attempt to exploit the opportunities and insert that vote into a structure of relationships which might transform the exchange relationship into another type of relationship, less instrumental and conjunctural. Needless to say, this process requires much determination and time, as well as adequate resources.

As to the capacity to strike the bargain and to guarantee its fulfilment, the prerequisite is the control over, or the creation and adaptation of, channels of communication and organisational networks capable of managing such a relationship. These problems bring out immediately the volatility of this element in the modification of the vote structure. Its concrete occurrences, in fact, presuppose on the one side political trends largely originating in the areas of previous voting patterns and, on the other side, the existence within the left or, more precisely, among the various party components, of electoral strategies which seem to offer a satisfactory outlet to exchange voters. Otherwise, as we have stressed in our analytical definition, this type of vote will find the need to address itself elsewhere or to transform itself into other related types of electoral behaviour—abstention or protest vote. In this latter case, which cannot be automatically ruled out, to the extent that the target of the exchange proposal is unable (or unwilling) to guide or lead the protest, then the very protest will turn against him manifesting the merely potential character of what we have defined as 'access' to this type of vote.

PERSPECTIVES

What are the consequences of these modifications for future Italian electoral behaviour? What kind of hypotheses can be formulated? Tackling first the question of the more or less mobile 'immobility' of the Italian electorate, if our reasoning is not completely unfounded, then it means that one should expect a considerable degree of electoral mobility rather than a return to conditions of stability (even though different in nature from those conditions of stability whose very existence in the past we questioned).

Whether this mobility brings about significant changes in electoral behaviour depends on whether those 'movements' cancel one another out or are of such size and political orientation that one tendency sharply prevails upon the others, producing net balances decisively in favour of one or more parties. It depends, too, on whether they will be widely distributed along the party spectrum or be concentrated, polarised on some parties only. There are several reasons to expect the non-cumulation of these likely changes.

First of all, there is the persistence of the crisis of *appartenenza* along the lines we have discussed above. This does not necessarily mean a crisis of the supportive organisations. It involves the fact that within them the meaning and the intensity of the commitment have qualitatively transformed themselves and have become more and more instrumental, specialised, and secular. This is true in the case of the organisations of the Catholic world, where the return to some traditionalist positions does not significantly counter-balance the fundamental trend at the mass level, at least not in the short run. And it is also true for the parties of the left. Trade union membership itself which has made such a great contribution to electoral expansion, channeling the overall political orientations toward the leftist alignment, has at the same time blurred individual party affiliations and has considerably weakened them. Similar considerations can be formulated with reference to the young voters. The sharpening of the socio-economic crisis, which seems sometimes to reinforce their already existing political orientations, also sets them apart and thus prevents the development of stable party identifications.

Fundamentally the product of the shrinking of the areas of the votes of *appartenenza* and of exchange, the expansion of the area of the vote of opinion goes hand in hand with an increase within it of the mobility of orientations. This mobility finds its origin in a plurality of factors. Among them, the leading one is certainly represented by the instability of the political situation: the precise variable to which this type of vote is highly exposed. It is also true that one can object that, if the conjunctural insecurity should reach the level of a major political crisis, then the vote of opinion might yield to the appeals of previous identifications and social embeddedness, the *appartenenza*, which might be quickly intensified again. Indeed, this process cannot be ruled out for some sectors of the electorate, though it must be immediately added that for most opinion voters this is no longer feasible because the old ties of *appartenenza* have definitely become both too weak organisationally and unviable in their structural and cultural assumptions. One might then want to think in terms of the emergence of new *appartenenza*, that might be coterminous with the old and obsolete ones, rather than to the simple revival of the old ones.

A certain role in the expansion of the 'opinion' area and in the consolidation of its specific features—in particular of its variability and specificity—can be found in the multiplication of the opportunities for electoral participation. From school boards to neighbourhood councils up to the very elections of the European Parliament, Italian voters have had many chances to cast a differentiated ballot. On the one hand, it is true that the multiplication of opportunities provides all the parties, and especially the mass parties, with a fundamental instrument through which to re-establish and deepen their contact with civil society (which might otherwise have found in the trade unions and other channels the fundamental structures of participation). And this contact had been severely impaired (particularly, but not exclusively, in the case of the Christian Democrats), following the crisis of *appartenenza* and, more generally, of territorially-based organisational structures (both revived in the case of the DC by the elections to the school boards, for instance). On the other hand, it is also true that the elections represent an additional opportunity for the vote of opinion to express the variability of its orientation with reference to the specificity of the choice and the event-related meaning it assumes. But at the same time this reinforces the proclivities which mark its specificity and pushes into the background the remaining residues of a relationship of party identification.

In order to bring to a close the assessment of this likely strengthening of electoral mobility in Italy, a look must be given to the vote of exchange. In this case, the decisive element seems to us to be the heightening of the economic crisis. The target or partisan initiator of the exchange proposal can be essentially identified with reference to his capacity to control resources. On the other hand, one should not forget that what identifies this type of voter is, above all, the existence of unsatisfied primary needs, beginning with that of employment. Apart from any strengthening of political preferences, the persistence and the deepening of the unemployment crisis will undoubtedly increase the availability of votes of exchange as well as their lack of concern with the partisan implications of the actual electoral behaviour. To the extent that the crisis reaches levels at which the control over resources which might somehow satisfy these needs is radically curtailed, it follows that the inclination of this vote to become a protest vote will increase, since the political counterpart will not be able to organise it, establishing and managing an exchange relationship. It will then remain extremely difficult to transform this type of vote by organising it, since even in the recent instances of leftist organisations of the unemployed, the major motivation behind the vote remained the acquisition of an immediate and individual (personal) advantage.

The emphasis we repeatedly put on the likely mobility of the electorate does not mean overall volatility or total unpredictability of future Italian electoral behaviour. The fundamental orientations of the electorate (especially in terms of the distinction left/right) are not susceptible to dramatic changes. Indeed, the very expansion of the area of opinion voters means that, to the extent that this type of vote is characterised by its endowment with a maximum of rationality vis-à-vis the electoral choice (even when the choice finds at its foundations definitions of the situation that carry the traits of 'fear' rather than 'hope', as it was in 1976), the underlying orientation which is congruent with the interests of the social classes of *appartenenza* and compatible with the cultural definitions and the symbolic representation to which they refer, should stand reconfirmed.

The same can be said for the vote of *appartenenza* which we considered by definition the most stable. The same cannot be said, however, for the vote of exchange. Lacking by definition its own specific orientations and being largely available (presently more than anytime in the past) to several options, comprising in its horizon leftist as well as rightist solutions, the vote of exchange may provide some surprises.

CONCLUSIONS

Having focused our attention on the relationship between parties and voters and having defined our central hypothesis to the effect that changes taking place in those relationships are the product of transformations in the overall structures of the types of vote and, at the same time have produced modifications in the pattern of electoral behaviour in Italy, we should like to conclude our analysis by pointing at some pieces of evidence as well as at some problems for the parties.

As anticipated, the electorate has shown its mobility in local elections, in the June 1978 referenda, and in the June 1979 parliamentary elections. To a considerable extent, even the direction and the nature of the changes seem

to lend support to our hypotheses. Without entering into details, it appears
that in the local elections, particularly those held in the South, but not
exclusively, there has been a rather conspicuous flow of votes away from
the PCI and toward the DC. It would be far-fetched to assume that all these
votes are votes of exchange returning to the DC, because of anticipated
difficulties of the PCI in dealing with them. Nevertheless, the magnitude of the
fluctuation which has reduced the PCI to its pre-1975 size, the areas where
these fluctuations have taken place and the reports of Communists and non-
Communists alike, from these areas, all point to the inability of the PCI to
'deliver the goods' and to a growing dissatisfaction of 'voters of exchange'
successfully courted by Christian Democratic organisers.[19]

It is interesting to note that where the PCI is organisationally and sub-
culturally strong, in the North or in Florence, for instance, either the fluctuations have not taken place or have been extremely limited, being maintained
within 'physiological' boundaries. It cannot be denied, however, that the DC
has successfully exploited the opportunities offered to it by a situation in
which the left is bickering, with the Socialists openly aiming at enticing opinion
voters as well as disgruntled Catholic voters. The struggle being waged by the
Socialists for greater visibility and better exposure is clearly intended to attract
opinion voters (while the required organisational efforts remain somewhat in
the background or amount to creating stronger ties with flanking organisations
such as with the trade unions UIL and with the League of Co-operatives).
The timing of the parliamentary elections, however, made it impossible for
the Italian Socialists to reap domestically the benefits they anticipated from
the mass media coverage of the 'Socialist victory' at the level of the European
Parliament.

If the purpose of an analysis of trends in electoral behaviour is to identify
above all the nature of the relationships which relate political parties and
social groups, then the June 1978 referenda offered abundant material. For
our present purposes, it is sufficient to stress a few points and draw some
conclusions. First of all, on major issues such as public order and State
financing of political parties, the voters have shown an unprecedented level
of disagreement with their parties. However, while the Communist organisational network and subcultural implantation have, on the whole, delivered the
vote in such a way as to clearly indicate the range as well as the limits of their
influence, the nature of the Catholic subculture and the characteristics of the
Christian Democratic organisational networks have proven to be less
mobilisable and less powerful on these issues.[20]

Opinion voters in the North—on the moderate side the bourgeoisie of
Milan, on the radical side some working class sectors of Turin—have shown
their autonomy from the parties and coalesced in casting a vote quite divergent from official party indications. Exchange voters in the South have found
an outlet for their dissatisfaction, resentment and preoccupations. In the
absence of a meaningful relationship with some political parties or candidates,
a vote of protest—against official party indications—was to be expected. The
results of the referenda represented the outcome of a complex vote whose
meaning is not univocal or unambiguous, that has many components and
many shades and might not be fully understood. Two lessons, nevertheless,

seem to derive from it. The first is some additional evidence that, indeed, electoral mobility might remain a major component of Italian electoral behaviour in the 1980s. The second is that strains and tensions are emerging vividly in the relationships between parties and voters, that major efforts at reorganisation of the parties are needed, that new flexible ties should be established between parties and flanking organisations, that a restructuring of the party system might be in order, that, indeed, a crisis of political representation may lurk in the background.

These trends have not been contradicted by the results of the June 1979 parliamentary elections. While a full analysis cannot be provided here[21] (see Tables 5 and 6 for the results and some comparisons), some aspects should be stressed. As anticipated, exchange voters deserted the PCI, especially in the South. Opinion voters indicated their ability to assess coolly the political situation. Sensing no danger of the DC being overtaken by the PCI, they felt free to return to minor centrist parties, as well as, within the leftist area, to reward the criticisms waged especially by the Radical party against both the PCI and the PSI. Finally, for the first time since 1948 the abstention rate went up by 3 per cent.

TABLE 5

RESULTS OF THE 1979 ELECTIONS TO THE CHAMBER OF DEPUTIES AND COMPARISONS WITH 1976

	Votes in 000's	1979 %	seats	1976–1979 %	seats
DC	14,008	38.3	262	— 0.4	— 1
PCI	11,108	30.4	201	— 4.0	— 26
PSI	3,586	9.8	62	+ 0.2	+ 5
PSDI	1,404	3.8	20	+ 0.4	+ 5
PRI	1,107	3.0	16	— 0.1	+ 2
PLI	708	1.9	9	+ 0.6	+ 4
MSI	1,928	5.3	30	$\Big\{$ — 0.2	— 5
DN	228	0.6	—		
PR	1,259	3.4	18	+ 2.3	+ 14
NSU	293	0.8	—	$\Big\{$ + 0.7	—
PdUP	501	1.4	6		
SVP	206	0.6	4	+ 0.1	+ 1

Notes NSU = Nuova Sinistra Unita' (United New Left)
         PdUP = Partito di Unita' Proletaria (Party of Proletarian Unity)
         SVP = Südtiroler Volkspartei

TABLE 6

RESULTS OF THE 1979 ELECTIONS AND COMPARISONS IN SEATS AND
PERCENTAGES WITH THE 1976 ELECTIONS (SENATE)

	1979		1976–79	
	%	seats	%	seats
DC	38·3	138	—0·6	+3
PCI	31·5	109	—2·3	—7
PSI	10·4	32	—0·2	+3
PSDI	4·2	9	+1·1	+3
PRI	3·4	6	+0·7	=
PLI	2·2	2	+0·8	=
MSI	5·7	13	—0·3	—2
DN	0·6	—		
PR	1·3	2	+0·5	+2
SVP	0·5	2	=	=

In conclusion, it would appear that renewed attention to the electorate and its behaviour, along the lines we have suggested above, may provide a useful framework for analysing, interpreting, and predicting some of the forthcoming changes in the Italian political system and of some of its future problems.

NOTES

1. For data and analyses see *Il comportamento elettorale in Italia* (Bologna: Il Mulino, 1968), which covers the 1946–1963 period; Mario Caciagli and Alberto Spreafico (eds.), *Un sistema politico alla prova. Studi sulle elezioni politiche italiane del 1972* (Bologna: Il Mulino, 1975); Celso Ghini, *Il voto degli italiani* (Rome: Editori Riuntii, 1975); Arturo Parisi and Gianfranco Pasquino (eds.), *Continuita' e mutamento elettorale in Italia. Le elezioni del 20 giugno 1976 e il sistema politico italiano* (Bologna: Il Mulino, 1977); and Howard R. Penniman (ed.), *Italy at the Polls. The Parliamentary Elections of 1976* (Washington, D.C.: American Enterprise Institute, 1977).

2. For a more detailed presentation along these lines, see Guido Martinotti, 'Le tendenze dell'elettorato italiano', in Alberto Martinelli and Gianfranco Pasquino (eds.), *La politica nell'Italia che cambia* (Milan: Feltrinelli, 1978), pp. 37–65.

3. Giorgio Galli and Alfonso Prandi, *Patterns of Political Participation in Italy* (New Haven: Yale University Press, 1970), p. 304, state the prevailing line. On the 'impression' of remarkable electoral mobility they write, 'The data analyzed in the present study indicate, however, that this impression is erroneous and that electoral behaviour in Italy, as in other democratic systems, has tended to become essentially stable after an initial period of adjustment'. Stability is also stressed by Samuel H. Barnes, 'Italy: Religion and Class in Electoral Behaviour', in Richard Rose (ed.), *Electoral Behavior: A Comparative Handbook* (New York–London: The Free Press–Collier Macmillan, 1974), pp. 171–225.

4. Barbara Bartolini, 'Insediamento subculturale e distribuzione dei suffragi', in *Continuita' e mutamento elettorale in Italia,* p. 137. For a different but complementary analysis see Arturo Parisi and Gianfranco Pasquino, '20 giugno: struttura politica e comportamento elettorale: il polo bianco', in *Continuita' e mutamento elettorale in Italia,* pp. 34–60.

5. For data and analyses see Arturo Parisi, *Referendum e questione cattolica. L'inizio di una fine* (Bologna: Il Mulino, 1974) and A. Marradi, 'Italy's Referendum on Divorce: Survey and Ecological Evidence Analyzed', *European Journal of Political Research* (March 1976), pp. 15–39.

6. Celso Ghini, *Il terremoto del 15 giugno* (Milan: Feltrinelli, 1976), and Giacomo Sani, 'Ricambio elettorale e identificazioni partitiche: verso una egemonia delle sinistre?', *Rivista Italiana di Scienza Politica* (December 1975), pp. 515–544.

7. For details and explanations see Giacomo Sani, 'Le elezioni degli anni settanta: terremoto o evoluzione?', in *Continuita' e mutamento elettorale in Italia*, pp. 91–96, and Gianfranco Pasquino, 'The Italian Socialist Party: An Irreversible Decline?', in *Italy at the Polls*, Table 6–10, p. 210.

8. Supporting evidence can be found in *Il comportamento elettorale in Italia*, and Giorgio Galli, *I partiti politici* (Turin: UTET, 1974).

9. Giacomo Sani, 'Political Traditions as Contextual Variables: Partisanship in Italy', *American Journal of Political Science* (August 1976), p. 381.

10. This and the preceding quotation are from the same article by Sani, respectively p. 397 and p. 399.

11. The evidence is still scanty, but see Maria Weber, *Il voto delle donne* (Turin: Centro di Ricerca e Documentazione 'Luigi Einaudi', 1977), and the data analysed by Giacomo Sani, 'Ricambio elettorale, mutamenti sociali e preferenze politiche', in Luigi Graziano and Sidney Tarrow (eds.), *La crisi italiana* (Turin: Einaudi, 1979), pp. 303–328.

12. For further discussion, see Arturo Parisi, 'Tra ripresa ecclesiastica ed eclissi della secolarizzazione', *Citta' & Regione* (July 1978), pp. 32–46.

13. Giacomo Sani, 'Le elezioni degli anni settanta', in *Continuita' e mutamento elettorale in Italia*, p. 79.

14. In the next four sections, we present in abridged form sections of the analysis more fully elaborated in our 'Relzioni partiti-elettori e tipi di voto', in *Continuita' e mutamento elettorale in Italia*, pp. 220–243.

15. A parallel can be found with issue voters and 'independent' voters. However, it is essential not to forget that in Italy we are dealing with a party system in which crossing the boundaries separating the centre-right from the left has never been easy. Therefore, there are clear limits to the range of fluctuations of opinion voters—intra-area fluctuations being far more common and likely than inter-area fluctuations.

16. It is very difficult to translate *appartenenza*. Bits of explanations can be found in these two quotations from Galli and Prandi, respectively p. 47 and p. 166 of *Patterns of Political Participation in Italy*. 'The competition for positions by the Christian Democratic and Communist parties is a variant of the wider patterns of contrast between the Socialist and the Catholic subcultures and of the right–left cleavage. Thus, the polarization of forces that has given the Christian Democrats and the Communists their position of leadership is not entirely political'. And 'By establishing organizations of many types—from those with local interests to those concerned with culture and leisure—or by acquiring some measure of control over already existing organizations, the Communist and the Christian Democratic parties, as mass parties, seek to give political direction to social actions of all kinds, at all levels of society'.

17. The reader might want to consult the following works: Anthony Downs, *An Economic Theory of Democracy* (New York: Harper and Row, 1957); R. L. Curry and L. L. Wade, *A Theory of Political Exchange* (Englewood Cliffs: Prentice Hall, 1968); and Stephen R. Waldman, *Foundations of Political Action. An Exchange Theory of Politics* (Boston: Little, Brown, and Co., 1972).

18. For a detailed sociological analysis see Arturo Parisi, 'La matrice socio-religiosa del dissenso cattolico in Italia', *Il Mulino* (July–August 1971), pp. 637–657.

19. The overall changes were as follows:

Local Elections (May 1978)

	Difference 1972–1976	Difference 1976–1978
	%	%
DC	+5·0	+3·8
PCI	+0·7	−10·1
PSI	−0·2	+4·1
PSDI-PRI-PLI	−1·9	+2·5
MSI-DN	−1·7	−2·1
DP-PR	+0·7	−1·3

1976 parliamentary elections
1972 previous local elections

Regional Elections in Trentin-Alto Adige
(November 1978)

	Difference 1973–1978	Difference 1976–1978
	%	%
DC	—5·8	—2·2
PCI	+1·5	—5·5
PSI	—1·8	—1·0
PSDI-PRI-PLI	—3·7	—0·1
MSI	—0·5	—0·7
New Left	n.p.	+1·8
PPT	+4·1	+6·2

n.p. = not present in 1973 (previous regional elections)

PPT = Popular Party of Trentino

20. Theoretically, the political alignment in favour of repealing the law on public order could count on 14·5 per cent of the votes (Radicals, Demoproletarians, MSI, perhaps 3/4 of the PSI). It polled 23·3 per cent. The respective percentages in favour of repealing the law on public financing of political parties were about 4 (Radicals, Demoproletarians, and PLI) and 43·7. For the first time abstentionism touched a high level: 18·6 per cent, the highest recorded in post-war Italian electoral history. For detailed analyses with reference respectively to the relationship between parties and voters and to the strength of the subcultures, see Arturo Parisi and Maurizio Rossi, 'Le relazioni elettori-partiti: quale lezione?', *Il Mulino* (July–August 1978), pp. 503–457; and Gianfranco Pasquinio, 'Referendum: l'analisi del voto', *Mondoperaio* (July–August 1978), pp. 18–24.

21. For an interview see Gianfranco Pasquino, 'Italy Tries Again: The Parliamentary Elections of June 1979', *Government and Opposition* (Winter 1980). For a detailed analysis: Howard R. Penniman (ed.), *Italy at the Polls. The Parliamentary Elections of 1979* (Washington, D.C.: American Enterprise Institute, forthcoming).

Muddling Through: Economics and Politics in Italy 1969-1979

Michele Salvati*

The 'Hot Autumn' of 1969 was much more than a particularly intense wage explosion: it was one manifestation of a great mass movement that has had a profound and enduring influence on Italian political life in the years that followed. The crisis and disintegration of the Centre-Left coalition, the electoral successes of the PCI in the seventies, and its movement toward the sphere of government would be difficult to understand without considering the severe shock which the 'Hot Autumn' administered to Italian society. Together with the student movement but with much greater force, the workers' movement expressed the privation and dissatisfaction of broad strata of Italian society with the political order of the Centre-Left. These strata were the most 'modern' and politically articulate in Italy, created or enlarged in the course of the 1950s and 1960s through the tumultuous processes of industrialisation, internal migration and education.

The inclusion in the government of political forces of the working class movement (if only with the obvious aim of isolating the Communist Party), a much broader and more innovative programme of social reform, and a more expansive domestic and international political climate—these were the characteristics which distinguished the Centre-Left from the Centre govern-ments of the 1950s. But precisely these 'openings', with their limitations and their contradictions, frustrated the expectations they had raised. Especially limited was the 'opening to the left', which divided the working class move-ment and excluded its most important component. The Centre-Left's widely publicised programme was courageous, but it was not even minimally realised. The greater relaxation of the political climate, and the disappearance of the atmosphere of religious war that had characterised the fifties now contrasted with the regular operation of the system of industrial relations. The de-flationary measures adopted in the winter of 1963–64 rapidly upset the 'sellers' market' which the unions had briefly enjoyed during the last phase of the 'economic miracle'; the middle of the sixties saw the return of significant industrial unemployment, while the unions were weak in the factories and were hardly recognised by their opponents.

The contradictions of this limited and hesitant 'opening' exploded towards the end of the decade. The student movement was the first to grasp these contradictions politically in the spring of 1968. However, they burst forth only with the collapse of the old system of industrial relations, a collapse which matured in the course of 1969 and culminated in the winter of 1969–70.

*Professor of Economics, University of Modena.

During the events of May 1968 in France an even more intense working class explosion was rapidly controlled and played out without effecting any profound transformation of industrial relations in the workplace. The political elections at the end of June, the divisions among the French unions, and the decision to divert militancy in most of the unions into political-electoral tasks, all help explain the rapid exhaustion of union activity after May's few weeks of near revolution; the electoral defeat became a union defeat. The pervasive influence of the 'Hot Autumn' on the Italian political system lies exactly in the fact that the movement did not set itself an explicitly political objective; rather, it collided with the existing system of industrial relations with such intense demands and sustained pressure that it could no longer continue as before.

We must refer the reader elsewhere for an analysis of the factors which provoked this wave of social mobilisation.[1] Here we propose to deal only with some of its effects, some of the ways it influenced and reacted to the political system. In particular we will concentrate on the initiatives taken in economic policy, because it is in the economic sphere that the 'disequilibrating' consequences of the breakdown in the earlier system of industrial relations were greatest.

Looking back at the past decade in this light, we can distinguish three distinct sub-periods: 1969 to mid-1972; mid-1972 to mid-1976; and mid-1976 to the present. From an economic viewpoint, the differences between them are clear enough. The first was a period of prolonged stagnation: exchange rates were stable; prices rose but not out of line with the European average; and the large wage increases of 1969–70 involved a significant redistribution of income in favour of wage-labour. The second was a period of great instability: until mid-1974 the Italian economy had become involved in the violent and inflationary world-wide boom which preceded the oil crisis; it was similarly involved in the deep recession of 1975; with the recovery in the winter of 1975–76, a new monetary crisis accompanied an inflationary wave. (Fixed exchange rates had been abandoned and a first wave of inflation had arrived during the winter of 1972–73.) The third period is once again a period of stagnation and of (relative) monetary stability: the drastic credit restriction of spring and summer 1976 blocked the growth of income until the second half of 1978; and the growth rates of the price indices started to decline—if quite slowly—until the end of that year.

Many of the events summarised above had international causes, and were visible, to some degree, in all the European countries. However, the extent varies and some countries were little affected. Thus, the economic policy adopted by the Italian authorities, and the response of the social system, had an influence in all these events. And since economic policy has an important weight in politics *tout court*, it is perhaps no accident that the periods we have drawn are also politically significant; they identify three *Gestalten* within which we can discover considerable coherence among economic, political, and social phenomena. The first period, for example, closes with the crisis of the Centre-Left and the elections of 1972. It was followed by a period of very unstable governments of the Centre or Centre-Left. The third period opened with the great advance of the PCI in the elections, also held early, of June

1976, which led to the formation of a government supported in parliament by the Communists. Naturally we must not overemphasise these distinctions and symmetries; there are also important continuities in the period and, in any case, our chosen dates fit some phenomena better than others. On the whole, however, the periodisation we have adopted picks out relevant transitions and is useful.

1969–1972

The monetary authorities reacted to the 'Hot Autumn' by toughening the restrictive measures which they had taken, beginning in the summer, to obstruct the exodus of capital and to bring the Italian interest rates—then comparatively very low—in line with those prevailing on the international markets. Later, in August of the following year, credit restrictions would be accompanied by a deflationary fiscal package, thus delivering the final blow to an economy which was already approaching recession. Private investment in fact stopped growing during the winter, and was not to revive until the second half of 1972, even though monetary and credit policy was relaxed in the second half of 1970; 'the horse refused to drink', as was said at the time.

A deflationary reaction by the monetary authorities and a consequent drop in investment characterise both the period 1969–70 and that of 1963–64. At the end of the 'economic miracle' in 1963–64, large wage increases had also coincided with widespread inflationary tendencies. There were, however, noteworthy differences, in the circumstances in which the monetary authorities intervened, and in the subsequent evolution of the economy.[2] It is very doubtful that in 1969 the Italians were faced with a situation of excess demand, (unlike the situation in 1963): from a purely economic standpoint, deflationary measures were much less justified than in the earlier case. These measures primarily reflect the monetary authorities' intention to hinder wage increases by weakening the labour market and reinforcing management's resistance to union demands, although a deflated economy did make it easier to defend the exchange rate against the current speculative attacks, and to hinder an inflationary explosion. Above all, however, the course of the economy after 1970 was very different from that after 1964, with respect both to the distribution of income, and to the growth and composition of demand.

Because the restrictive measures of 1969–70 were less drastic, and because the unions and the 'mass movement' were stronger than in 1963–1964, 1970 did not bring as rapid and violent an upset of the power relations in the factories as there had been in 1964. On the one hand, as we have already mentioned, strong wage-pressure continued, spreading from the national contracts into a far-reaching net of negotiations, firm by firm. On the other hand, the weight of the new representation of the workers in the factory, their influence on the organisation of time and of work, hindered the reduction of personnel and the intensification of work rhythms that had been introduced during 1964–65. After 1970, despite the stagnation of production, employment did not fall, and the increase of productivity was interrupted. Sharply increased money wages, low productivity, low levels of activity, and prices held down by stable exchange-rates led to a strong profit squeeze: the distribution of income in industry altered noticeably in favour of wage-labour, and visibly raised real wages, given the still moderate growth of consumer prices at the end of 1972.

Looking at the composition of demand, the differences between the period after 1970 and 1964–69 are just as striking. If the economic authorities hoped that the deflation of domestic demand would trigger a rapid development of exports, as they had before, these expectations were not to be realised. Partly because of the low dynamics of world trade between 1969 and 1972, but largely because of domestic difficulties (limitations of supply, lower competitivity, lower stimulus to exports), the growth of exports was quite modest in this period, and Italian manufactured exports as a percentage of world trade decreased remarkably from the high point reached in the first half of 1969. In the absence of a strong growth of exports and with sagging investment, the stagnation of demand between 1970 and 1972 becomes comprehensible: although multi-year spending decisions were initiated in this period— (which would weigh heavily on the public budgets of the years to come)— public spending remained relatively modest, and was not sufficient to offset the depressive effect of low growth in other components of demand.

To understand the significant shift in the distribution of income favouring wage-labour in the first years of the 1970s, we must also consider an analogous shift in the political system. Like the first shift, this, too, had its origins in the transformations which occurred in 'civil society' and which were expressed principally, though not exclusively, in the great mass movements at the end of the '60s. The unions constituted the most important institutional intermediary through which the new social demands were channelled and articulated. This profoundly shook the fragile equilibrium of the Centre-Left. The two major parties of the coalition, the DC and the PSI, especially the latter, were very vulnerable to the changed social climate. They were in no position to temper the new demands and render them compatible with the main goals of economic policy: a high level of employment, economic activity and investment, and a moderate level of inflation. We shall look at this more closely.

There was an unusually intense wage push throughout Europe in the 1970s, but this cannot explain the Italian experience, in which the wage increases of 1969–79 were exceptionally high, and completely incomprehensible in terms of the factors normally invoked to explain them.[3] What is particular in the Italian case is the persistence of this wage pressure over time, and the lasting alteration of the power relations between management and representatives of the workers in the workplace. If we look at the events of those years from a distance, we may conclude that the unions profited from the explosion of the masses to impose, from a position of strength, a far-reaching reform of the system of industrial relations which had existed up to then.

Organisational weakness, scant presence in the factories, marginal recognition as negotiating partners, ideological divisions, centralisation of contract-making—these were traditional characteristics of Italian unionism. Some of these features were mitigated and others disappeared during the period we are considering: ideological-organisational divisions lessened, and effective unity of action led to the formation of new unitary organisational forms. Unionisation was notably strengthened in the factories; the struggles produced hundreds of new representative bodies in the workplace, which the union transformed into its permanent local structures, the delegate councils. The incorporation of broad sections of the working class into the unions, with priority given to peripheral or unrepresented sections along with a simultaneous transformation of union structures and the previous rules of the game in industrial relations, could hardly develop without upsetting the management of economic policy. Active local bargaining now supplemented national labour contracts which already guaranteed very high wage increases; greater union control over the organisation of work—reduction of hours, bargaining over the speed of work, hindering layoffs—rendered impracticable the easier routes which management might have taken to a rapid recovery of productivity and a reduction of unit costs. But it was in guiding this process— stimulating it, extending it, consolidating it—rather than in hindering it, that the union could pursue its aim of organisational reconstruction.

For this to happen, of course, the unions needed a favourable political situation: a strong, hostile government with an economic policy decisively oriented to 'teaching labour a lesson', would have been incompatible with the great reinforcement of union power in those years. The moderate deflationary policies which are described above were completely inadequate in realising goals. They succeeded only in depressing economic activity without seriously impairing labour's consolidation of its position: to pursue a deflationary strategy an even greater dose than in 1963–64 would have been necessary in 1969–70, to obtain the same result. It is enough to pose the problem in these terms to be aware that no alchemy of economic technique, however sophisticated, could make up for the absence of a political will definite enough to contain union action within the main goals of economic policy, and the absence of power sufficient to impose this aim. Unlike the de Gaulle and Pompidou governments after May 1968—the Italian governments of the IV Legislature (1968–72) lacked the political strength to pursue an anti-union strategy; and, unlike Heath's Conservative Government in England they lacked a clear political will to follow such a strategy. We shall see why.

The Socialist Party, just recently unified with the Social Democratic Party, emerged quite battered from the political elections of 1968: the two parties lost around a quarter of the votes they had obtained in the previous elections. The collapse of the reform plan which constituted the Centre-Left's programme was not compensated for—in terms of electoral approval—by the modest share of patronage which the DC had conceded to the PSI. The emergence of widespread frustration in society, and the criticism—incessant and well-founded—by the PCI, which was excluded from the governing coalition but was far stronger and more influential in the unions, were the roots of this failure. Within the PSI a process of reflection and self-criticism began, which was to dominate Italian political life for the next ten years. The PSI grew reluctant to form a governing majority with the DC, while the PCI was in a critical position outside the government. As a consequence, stable majorities could not be formed during the middle 1970s, and the conditions for the PCI's participation in the governing majority were created after the political elections of 1976. During the period under consideration, the immediate effects of the electoral upset were demonstrated by a visible swing to the left by the PSI. In addition, this led to the breakdown of the unhappy union with the Social Democrats, and to a sharp rise in the price demanded for participation in the Centre-Left. This price included a favourable attitude toward the unions and the rapid realisation of some of the 'reforms' promised in the original programme of the Centre-Left but never put into practice.

The dominant party of this coalition, the Christian Democrats, was in no position to resist the increased pressure of the Socialist Party. After all, given the election results, the Centre-Left still remained the most practicable coalition government; a coalition with the parties of the Right was not possible, given the nature of those parties (fascist and monarchist), so that alliance with the PSI constituted the only dependable way to deny the PCI access to government responsibility. In addition, the change of social climate during the end of the sixties also made itself felt within the *Democrazia Cristiana*. In the shifting balance of currents and interest groups which competed to determine the political goals of this party, the Catholic Labour Union and the ACLI contributed to move the centre of gravity to the left.

Thus the government respected the demands of the unions, and was incapable of imposing an economic policy objective which could simultaneously secure the goals of increased economic activity and of moderate development of wages and prices. The frequent interventions of the Christian Democratic Minister of Labour—an ex-CISL unionist, Donat-Cattin—into collective bargaining generally aimed at preventing excessive industrial conflict, which threatened the stability of the political structure, rather than at insisting on a more modest increase of money wages. Likewise, there was greater activity in the field of public spending, and the interests of wage-workers were favoured by new laws on pensions and the health system. This was done, however, without challenging the interests of the classes tied to the Christian Democratic power structure, and above all without modifying the system of pay-offs as a way to find the funds needed to cover the increased spending. It was in this period that the foundations were laid for the fiscal crisis which was to explode in the following years.[4]

1973–1976

After two years of stagnation—a long enough period for the Italian economy, which has always reacted nearly as fast as that of Japan to measures restricting credit—the recovery began in the second half of 1972. There was, however, an unexpected aspect to this recovery. In 1958 and in 1964 exports had led the other components of demand, thus guaranteeing a long period of development without balance of payments worries. This time, despite the worldwide boom of 1973, exports increased at a relatively modest rate. The recovery was fuelled by domestic demand, above all by a rapid reaccumulation of stockpiles, with a strong speculative component, though an intense but brief wave of fixed investments in industry and a sustained development in public spending and private consumption also contributed to the recovery.

The vigorous revival of domestic activity, the relatively disappointing increase of exports, the continual speculative flight of capital—which never slowed down by really incisive administrative measures—rapidly dismantled the conditions which had permitted the stabilisation of the exchange rate during the preceding two years. In the face of an increase in unit costs higher than those of Italy's principal trading partners, only the assets of the balance of current accounts, due to the low level of domestic activity, furnished the economic policy authorities with the resources to combat speculation against the lira. During the winter of 1972–73 the first payments deficit appeared. It was not a very serious deficit, but Italian unit costs were already out of line relative to those abroad; such costs threatened, in addition, to increase before long, as a group of important labour contracts were under discussion, and the unions' demands were very high. To restrain and counteract speculation against the lira was practically impossible under these conditions; the lira was allowed to float at the beginning of February and fell rapidly with respect to the currencies of Italy's principal trading partners. Naturally this gave Italian industry a chance to increase domestic prices and profit margins: with these increased margins and an increase in economic activity, total profits jumped significantly in the boom from the second half of 1972 to the first half of 1974, coming back from the extremely low levels of the two previous years. But, not surprisingly, the increase in prices did not create ideal conditions for preaching moderation to the unions: the wage negotiations of the winter of 1972–73 ended, in April 1973, with very high wage increases, which were in fact smaller in real terms than the previous contract. This provided the starting point for the continuing spiral of prices, wages, and exchange rates through even higher levels of inflation which characterised the Italian economy up to the first half of 1976.

This picture is not very different from that of the other countries—the United Kingdom, for example—which found themselves, at a time of fluctuating exchange-rates, in more than average inflationary conditions. As far as the level of economic activity is concerned, it is a picture dominated by the international cycle, never completely synchronised amongst the different capitalist countries: the great boom of 1973, the oil price rise, the deep recession of 1975, and the slight recovery of 1976. It should only be mentioned that the Italian authorities—like those of the United Kingdom and unlike, for example, the German authorities—were rather reluctant to impose restrictive measures when faced with rising inflation and the aggravation of the trade deficit; after two years of stagnation, both business and organised labour were deeply hostile to a new deflation. Under the conditions of 1973–74, of course, a loose monetary policy permitted a very rapid inflationary spiral and opened the way for an enormous foreign debt, so that, by mid-1974, a drastic monetary restriction could no longer be avoided.

The United Kingdom provides an obvious point of comparison with the Italian experience, since both countries were then facing far higher rates of inflation than the other important European economies. Both economies were characterised by strong wage pressure, and a relatively low sensitivity of wages to variations in the conditions of economic activity. Nevertheless, two differences may be noted, which became especially important from 1975 on. With the fall of Heath's Conservative government, the foundations were laid in Great Britain for an agreement between government and unions, widely known as the 'social contract'; movement in this direction has been much slower in Italy. The conditions required for such an agreement were still lacking in 1975, and the government did not intervene when union and employers agreed on a cost-of-living escalator—the most extensive, automatic, and favourable to labour of any in the advanced capitalist countries—that has yielded appreciable real gains to wage-workers in its first phases, and today hinders any anti-inflationary strategy based on a reduction of real wages.

A second difference—quantitative in nature, but still significant—was the larger State deficit in Italy. We have already mentioned how the final, and most 'activist' phase of the previous legislature had laid the basis for an extensive increase in public spending, which was not followed by an analogous increase in revenues. This was not at all what the proponents of the 'reforms' wanted: the reforms were intended as redistributive measures financed by an increased levy on those classes with greater fiscal capacity. But increased public expenditure was all they could win, given the political and administrative resistance to a truly redistributive strategy. No wonder, therefore, that a Public Administration deficit emerged, rising to 10 per cent of the GNP in 1976—in the seriously inaccurate estimates of the OECD—in contrast with 5 per cent in the United Kingdom which was already a very high figure for a European country.

Beyond the long run consequences of this distorted use of revenue and disrupted financial structure, one short-term consequence must also be emphasised. Such large financial demands by the Public Administration need not have been inflationary. But in managing monetary policy when financial markets are permanently clogged by the public sector's need for credit, it is very difficult to pursue a middle course between excessive creation of liquidity, and over-restriction of credit which would injure the private sector and discourage investment, especially considering the very high dependence on bank credit that typifies Italian business. The growth of liquidity in the winter of 1975–76 was stimulated by a situation in which business was hard pressed by the credit restrictions of the year before and by the recession of 1975. With this 'excessive' liquidity, and a revival of economic activity, a serious currency crisis developed, leading to a sharp drop in the exchange rate and a new inflationary wave. A few months after restrictive monetary and credit measures had been abandoned, they had to be revived with greater force: from mid-1976 to mid-1978 there was a new phase of declining investment and stagnant economic activity.

The violent oscillations of economic activity that we have described, and the strong inflationary impulses which accompanied them were due largely to international causes. But it must be said that in the majority of industrial countries this turbulent period of international economic relations saw better performances in basic economic indicators, such as the level of activity (either employment or investment, which usually follow similar courses) and price increases. France maintained a very high level of activity and investment from May 1968 until the world recession of 1975, and succeeded in containing price increases within acceptable limits. The FRG deliberately sacrificed domestic economic activity, a path not dissimilar to that taken in

Italy and Great Britain, but in return obtained an exceptionally low level of inflation. It can, therefore, be concluded that, to no small degree, we must seek domestic causes for the economic disequilibria which we have described.

We have already seen how these disequilibria were produced in the last months of the parliament which ended in 1972. The elections held ahead of schedule in 1972 led to an even more unstable political situation, with governments even less able to carry out a coherent economic policy than those of the preceding parliament. The general elections of June 1968 in France eliminated the forces that could have led to an alteration of the previous political equilibrium when they first appeared. In Italy, however, after four years of social unrest—characterised by continuous worker and student protest on the one hand, and by obscure terrorist manoeuvres, on the other—the electorate did not give its favour to any 'law and order' coalition, and indeed reversed the slight shift to the right, which had harmed the DC in the elections of the year before. The cautious policy of the PCI, its distance from the more extreme manifestations of the 'mass movement', on the one hand, and the low credibility of the DC as a party capable of good government and honest administration, on the other, impeded a polarisation of the alignments: the equilibrium of the parliamentary groups thus remained the same as that of 1968, and the options open were identical.

The governments of the fifth legislature clearly demonstrated, by the very variety of the majority coalitions on which they were based, an inability to pursue a political plan, and therefore also an economic policy, with continuity and coherence. The legislature opened with a return to a coalition abandoned ten years before: the tensions between the DC and the PSI, aggravated during the electoral campaign, and the latter party's uncertainty about continuing its alliance with the DC, impeded an immediate return to the Centre-Left and produced a Centre government, weak in parliament and very weak in the country. Obviously this was not the political alliance to ask labour's aid in the fight against inflation; on the other hand it was a government too weak to govern against the unions. In fact, it was the government of the 'doctored recovery', of the monetary accommodation of the demands both of labour and of business, the government of double figure inflation.

Once a coalition of forces favouring a return of the Centre-Left was put together in the PSI, the middle years of this legislature were characterised by a rerun of the political formula of the 1960s, which at least made a solid majority in parliament available. In the presence of scarcer resources, with a more difficult international situation, this effort too was destined to fail. Learning from their past experience with the discredited 'two stage' strategy of the 1960s (first, put your house in order, then make reforms) the Socialists were firmer in demanding a programme of ample and courageous state intervention. Meanwhile, in the face of galloping inflation, the voices in the government which called for a return to rigorous financial orthodoxy were strengthened: the recommendations of the IMF found supporters not only in the small Republican Party, but also in important sections of Christian Democracy.

During its final phase this parliament was ruled by the two minority governments of Aldo Moro, first the DC with the Republican Party, then the

DC alone. These governments were made possible by favourable votes by the Left, in a situation which saw the DC in great difficulties and the left parties, especially the PCI, in a period of significant ascendancy. The vote favouring divorce in the referendum of May 1974, and the very strong leap forward of the Communist Party in the elections of June 1975 indicated a most important shift in the stable Italian electorate. The Communist Party, after a first moment of uncertainty when social mobilisation was at its high point in 1969–70, profited from the PSI's shift to the left and its increasing reluctance to form a coalition government with the DC; it advanced its own candidature as a governing force continuously and diligently. Innumerable laws and measures were passed in parliament with the support or the 'constructive' opposition of the Communist Party during this period. The image of an efficient and honest party, and the conviction that the country's difficulties would be surmountable only with the collaboration of the PCI, gained wide currency, skilfully fuelled by the PCI itself, which since 1973 had declared its availability for a coalition of national emergency with the DC and the PSI, coining the term, 'historic compromise'.

With the persistent objections posed by the DC to a government with the Communists, the PCI's proofs of moderation, as an opposition force, certainly did not suffice to define an effective programme of economic policy. The PCI openly declared its availability for an austerity policy; but it was obvious that the type of austerity proposed by the government did not sit well with the Party and that it intended to manage its austerity programme itself, as a part of the government. It was just as obvious that it did not intend to use up its influence over the unions—by favouring a programme of wage moderation—while remaining in the opposition: such a policy is difficult and unpopular even when a party is in government and can directly control the *quid pro quo* offered to the unions and the workers.

Faced with weak and unstable governments that yielded in confrontations with labour, and also to any group with channels of representation and sufficient pressure, incapable of effective administration, let alone courageous redistribution, the unions found themselves in a rather difficult situation. Worried that labour conflict would add to political and social instability, the governments did not put serious obstacles in the way of union activity in the framework of industrial relations: we have already mentioned the high wage settlements of 1973 and the 1975 agreement on the cost-of-living escalator. On the other hand, the unions became increasingly aware that successes obtained with respect to wages were being nullified by inflation. They had to consolidate the strength won in industrial relations with political and institutional conquests to influence economic policy, even though this was not an alternative to pressure on wages. These objectives, obviously, became even more relevant when, towards the end of the period we are considering, unemployment and inflation emerged as the central problems facing the unions.[5]

Pressure in the area of industrial relations was thus accompanied, beginning in 1970–71, by intense activity in the political market, through continual meetings with the government and through mass mobilisation concerning problems of general political interest: urban and housing policy, Southern development, health, investment, etc. The nature of the subjects dealt with, the strength and activism of the unions, and the weakness of the parties and the government led some people at the beginning of this period, to believe that organised labour had conclusively established itself as a substitute for the parties in expressing and channelling a significant portion of political demand. This period, however, was of limited duration; the very weakness of the governments, their incapacity to pursue a reform programme, though it had damaged the parties' image, quickly weakened the unions' momentum. This led to a widespread sense of frustration in the unions with regard to top-level relations with the government and to the great mass mobilisations for reforms; it led to an attempt to reduce some of the great problems of national interest to a scale which could render them susceptible to the traditional procedures of union action: between 1973 and 1977 the unions introduced demands for the location of business investment in the South into their local bargaining platforms.

It should be emphasised that in this period labour's activity on the political market was never accompanied by explicit self-limitation in the field of wages: the very metaphor of 'political market' present in much of the talk of the period by both sides but absent in the bargaining process is not very relevant during these years. The question of bargaining, of explicit and significant self-limitation and the demand for precise equivalents received in return, was first posed only in the following period, when the aggravation of the economic situation and the PCI's movement towards governing would create the conditions for it.

1976–1979

From mid-1976 to the end of 1978 the Italian economy again experienced a long period of stagnation, from which it has been re-emerging, apparently with considerable vigour, only in the last few months. The currency crisis of the first part of 1976 was combatted with a violent credit squeeze; the currency supply was rigorously stabilised and credit supplied to the private sector in tiny drops. This economic strategy, which deliberately sacrificed the goals of growth, investment, and employment to the objective of achieving a surplus in current accounts, repaying the debts contracted in the previous phase, stabilising the rate of exchange, and controlling inflationary tensions some-what, was formulated with clarity by the Governor of the Bank of Italy in May 1976. It was consistently pursued for the following two and a half years, and crowned with notable 'success'. GNP did, in fact, increase by less than the average of the other Western European countries (1·7 per cent as against 2·2 per cent in 1977, and 2·4 per cent as against 2·8 per cent in 1978), and unemployment fluctuated around a million and a half, 7 per cent of the labour force. The reversal of the balance of payments situation of the beginning of 1976 was, however, surprising: a large part of the debts contracted with official institutions were repaid, and in 1978 current accounts registered assets of around three billion dollars, among the highest in the OECD. In contrast to the experience in the years following 1969, from the end of 1976 the traditional elasticity of Italian exports relative to depressed domestic demand reappeared with strength, and the Italian economy regained a good part of its share of exports on the world market, which had been lost in previous years. This period saw a striking 'adaptation' to the upheavals—both in industrial relations in terms of trade—of the first part of the '70s, in ways which have given rise to controversy in recent years.[6]

During the period as a whole, the authorities followed a shrewd foreign exchange policy: they were aware that the growing costs of production in Italy did not permit linking the lira to the strong currencies of Western Europe. The Italian currency was tied to the dollar throughout 1977, which made possible a stabilisation of imported raw materials costs, in dollar terms, and the maintenance of a margin of competitivity on manufactured exports, largely directed towards countries with strong currencies. The dollar, however, was not followed in its later decline, and the reserve situation and the balance of payments appeared so favourable, towards the end of 1978, that—with some hesitancy—the monetary authorities lined up behind the political decision to participate in the European Monetary System.

The main reasons for this hesitancy about an international agreement which apparently favoured one of the monetary authorities' institutional goals are easy to understand. The full success of the stabilisation measures with respect to foreign obligations was not matched by an equal success in dealing with the problem of prices. The slowing down of inflationary pressures has been very slow: in 1978 consumer prices were still increasing at a rate (12–13 per cent) nearly double that of the main European countries; money wages in industry, tied by the cost-of-living escalator to the consumer price rises of the previous trimester, increased about 15 per cent in 1978. Given the modest growth of labour productivity (if we exclude the last trimester, 1978 was a year of stagnation), this has entailed an increase of unit costs in industry on the order of 12 per cent. Establishing a fixed exchange rate with a country like the FRG, Italy's main trading partner, where unit costs were increasing by around 2 per cent in 1978, would appear risky and counterproductive even to a central banker: there can be no durable band of fluctuations—and Italy has obtained a relatively wide one at 6 per cent—if these divergences continue for very long.

In fact, it was a risky decision—above all for the goals of growth and employment: It can yield good results only if the main domestic sources of inflationary pressure are rigorously controlled: above all, the growth of wages, but also public spending and deficits, if room is to be left for a sufficient distribution of credit to the private sector. It seems that the economic authorities are convinced that the political conditions exist for attempting a further, and more decisive, turn of the anti-inflationary screw. Increased growth of productivity with recovery underway, greater inflationary pressures among the principal trading partners, and greater political stability in the past two years have helped make adherence to the European Monetary System possible. The unions have been moderate in their demands and the political parties are amenable to a more severe programme of monetary stabilisation.

The document outlining the principal features of the stabilisation programme was published in September 1978 (the Pandolfi Report, named after the Treasury Minister who drew it up). It was reworked and enlarged as the 'Three Year Plan', published in mid-January by the Minister of the Budget. Essentially, it proposes an Italian version of the McCracken Report's 'narrow path':[7] its central point, as a programme against inflation, is that real wages in industry will remain constant for the next three years: money wages will rise very little beyond what the cost-of-living escalator already guarantees. It involves a significant restriction of bargaining freedom, and the least to be said is that it will be respected only under very 'favourable' political conditions. In recent months, the political situation has once again become perilous.

As numerous indices predicted, the general elections of June 20, 1976 marked a great leap forward for the PCI: from 27·1 per cent in the previous general elections to 34·4 per cent, (compared to 38·7 per cent for the DC, the same percentage as in the elections of 1972). Equally predictable, in the light of the last two Moro governments, was the lasting reluctance of the PSI to resume the Centre-Left experiment, the drastic shrinkage of the smaller parties in the middle, and the refusal of moderate forces to join a *grosse Koalition* with the Communist Party. The only remaining possibilities were such byzantine solutions for 'close encounters of various kinds', such as minority Christian Democratic governments sustained with abstention or support in parliament by the left-wing parties. While the abstentions were voluntary during the last governments of the previous legislature, they were 'contracted for' with the governing programme of the third Andreotti government (August 1976–January 1978) and were transformed into favourable votes during the fourth Andreotti government (March 1978–January 1979). Thus the PCI was explicitly included in the governing majority, though not in the government.

Beyond the obscurity of the proposed coalition formulae the problem is very simple: on the one hand, the impossibility of extending the governing alliance to the extreme right, which includes the still solid group of neo-fascist Deputies, leaves a minority to any conservative government which wishes to exclude Socialists and Communists on its left. On the other hand, a government of the left which excluded the Christian Democrats on its right, would also be in a minority, since some of the small centre parties are even more anti-Communist than the DC and would never participate in this kind of government. Thus the importance of the Socialist Party's decision: as we pointed out at the beginning of this account, in parliament it was the leftward shift of the PSI, and its growing unwillingness to join the Christian Democrats in governments excluding the PCI, that generated the political instability of this decade and offered the Communist Party its chance to approach the threshold of government. The social causes and organisational expediencies which have induced this behaviour deserve to be noted once again, since we are perhaps near a turning point.

The great difficulties experienced by the PSI in trying to reform the Christian Democratic style of government and the wave of unrest and dissatisfaction expressed in civil society by the social mobilisation of the end of the '60s, profoundly damaged the image of this party. Important segments of its electorate had moved towards the Communist Party or minor groups of the extreme left, while moderate voters remained alienated from the PSI by its continuing symbolic identification with the left and by the scanty proofs of its administrative efficiency and honesty. The PSI's shift to the left is comprehensible, therefore, as a long-term choice despite its electoral and organisational drawbacks. The move to the left, in fact, did not pay off in the elections of 1972 and 1976, and it appears to have aided the PCI rather more than the PSI. Thus we can explain the increasing political instability of the PSI in 1978, and the deliberate accentuation of its polemics against the Communist Party. Whichever big party the PSI has collaborated with, be it the DC in a Centre-Left government, or the PCI in a strategy of joint opposition ('collaborative abstention') the larger party has enjoyed the fruits. The PSI is still seeking an independent image which can win elections, and, therefore, violent fluctuations of strategy cannot be ruled out in the near future.

Nevertheless, there is little doubt that the period from the end of 1976 to the beginning of 1979 saw one of the most stable governmental formations of the whole decade which we have been considering. This government fell because in the end a wall had been erected against the 'progressive displacements' of the PCI towards the government, even if the byzantine imagination of the Italian political system could have invented still more intermediate steps for the PCI to take toward full governing rights.[8] Such further displacements were required to compensate the PCI for the price which it had been paying to stabilise a difficult social situation. But as long as the Andreotti government remained alive, it created the stable political situation which, together with greater moderation on the part of labour, was the premise for the Central Bank strategy we described above, the only true and coherent economic policy (in contrast with those discussed in parliament) followed in Italy in the last two and a half years.

Increased political stability, however, has not been matched by greater effectiveness in making decisions or greater ability to order priorities in a coherent plan for reform; if anything, these have diminished. It is not possible to give a detailed appraisal here of the principal legislative and governmental measures passed (or still under discussion) in this period, such as industrial restructuring, youth employment, rent control, proposals for the reform of agrarian contracts, for university reform. These are technically skeleton laws and proposals, often so ill-written as to be unenforceable; and even when they are enforceable they require a competence, an impartiality, and an efficiency which do not exist in the Italian administration and so they will all remain dead letters. This is because they are always the fruit of long and exhausting compromises worked out between forces with profoundly different orientations. The public authorities' already low capacity for government and innovation can only be diminished by the entrance of still more interest groups in the legislative game, and by the increased resistance, in a climate of deep economic crisis, of the interest groups traditionally defended by the government.

Yet a favourable attitude toward the government on the part of the unions and of the Communist Party can be justified only if there is a new momentum and incisiveness in passing reforms and if the government can protect the interests harmed by its macro-economic stabilisation measures, with redistributive and micro-economic measures.[9] The Communist Party will encounter increasing difficulty dealing with a situation where it is held ever more responsible for the activity (or inactivity) of the government, without in fact really sharing in executive responsibility and without a sure perspective of participating in the government in the near future. And the unions have had an ever harder time maintaining a line of moderation and self-control, with pressure developing among broad sectors of the rank and file, in the absence of any political returns.

The high point of the unilateral commitment to self-control on the part of the unions was reached in the EUR congress of the three federations, in February 1978. This commitment is rather more vague and bland than that which the British unions made in the 'social contract', and, in fact, the average real wage has never actually stopped rising in recent years. The Communist side of the labour movement, and especially the Secretary of the CGIL, Luciano Lama, have, however, made serious efforts to turn the EUR declarations into an effective policy of wage self-limitation. Whether the reduction of confrontation and of contractual pressure in the last two years owes more to this political line or to greater market difficulties is not yet clear. What is certain is that the 'Lama line' has come into ever more conflict with other political components of the labour movement, the Catholics of the CISL, the Socialists of the UIL and members of the CGIL itself, who see it as a subordination of the union's needs to the PCI's need for political legitimation. But, above all, it has come into ever greater conflict with the demands expressed by the rank and file.

The ties between the union organisations and the ranks established at the height of the movement appear significantly weakened; cost of living index-ation, which today provides for most of the increase in money wages, in the absence of a positive wages policy damages the union's credibility. The unions are not pushing for continual improvements and appear in the eyes of many workers as an external power, much like the government, preaching moder-ation and 'austerity'. This slogan does not express the profound sentiments of a mass movement roused by the menace of a foreign enemy or by intense social transformation; it is only the tired refrain of 'the organisations', in a situation in which no significant change of authority seems possible.

1979 AND BEYOND

The social mobilisation of the late 1960s was still fundamentally able to alter the electoral equilibria amongst the main parties in the mid-1970s, and has affected a political and administrative system that is singularly resistant to change. This system has been very malleable in the short run: that is, incapable of rigid responses and unable to discipline demands in the name of well defined priorities. But it is also a system which, finally, is very resistant and slow-moving. Thus Italy has seen only an extraordinary inflationary push, with no steps toward the solution of political and social problems that were already on the agenda in the days of the Centre-Left.

As the events of these years have clearly shown, we are dealing with problems that demand a coherent and long-term commitment; the very instrument with which to confront them, the public administration, must be practically rebuilt. Hence they require a stable political equilibrium, which would make it possible to devote significant resources to ends which will not pay off in the short run. Such an equilibrium seems more distant than ever: the electoral progress of the PCI has ended, but has not led to a great electoral victory for the Christian Democrats and other centre parties. The resulting parliamentary equilibrium is just as unstable as ever. This instability is inevitable unless the DC removes its veto on the PCI's participation in the government, or unless the Socialists accomplish a further inversion of their strategy and return to the Centre-Left.

The crisis continues, an endemic crisis, a 'multiform' crisis, as Sidney Tarrow has described it,[10] whose various aspects have not (yet?) taken on the more menacing form of an organic crisis, a crisis of the regime. It may be possible to read, in 2021, this short '*Au jour le jour*' which appeared over the signature of Gilles Ceron in *Le Monde* of 6 May 1978. Under present circumstances, this hardly enrapturing perspective is almost a hope:

Bad News from Italy

Rome, late April 2021. As a result of the tragic events which have been occurring here, the seventy-fifth anniversary of the Italian Republic has been very soberly celebrated. It will be recalled that the Italians have never had a sense of the State, because of their long history of invasions and divisions, and that, in the climate of institutional disintegration, the days of the Italian Republic are numbered. On this occasion, the President of the Italian Republic received numerous messages of sympathy, notably from the Prime Minister of the XII French Republic, the Presidents of California, Wyoming, and forty other North American republics, from the kings of Murcia and of Wales, and from the Grand Duke of Schleswig-Holstein.

NOTES

1. The best known analysis is that of A. Pizzorno. For a formulation of its most general lines in English, see this author's essay in C. Crouch and A. Pizzorno, eds., *The Resurgence of Class Conflict in Europe* (London: Macmillan, 1978); in the same volume the essay by I. Regalia, M. Regini and E. Reyneri describes the Italian situation in detail. The research on which Pizzorno's interpretation is based has been published in many volumes between 1974 and 1978 by Il Mulino in Bologna; in the last volume (A. Pizzorno, E. Reyneri, M. Regini, I. Regalia, *Lotte Operaie e Sindacato: il Ciclo 1972–1978 in Italia,* 1978) are collected the conclusions of this research. It should be said here that this interpretation is not universally accepted: it suffices to compare the essays of A. Pizzorno, B. Trentin, A. Accornero, and M. Tronti in the XVI volume of the 'Annali della Fondazione Feltrinelli' (*Problemi del Movimento Sindacale in Italia, 1943–1973,* Milano: Feltrinelli, 1976) to be aware of the strong disagreements that exist. For a critical comparison of the various interpretations see B. Beccalli, *Sindacato e Politica: un Caso Italiano'?* in *Quaderni Piacentini* 65–66 (February 1978).
2. A detailed analysis of the turning points of these two economic cycles can be found in M. Salvati, *il Sistema Economico Italiano: Analisi di una Crisi* (Bologna: Il Mulino, 1975).
3. There are innumerable works by economists on the wage and price explosion which began at the end of the '60s: both from a theoretical and from a descriptive point of view. Two of the most useful and most easily consulted are: G. Maynard and W. Van Ryckeghem, *A World of Inflation* (London: Batsford, 1976) and L. B. Krause and W. S.

Salant, eds., *World-wide Inflation* (Washington: The Brookings Institution, 1977). These authors correctly emphasize the common, and international, factors in the generation of the great inflationary wave of the 1970s; however, we are also interested in ascertaining the origin—political and economical—of the very different national 'responses': see below (the text), p. 14. Economists have done very little comparative work on this question, predominantly tending to find the single cause of the various national rates of inflation in the differing propensities of the national authorities with respect to the money supply. For a more complex perspective, and one more useful for a sociologist or a political scientist, see the essay of D. Soskice in C. Crouch and A. Pizzorno, *The Resurgence of Class Conflict*, and R. J. Gordon, *World Inflation and Monetary Accommodation in Eight Countries*, Brookings Papers on Economic Activity, 1977, No. 2.

4. A short and balanced description of the Italian 'fiscal crisis' is contained in A. Pedone's article, 'Aspetti della Crisi Finanziaria del Settore Pubblico', in L. Graziano and S. Tarrows, eds., *La Crisi Italiana*, 2 vols. (Turin: Einaudi, 1979). Much ample and more informative are the works of F. Reviglio, *Spesa Pubblica e Stagnazione nell'Economia Italiana* (Bologna: Il Mulino, 1977) and E. Gerelli and F. Reviglio, eds., *Per una Politica della Spesa Pubblica in Italia* (Milano: F. Angeli, 1978).

5. On this most recent phase of union activity, not covered in the works which we mentioned in footnote 1, see E. Reyneri, 'Movimento Sindacale, Crisi Economica e Sociale, Compromesso Storico', *Il Mulino,* July–August 1977, and G. P. Cella, 'L'azione Sindacale nella Crisi Italiana' in L. Graziano and S. Tarrow, *La Crisi Italiana*.

6. The discussions refer to the non-'orthodox' nature of some of these adjustments, in particular to the development of 'wildcat restructuring' and of the 'underground economy', to use the journalistic terms with which they have been designated. On the two closely linked phenomena there are many journalistic investigations, but few studies on particular aspects, and no general work. On the first, which refers to activities of businesses with a view to regaining the flexibility in the management of labour that they have lost in the big factories (sub-contracting, putting-out . . . up to black labour), see A. Graziani, ed., *Crisi e Ristrutturazione nell'Economia Italiana* (Turin: Einaudi, 1975). On the second, the development of economic activity unseen by any official statistics, a large scale investigation on 'double labour' is being completed by the Istituto di Sociologia, Facolta di Lettere, Universita di Torino. These non-orthodox adjustments are naturally not an exclusive prerogative of the Italian economy: judging by what one reads in the press, a vast underground economy also exists in the United Kingdom; however, given the greater weight of small enterprises and of independent labour, it can be presumed that the dimensions and the development of the underground economy are greater in Italy as well.

7. OECD, *Towards Full Employment and Price Stability*, Paris, June 1977. It is unnecessary to say that R. Keohane's observations on the McCracken Report ('Neo-orthodox Economics, Inflation and the State: Political Implications of the McCracken Report', *World Politics*, October 1978) can to a great extent be applied also to its Italian emulators.

8. An intermediate step, discussed at length and then discarded by the Christian Democrats during the recent crisis was that of admitting into the government as ministers some non-Communist personalities elected on the PCI list, the so-called 'left independents'.

9. The problem of the 'quid pro quo' (wage moderations *vs*. . . . what?), obviously, is not so simple. For a brief analysis of some of its complications, see G. Brosio and Michele Salvati, 'The Rise of Market Politics: Industrial Relations in the Seventies', *Daedalus*, April 1979.

10. 'Aspetti della Crisi Italiana: Note Introduttive', in L. Graziano and S. Tarrow, *La Crisi Italiana*.

A much more extended political commentary on the same period that we have dealt with, up to the kidnapping and murder of Aldo Moro, can be found in the latest edition of G. Mammarella, *L'Italia dalla Caduta del Fascismo ad Oggi* (Bologna: Il Mulino, 1978). Up to 1972 one can use G. Tamburrano, *Storia e Cronaca del Centro-Sinistra* (Milan: Feltrinelli, 1973), which has a similar tack to the one we have adopted. To go deeper, the collection which we have just cited is indispensable: L. Graziano and S. Tarrow, eds., *La Crisi Italiana*, 2 vols. (Turin: Einaudi, 1979). It is also useful to consult the collection edited by S. R. Graubard and F. L. Cavazza, *Il Caso Italiano*, 2 vols. (Milano: Garzanti, 1974). From these works, and from their references, one can reconstruct all the best known political-scientific and sociological interpretations of the Italian crisis.

For economic affairs, there are no up to date general works that are moderately readable by non-economists. The best known readable accounts (e.g., M. D'Antonio, *Sviluppo e Crisi del Capitalismo Italiona, 1951–1972*, Bari: De Donato, 1974; A. Graziani, *L'Economia Italiana, 1945–70*, Bologna: Il Mulino, 1972; M. Salvati, *Il Sistema Economico Italiano: Analisi di una Crisi*, Bologna: Il Mulino, 1975; V. Valli, *L'Economia e la Politica Economica Italiana, 1945–1975*, Milan: Etas Libri, 1976; G. Podbielski, *Italy: Development and Crisis in the Post-War Economy*, Oxford: Clarendon Press, 1974) all leave out the 1975–79 period. For this period it is necessary to rely on periodicals or on official reports: of these the best are the *Relazioni Annuali* of the Bank of Italy, published in May of every year. On the 'Pandolfi Document', and, more generally, on the economic policy of the last two years, one can read the interesting series of commentaries by numerous Italian economists, published between September 1978 and January 1979 in the weekly *Mondo Economico*.

Labour Unions, Industrial Action and Politics

Marino Regini*

In the last ten years, observers of the Italian scene have twice been struck by the apparently dramatic changes in labour unions' behaviour and by their consequences.

The 'hot autumn' of 1969 provided the first shock, but it was just the high point of an intense and radicalised period of industrial conflict. By strengthening union organisations, it caused the breakdown of the system of industrial relations slowly developed in the sixties, which had been based on a mixture of union weakness and managerial authoritarianism. It also gave rise to the most dramatic change in the relative strength of political actors since 1947–48: labour unions (and the PCI) became the emergent actors in Italian politics.[1]

By contrast, what has come to be known as the *svolta sindacale* ('union turning point') of 1977–78, has been interpreted as a major reversal of this trend. Commentators either disturbed by Italy's persisting high level of labour militancy or seriously concerned with the poor performance of its economy, applauded the unions' unusual willingness to moderate wage demands and to allow for more 'flexibility' in capital's use of labour as well as for cuts in public expenditure. This type of union behaviour, actually, was not totally new, as by then it had been practised for a few years. In the so-called 'EUR document' of 1978, however, the unions tried more consistently to justify it as part of a strategy to restore capital accumulation in exchange for control over investments and for participation in economic policy formation.[2]

How were such changes brought about? What precisely was their content, apart from the most glamorous and noticeable aspects? To what extent can we discern basic continuities in union behaviour behind the more visible and dramatic breaks?

To answer these questions, I shall analyse the development of the labour unions' behaviour in the context of two different, though connected, systems in which they operate: the industrial relations and the political systems. In the first, union organisations deal with such actors as the workers they represent, employers, and the State (to the extent that it 'intervenes' in industrial relations). In the second, they deal mainly with government, other State institutions, and political parties.

In Italy, the unions' action in the latter system has traditionally been viewed as more important than in the former, but this hierarchy changed during a long period in the late sixties and early seventies. Within both systems, the relationships between unions and the other actors have been patterned in

*Associate Professor of Sociology at the University of Milan. I wish to thank Peter Lange for many stimulating discussions on this subject at the Centre for European Studies, Harvard University.

different ways during different periods, stressing conflict at certain times, bargaining or co-operation at others.

I will, therefore, briefly describe the change in the unions' action in both systems through time before proposing a general interpretation. The focus will be on the last ten years, although a very short description of the fifties and sixties is offered.

1. THE UNIONS IN THE INDUSTRIAL RELATIONS SYSTEM

1.1 Industrial relations up to 1968–69

Industrial relations and unions' action show quite different characteristics in the two phases in which the 1948–1968 period is conventionally broken down: grosso modo, the fifties and the sixties. Changing labour market and political conditions to a large extent determine these differences. But union strategy is only slowly modified by them. In fact, the basic assumptions on which strategy was originally built act as a constraint upon subsequent change.

In the fifties, both the labour market and the political conditions were highly unfavourable to the workers. Due to the lay-offs which had taken place during the 'reconstruction' years, and to the labour-saving character of capital accumulation in the fifties, unemployment remained high and labour demand quite limited throughout this period. Permanent employment in manufacturing rose in the 1952–58 cycle by only 8 per cent; as to unemployment, the official (notoriously underestimated) 1959 figure was still 1,135,000, against a total employed labour force of about 20 million. The political situation was characterised by the exclusion of the communists from government (which was instead dominated by the Christian Democrats) and by the Cold War climate.

In these conditions, strike activity remained at low levels; unionisation declined slowly but sharply through this period (see Appendix), while ever fewer workers were participating in union activities. After a short period of union unity (the CGIL had been reorganised by the anti-fascist parties during the Resistance period as a unitary union, but it then split in 1948), acute division among the three labour confederations (CGIL, CISL and UIL)[3] prevented them from pursuing any common policies. None of the three confederations succeeded in building (or was willing to build) union organisation at the workplace level; union activity, and collective bargaining in particular, remained very centralised. In such a situation of the labour market and of the organisational weakness of the unions, employers could enjoy almost total freedom of action. They could fire union activists, as well as pay 'black'[4] wages where market conditions for wage drift occurred. Formal industrial relations were, therefore, practically absent at the workplace level. Employers granted a very low degree of recognition to the unions, and the unions in turn assumed a generally conflictual attitude.

This very situation made labour unions particularly dependent on support from the political parties to which they were connected (see section 2.1 below). The system of industrial relations in general was a 'centralised and predominantly political' one.[5]

At the end of the fifties, however, external conditions began to change; this forced some modifications in the unions' strategy as well. Consequent upon the high rate of economic growth, labour market conditions became more favourable throughout the sixties (except during the recession of 1964–65). Permanent employment in manufacturing in the 1958–64 cycle rose by 20 per cent, well above the rate of the previous cycle.[6] Unemployment gradually fell from the 5.2 per cent rate of 1959 to as low as 2.5 in 1965, and floated around a 3.5 rate in the following period. On the political level, the opening to the left and the series of centre-left governments created more favourable conditions for union action.

Strike activity increased significantly in this period (see Appendix). The index of volume of conflict in the whole economy rose from 3·46 (hours lost per employee) in the 1952–58 period, to 7·26 in the 1959–67 one.[7] The first big strike wave since the war swept the country in 1962, leading to substantial wage increases. The rate of unionisation showed, by contrast, very little change, signalling persistent difficulties in the relations between workers and union organisations still based outside the factory; but the previous downward trend came to an end (see Appendix). Relationships between CGIL and CISL became closer, while both unions made some (unsuccessful) attempts at building organisational structures in the workplaces.

While union organisation remained centralised, some decentralisation took place in collective bargaining: the national industry-wide agreements were still the most important, but some bargaining was allowed at the plant-level on specific issues.

This evolving situation forced the unions to make some timid attempts to gain more autonomy from the political parties. Industrial action at the factory level was given a somewhat greater role in the unions' strategy. This strategy, however, did not undergo major changes. Bargaining at the factory level was mainly concentrated on such traditional issues as piecework and especially productivity bonuses. At the industry level, it dealt only with minimum wages, working hours, and union rights. At the confederal (i.e. inter-industry) level, wage equalisation was still the main policy objective.[8]

As union activity and strategy did not undergo major changes, the unions could not match the growing discontent of large sections of the working class, especially of the emergent groups: the semi-skilled, usually immigrant, workers. From 1968 on, these 'under-represented' groups of workers were the protagonists of the biggest wave of conflicts in the last thirty years[9].

1.2 Changes in strike actvity and demands

May 1968 was, for the French, a sudden shock or hope which, however, lasted only *l'espace d'un matin*. General strikes, sit-downs and rallies were so intense and involved such a large part of the working population (beside the students), and produced so much radicalised ideology and expressive behaviour that many believed France to be on the verge of a revolution. But a few months later, both the industrial relations and the political systems in France were again working in much the same way as before 1968. The strike wave had left few signs.

In Italy, on the other hand, the strikes which took place at approximately the same time were at first less conspicuous. The 'sweeping May' which made its appearance in some key factories of the North in 1968, however, slowly developed into the 'hot autumn' of 1969 and gave rise to a period of intense conflicts with new characteristics, which was to last for a few years. Some of these characteristics receded soon after 1969, others became a permanent feature. From 1963 on, union behaviour and industrial relations actually underwent a process of re-institutionalisation; but the changes brought about by the 1968–72 cycle of conflicts were so deep as to make this process a very slow and contradictory one. At any rate, the industrial relations system of the sixties was deeply and permanently transformed.

To begin with, the volume of conflict rose from the 7·26 (hours lost per employee) rate of the 1959–67 period to a 11·55 rate in the 1968–75 period, reaching a peak of 23·0 in 1969. This increase was due to both an intensification of conflict in the traditionally stike-prone firms and industries, and a spreading of conflict to industries, firms, geographical areas, and groups of workers which had been usually less conflictual in the past.[10]

If we turn to the most striking features of conflictual activity in the 1968–72 period, we can summarise them as follows. First, a large proportion of conflicts was not initiated or fully controlled by the unions: wildcat strikes took place, agreements were rejected and a tougher attitude toward employers was often forced upon the unions by the rank and file. Second, more radical forms of struggle were adopted. Articulation of strikes over time and across space as well as go-slow were used systematically to disrupt production. Shipments were blocked and plants were occupied in many instances. Third, new demands were raised, which we can summarise as being egalitarian, and being disruptive of the traditional organisation of production. Fourth, both the forms of struggle and the demands were heavily ideologised. The creation of new ideologies to justify conflictual activity led to many 'expressive actions', that is actions not rationally directed towards a given end, but meant to reinforce the identity of the group in conflict.

While the intensification and diffusion of strikes may be accounted for by the tighter labour market and the need to break the wage restraint practised since the recession of 1964–65, the particular features these strikes took could only be a consequence of other factors. Without discussing their relative importance and the relations among them,[11] we can point to the following factors: the role of the immigrants from the South—socialised neither to factory and urban life nor to unions—in the industrial labour force; the under-representation of the interests of semi-skilled workers in general by the unions; the organisational weakness of the labour unions, which had prevented an institutionalisation of industrial relations.

Both the increase in strike activity and the new features of conflicts gave the period 1968–1972 the character of an unprecedented 'cycle of struggles', and profoundly transformed union organisation as well as industrial relations (see 1·3 below). Slowly, however, these conditions changed. While strike figures remained high, the pattern of conflict and of relations with employers in general showed signs of institutionalisation and self-restraint. Strikes became less diffuse and unpredictable; rank-and-file participation in union activity diminished; radical forms of action tended to be abandoned. Demands in pursuit of egalitarianism and control over the organisation of production formally remained the basis of unions' strategy. But wages and working conditions were subordinated to other objectives, such as an increase in employment, control over investments, industrialisation of the South.

With the so-called 'turning point' of 1978, some union leaders even went as far as to criticise the former union strategy as a whole, maintaining that labour unions should practice wage restraint and allow 'flexibility' in the use of the labour force, if the economic crisis was to be overcome.

1.3 Changes in union organisation and in collective bargaining

The period 1968–1972 was also one of growth and of decentralisation of the union organisation. A new generation of activists led the strikes, often informally grouping in committees either to help the unions or to take their place. They became available as the first potential network of union representatives at the plant level. To exploit this potential, the unions by and large chose to shift some power to these rank-and-file activists; they also created such networks where none existed, and later institutionalised them.

Building the organisation at the shop and plant level carried with it a decentralisation of control over union activities in general, and of collective bargaining in particular. This process of decentralisation was largely an informal one. Union assemblies in the workplace were held frequently. This *assemblearismo* meant that the most militant workers could actually use the assemblies to influence the formation of union policies, and then often join the official union representatives in collective bargaining. For the first time, plants and shops became the main centres around which union activity and bargaining were built. Plant-level agreements in industry rose from 3,870 in 1968 to an estimated figure of 7,567 in 1971.[12] National industry-level contracts retained their importance both as occasions of generalised conflict and as the means of involving the smaller and weaker firms in union activity. But the distinctive feature of this period lies in the almost continuous industrial action at the plant level; in fact, this came to be known as a phase of 'permanent conflictuality' precisely because no overall central co-ordination seemed to exist.

At the same time that this decentralisation was taking place, however, the labour confederations sought to regain the initiative by launching the 'strategy of social reforms', which could be pursued only at a centralised level and by stressing the priority of political over industrial action (see section 2·2 below).

Even after 1972, decentralisation continued: the number of shop delegates elected by the workers, in fact, kept growing; so did the number of factory councils formed by such delegates (see table below).

Year	Number of existing factory councils	Number of elected delegates
1972	8,101	82,923
1973	9,813	97,161
1974	16,000	150,000
1978	32,000	210,000

Sources: *Quaderni di Rassegna sindacale*, n. 51 and *La Repubblica*, November 28, 1978.

While these data show the spread of such decentralised structures to small firms, less unionised industries, and less industrialised areas of the country, a more general process of re-centralisation of union power and bargaining activities was however taking place.

Collective bargaining was re-centralised even at the plant level. Only the formal power of ratification of decisions, usually taken elsewhere, has been left to assemblies, shop delegates, and factory councils. The very small 'executive body' (*Esecutivo*) of the factory council is instead involved in the bargaining process. Most of the time, even the executive does not have the power to make decisions alone. In any important negotiation taking place in firms of some size and importance, other union structures are likely to join in: either one coordinating firms in the same industry or corporation, or the union organisation at the 'province' level, or the national industrial union. In any case, the decision-making mechanisms are shifted outside the factory. Also, the 'strategy of demands' which may be addressed to the employers in plant-level bargaining is increasingly set at the centre, i.e. by the national industrial unions.

The most important part of collective bargaining, however, no longer occurs at the plant level. As was said above, the labour confederations at first tried to regain the initiative by launching the 'strategy of social reforms'. Although this strategy basically failed, the confederations were nonetheless able to centralise an increasingly larger part of union activity subsequently. State economic policy (pursuing such objectives as more employment, investments, industrialisation of the South) became the main target of union action (see section 2·2 below); ability to influence them has been consistently given higher priority than plant-level bargaining since the 'turning point' of 1978. Moreover, even on more traditional issues of plant and industry-level bargaining, such as wages and job security, the most important agreement (providing for higher cost-of-living compensation and better security against lay-offs) was reached by the labour confederations with the employers' association in 1974–75.

Other aspects of union activity have been re-centralised in much the same way as collective bargaining. The delegates elected by all workers have, by and large, lost power to the union apparatus, which has kept growing (CGIL officers were estimated to be about 50,000—6,500 full-time among them—in 1978). Also, the process of unification among the three confederations, which proceeded extensively at the local and industry level, has been blocked more recently by the priority given to action by the confederations, and by the greater difficulties to overcoming the divisions amongst them.

1.4 *An interpretation of the change of union behaviour in industrial relations*

In the last decade, as we have seen, union action in the industrial relations system has gone through different phases.

To summarise, in the years from 1969 to 1971–72, the unions fostered a 'diffused' rank-and-file mobilisation; they informally decentralised organisational power and supported a major and rapid turnover of rank-and-file leaders and union activists; finally, they tried to interpret and push demands coming from the core industrial workers (the semi-skilled), with little effort to mediate them with the ones from other groups of workers.

Starting from 1971–72 (sometimes later, depending on the firms or industries), however, the unions tried to confine strike activity and rank-and-file mobilisation to only limited periods, when they were strictly necessary; they re-centralised organisational power by giving priority to detailed bargaining and to the work of committees, in which technical expertise is more important; they tried to co-ordinate demands, by mediating the more radical and innovative ones of the 1968–72 period with more traditional demands coming from different groups of workers (e.g., white collars, skilled workers, etc.) or from union officers.

In the last four years or so, the unions have become more involved in the management of the industrial system, and their emphasis is on co-operation with government to solve problems related to the economic crisis, as well as on control over the solutions given to these problems (most important among them is the control over the type and location of investments as a solution to the problem of creating new employment). Characteristic of this period is the practice of self-restraint in wage and other demands impinging on productivity, as a trade-off for more control over the ways in which economic policies are formed.

Why has union action changed so dramatically in the course of the last ten years? An interpretation of these changes must focus on the type of resources that the unions have and the constraints they face in pursuing actions suited to their interests.[13]

In 1969–71, the unions, as institutions, were very weak and confronted with rank-and-file unrest. Their main objectives in that period were to regain the loyalty of the rank-and-file and win the competition with unofficial radical leaders, to force the employers fully to grant them recognition as representatives of the workers and to root union organisation in the workplaces. To pursue these objectives, unions had to behave in the ways described above (supporting mobilisation was the main resource they could use to that end). They could not, instead, rely on such other resources as employers' and State recognition or organisational strength, as these were available only to a very limited degree.

As a consequence of their own action, however, all objectives were basically achieved. After 1971–72 there was, therefore, no longer any point for the unions to keep behaving as in the former period. They could rely on new resources such as full recognition, organisational resources, and control over the rank-and-file. Their action, therefore, could change. Not only were their resources different, but the constraints upon their action increased. New problems faced them. Economic crisis, shrinking employment, and inflation were a potential threat to their members, although their market power was not decisively affected. The lack of new investments, growing youth unemployment and labour market segmentation were instead a threat to potential or non-organised workers: by reducing the size of the unions' potential membership, they were undermining the unions' political power.

After 1975, the unions increasingly responded to these problems by practising forms of self-restraint, which then were fully elaborated in 1978.

What were the decisive factors behind this choice? One line of interpretation focuses on the persisting ties of the CGIL to the PCI; self-restraint in demands would be related to the gradual entrance of the PCI into the government coalition, which requires it (and the unions) to be concerned with the problems of capital accumulation and economic efficiency. This interpretation, how-ever, does not explain why similar trends develop in other countries as well. More important, it does not explain why the 'turning point' of 1978 was, in the end, also backed by CISL and UIL (even though with many differences and contrasts), which do not have ties with the PCI.

A second type of interpretation focuses instead on the aggravation of the economic problems discussed above. To confront these problems, the unions think it is in their interest to moderate their demands in order to allow an expansion of employment to take place; to this end, capital accumulation must be supported while the unions must be able to control the investment process. Why, however, should this policy be in their interest, as it compresses the wages of its own rank-and-file, which is not instead directly threatened by unemployment for the time being (in fact, actually damaged are only the unemployed, youth and unorganised workers)? The answer probably lies in the recent exceptional expansion of the secondary labour market, which is not organised by the unions. This expansion is not actually threatening the market power of workers in the primary sector (who are effectively protected by unions and by legislation). It does, however, threaten the political power of the unions, which is based on the proportion of the active population they can organise, on their ability to speak as representatives of more general interests (or, in other words, to act tacitly on behalf of other groups besides their members), on the mobilising power of their ideology as a class-based union. This makes it inconvenient for them to adopt a business unionism type of strategy, and largely explains the reasons and the limits of their willing-ness to practise moderation in industrial relations.

2.0 THE UNIONS IN THE POLITICAL SYSTEM

Labour unions in Italy have traditionally attached the greatest importance to their role in the political system. Since they were rebuilt by the parties of the anti-fascist coalition in 1944, their relation with them has always been very close.[14] The strategy of the majority union (the CGIL), moreover, has traditionally put an emphasis on relations with the State rather than with employers alone[15] (see section 3 below).

2.1 Unions and the political system until 1968–69

The close relationship between the unions and the parties was demonstrated and reinforced by the splits of 1948 and 1949, which eventually led to the formation of CISL and UIL in opposition to the formerly unitary CGIL (see note 3). These splits, in fact, took place over political issues and were the result of the divisions amongst the parties of the anti-fascist coalition.

In the fifties, the ties of the unions to different political parties were further reinforced by their very weakness in the labour market and by their lack of organisation in the workplaces. CISL and UIL were minority organisations, with little support especially from the core working class (the industrial blue collars). Their only advantage over the CGIL—i.e., their ability to secure some recognition by employers—stemmed not so much from their actual behaviour as yellow unions, but from the political guarantee they could offer to employers. The strategy of the majority labour confederation—the CGIL—on the other hand, was shaped by its organisational weakness and isolation. It could not rely on resources such as recognition by employers and by the State, ability to mobilise and to control a large portion of the potential members, organisational strength. It tried, therefore, to maximise its ties with the PCI (and the PSI), from which it drew militants, funds, ideology and political support. To that end, the CGIL had to emphasise the value of political action over economic action for wages. The rank-and-file was, therefore, called to strike or to co-operate mainly on political grounds.

Toward the end of the fifties the situation changed slightly. The CGIL criticised its own failure fully to meet workers' demands. The CISL (and especially its metalworkers' organisation—the FIM), on the other hand, turned to a more co-operative behaviour with CGIL, therefore loosening its ties with the Christian Democratic Party. By and large, however, the position of dependence of both major unions on the political parties was not challenged until the late sixties.

If we now turn to the relation between the unions and the State in the fifties, we may call it one of labour exclusion from the social bloc which was to control economic development. In fact, the unions' weakness permitted a strategy of labour isolation to be undertaken. Economic development could be based on low wages and high labour supply and flexibility, rather than on winning support from the working class; accordingly, the process of the formation and the implementation of economic policies was such as to exclude labour from any influence. It was much easier for the ruling class to use job insecurity and an anti-union repression as means to oppose union demands, than to pursue paths leading to some form of social contract. Also, after the split in the Resistance coalition (1947) and the unions (1948, 1949), the CGIL could no longer be involved in State policies because of its links with the PCI, its character as a class-based union, its refusal of relationships which might resemble the corporatist structures under fascism. The CISL, on the other hand, was politically 'safe' and willing to participate in public consultative bodies; but it could not claim to represent a large portion of the industrial working-class in such a design. As a result of these trends, union involvement in the State remained low throughout the fifties, as did the degree of State regulation and of institutionalisation of industrial relations.

In the early sixties, however, we have seen that both the labour market and the political conditions previously making the unions weak began to change. As a consequence, governments tried to involve the labour unions in the labour market and in economic policies.[16] In 1961, tri-partite meetings were convened to deal with the problems of employment, and with various economic policy issues. In the following years, a consultative tri-partite body, the 'national committee for economic planning' (Comissione Nazionale per la Programmazione), was established to discuss the five-year plan. The centre-left governments tried, in this way, to secure labour participation in the first attempts at planning. The CGIL took an unprejudiced attitude toward planning policy; the PCI was generally opposed.

But this attempt at involving the unions in the State proved short-lived. The results of consultations were never binding on the government. Recession, rather than planning, was the instrument eventually chosen by the government to respond to the threat posed by labour's increasing demands.

2.2 *Changes in the relations between unions and the State*

From 1969 onwards, the unions sought to take advantage of their new strength by addressing demands directly to the government. There was almost complete agreement within the unions on the need to channel working-class mobilisation towards social objectives beyond the workplace. Various factors account for such a decision: the great increase in union power at a time when the mobilising and innovating capacities of the parties were in severe doubt; the need to ensure that the living conditions of workers' families did not worsen, thus cancelling out the benefits won in factory-level bargaining; and the confederations' desire to react to centrifugal and divisive tendencies in the movement, to aggregate and co-ordinate various types of demands, and bring them together at the national level. From 1969 to 1971, the unions therefore pressed the government for reforms in pensions, housing, health services, education, transport, and the taxation system. These demands were backed up by general strikes articulated on a regional basis, by meetings with the political parties, and, particularly, by frequent meetings with the government. But the results were very disappointing, amounting merely to a change in the pension system, a general, and not particularly progressive, new law on housing, and certain promises about the health service. Although it was never in fact officially abandoned, by the middle of 1971 the 'struggle for reforms' could no longer generate rank-and-file support, and ended in failure as far as the unions were concerned. This failure was in marked contrast with the striking successes obtained during the same period in plant-level industrial disputes.

As early as 1971, but much more so in 1974–5, the economic crisis and the high rates of inflation gave questions of economic policy priority over issues of reform. In 1971, the three confederations launched a campaign to defend employment levels and to develop the South; at the same time they began to insist upon the need for what they called 'a new model of development'. The following year, facing large rises in the cost of living, they called on the government to hold down charges for major public services, and to control prices. But, given the worsening political situation, and the paralysing crisis of trade union unity, these demands—like those for reforms— met with no real success.

From late 1972 to early 1974, during the partial economic recovery, the major industrial unions (especially in the metal-working sector) regained the initiative.

By 1975, however, the basic problem of the government's economic policy returned to the centre of the stage, and the confederations once again came to play the major role. They sought economic and social policies through direct bargaining with the government. Political demands were directed to it in much the same way as economic demands are to companies. As to the government, while forced formally to negotiate with the unions, it tried to resist their demands on a day-to-day basis as in any bargaining relationship, rather than to secure their co-operation in some longer-term policy. We can, therefore, say that in the 1969–75 period a 'conflict-negotiation' pattern of relationships prevailed.

This pattern applied to economic policy formation. In those same years, however, the unions became involved in policy implementation in a 'creeping' way. Union representatives entered more and more public agencies designed to implement economic and social policies. The most important example, since 1970, is their majority participation in the *Istituto Nazionale per la Previdenza Sociale* (INPS), the national public agency which administers pensions and unemployment insurance. Also, union representatives have been co-opted into hundreds of national and local committees through which the public administration intervenes in the economy. In the public sector (such as railways, postal service, etc.) they join public managers on the boards of directors, with mixed tasks of personnel administration and control over expenditure.

In the last five years or so, the unions have increasingly been involved in the process of policy-formation as well. On the one hand, primarily as a consequence of the deep economic crisis, they have sharply moved from a conflict-negotiation strategy to a co-operative attitude, although in the face of strong internal opposition and with some changes of line. This new co-operative approach was linked to the unions' 'self-criticism', spelled out in the 'EUR document' voted in February 1978 by the delegates of the three confederations, and in many interviews given by prominent labour leaders to newspapers. It confirms and rationalises the existing co-operative attitudes in labour market and wage restraint policies. It also advocates participation in the formulation of an economic plan.

The government, on the other hand, has systematically consulted the unions—or even granted them privileged access—in the process of formation of bills on such important issues as subsidies to firms, industrial restructuration, youth employment, etc.[17] Also, from time to time (and most recently in the five-year plan presented in 1978) it proposes to establish tri-partite bodies which are to play an advisory role on economic policy and planning. However, the unions have so far rejected tri-partite institutions and asked for separate consultation of labour and employers by the government instead.

A new pattern of relations between unions and the State is, therefore, emerging. The degree of co-operation in shaping and implementing economic policy has certainly increased sharply. The institutionalisation of these relationships is, however, on the whole rather low. More precisely, as has been shown above, institutionalisation is quite high in policy implementation, but very low in respect to the process of policy formation. Union representatives have been co-opted in public agencies and boards of directors; but consultation in the formulation of policies has remained informal, though constant.

2.3. *An interpretation of the change of the unions' role in the political system*

As we have seen, relations between the unions and the State in post-war Italy have gone through different patterns in different periods: a pattern of labour isolation in the fifties; a short-lived neo-corporatist attempt followed by a return to labour exclusion in the early sixties; a conflict-bargaining pattern in the late sixties and early seventies; finally, in the last five years or s o, a new type of relationship which is based on union co-operation in the formation of economic and social policies, and on union participation in public agencies designed to implement them. In this way, the labour unions have won a privileged status, as compared to other interest groups, in access to government policy. While many interest groups can exert veto powers against specific decisions, the government and the political parties increasingly try to co-ordinate general economic policies with the 'producers' groups' (employers and unions) only. In fact, these groups claim to represent general interests, by aggregating smaller sectional interests into wider strategies.

What factors have pushed the unions in this direction, and what constraints do they face?

The interests leading the Italian labour unions to give priority to their co-operative relations with the State over collective bargaining with companies are bound to the following factors:

(a) Their awareness that private companies in Italy (even the largest ones) tend to become increasingly dependent on political decisions. For the unions, therefore, preserving the power and recognition won in plant-level industrial relations is no longer sufficient. Thus, union leaders develop an interest in increasing the degree of their political recognition and influence.

(b) The economic crisis and greater political instability, which negatively affect the wage strategy of unions. For them to pursue higher wages and better working conditions with no concern for the economic and political consequences of their action, is becoming more difficult (see section 1.4 above). A strategy of self-restraint, however, requires the unions to have an ability to offer long-term goals (such as influence on economic and social policies) to their rank-and-file, in exchange for their lower ability to deliver immediate and visible benefits.

(c) Finally, the need to appear as representatives of general class interests (namely of the marginal workers, the unemployed and surplus labour as well as of the regularly employed workers), which is crucial for the Italian labour unions. This need stems not only from the traditions and the ideology of a class union, but from an economic dualism and a segmentation of the labour market which, as we discussed in section 1.4 above, threatens the unions' political power. The unions, therefore, have a stake in representing the interests of these social groups as well and in winning their consent. To this end, the government becomes the natural counterpart, even though demands to protect marginal workers and to invest in order to create more jobs have been directed to private companies as well.

All these factors, therefore, foster unions' willingness to co-operate with the State. But many constraints work against it. The most commonly noticed limitation is the dissatisfaction likely to develop when workers are offered such long-term and hard-to-assess benefits as the ones stemming from influence over economic policy, as a substitute for immediate and certain gains. In Italy, strains arising inside the union organisation and in its relations with the rank-and-file have frequently emerged in recent years. In the public sector especially, wildcat strikes have increased, as has the strength of small 'autonomous' unions representing sectional interests and demands. This has put limits on the confederations' ability to deliver a policy of wage restraint as something to exchange in relations with government. Also, it has refuelled the differences amongst the three confederations, and between them and the industrial unions, on general union policy. A recent example has been the conflict on the reduction of work time as a legitimate union demand.

Rank-and-file opposition to policies of wage self-restraint or to the slender results of political action carried on by the confederations, can frequently express itself through the institutions of plant-level bargaining and of workers' councils. An outcome of the mass mobilisation of the 1968–1972 period, these institutions retain a high degree of legitimacy and autonomy. They act, therefore, as a constraint on attempts to shift all union power to the confederations and to subordinate industrial action to a purely political strategy.

Even more delicate for the unions in Italy is the problem of effectively protecting the interests of marginal workers as well as of part of the surplus labour force (such as employees of crisis-ridden firms subsidised by the State, unemployed, 'superfluous' public employees, pensioners, etc.). I argued above that the union interest in exercising general class representation is one of the reasons forcing them to give priority to the relations with the State over those with companies. However, this very interest is at the same time a constraint on greater co-operation in shaping and implementing a consistent economic policy. For, while it is possible for the unions to speak against 'Welfare Statism' (or even against freezing employment in crisis-ridden firms), it is then difficult for them actually to help dismantle the network of subsidies and of surplus jobs, as an effective economic policy would sometimes require. In fact, the Italian unions have shown contradictory attitudes in relation to problems such as reducing the number of disability pensions, widely used as mere subsidies in the poorer areas of the country. The public employees' unions, while formally sticking to the confederations' strategy of reforming and making public administration efficient, have in fact often helped the expansion of 'superfluous' jobs. As to industrial unions, they have sometimes supported poorly-grounded employers' claims of firm crisis, in order to get public subsidies (*Cassa integrazione straordinaria*).

3.0 UNIONS' STRATEGIES, AND THEIR BEHAVIOUR IN THE SEVENTIES

The following chart summarises the overall direction of union behaviour in the last ten years. The first horizontal line shows the way in which union action and structure have developed in the late sixties and early seventies. Taking advantage of a favourable labour market, the unions were able to support the mobilisation and the demands of the core industrial workers. In doing so, they decentralised their action and their structure, and gave priority

E

CHART 1

PATTERNS OF UNION BEHAVIOUR IN THE SEVENTIES

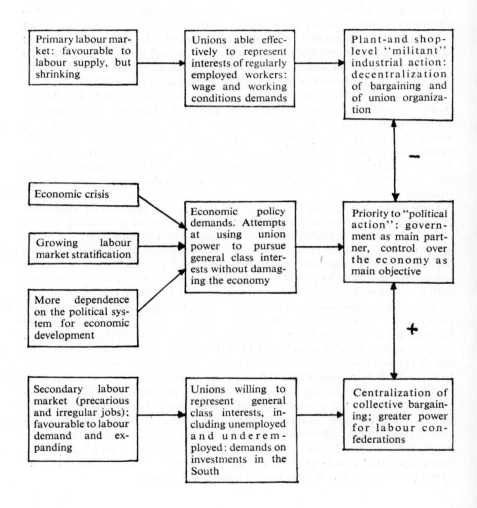

+ means mutual reinforcement
— means mutual constraint

to their power in the work-place over political action. This process has never been fully reversed, as some of its causes (i.e. a primary labour market favourable to labour supply, and a high level of rank-and-file mobilisation) persist. Rather, it has recently been paralleled and then overcome by new developments, which we may label as re-centralisation and re-politicisation of union action (see second and third horizontal line). The causes of this evolution are many, as the chart shows.

Economic or political factors, however, never directly determine organisational behaviour. They are mediated by a strategy which the organisation provides itself with, and which often survives the needs that gave rise to it.

Is there any long-lasting strategy of the Italian unions which may have determined their response to new problems facing their action? How can it be analytically discussed?

Looking at a longer period of time than the last ten years, one is struck by the substantial continuity in the long-term objectives pursued by the unions. These may be characterised as follows:

(a) A central and constant objective in union strategy is what may be referred to as *public/social control of the economy*. The capitalist economy is never called into question as such. An attempt is continuously made, however, to subject major aspects of it (depending on the circumstances, management prerogatives, patterns of income distribution, or economic policy) to a political control somewhat shared by public institutions and by 'workers' democratic organisations', namely the unions. Well-known policies (or slogans) pursued by unions such as planning in the late forties and in the sixties, a 'new model of development' in the early seventies, or industrial restructuration in more recent years, may all be seen as aspects of that more general objective. In fact, they all signify an attempt at political control, at first of the process of income allocation, then of income distribution and finally of income formation.

In the particular conditions of labour market (later of political as well) weakness in which union strategy was shaped, and through the filter of the traditional ideology and of the knowledge available, this choice perhaps appeared to be one allowing for the greatest distribution of benefits to members in the long run (or for a major modification of the distribution system) compatible with the degree of unions' organisational power. At the same time, it was seen as a condition to guarantee economic development and expansion of 'productive employment', which a weak and backward capitalist class was not (in unions' opinion) willing or able to secure.

Two other objectives are strictly related to the first crucial one (as they are both a cause and a consequence of it).

(b) The objective of *influence on the political system*, as a priority over maximisation of gains which can be won in collective bargaining, stems directly from the former. Except during the so-called 'pan-syndicalist' period of 1968–1972, ability to force the State and the political parties to issue favourable policies or to recognise and support the unions and their demands, has been traditionally considered more important than winning greater benefits for the members from employers. The unions have, therefore, usually underexploited their market power in order to increase their political power.[18]

(c) The objective of gaining or maintaining general *class representation* besides representing their own members, is also related to the first objective. The CGIL, at least, has constantly aimed (and claimed) to be able to represent effectively the interests of the working class as a whole (and more general interests as well), while the CISL is usually closer to the demands of the regularly employed and better-off industrial workers. In fact, a strategy of control over the economy by the unions requires them to be able to speak as representatives of wider interests than those of just their members. General class representation often implies centralisation of the union organisation. This trend is consistently found in the unions' strategy as well, except in the 1968–1972 period, when they had to shift more power to rank-and-file activists in order to root union organisation in the plants and shops.

In a sense, then, the unions' behaviour in the last few years must not be seen as a major departure from their traditions. Certainly, it has been adjusted to the differing conditions in which the industrial relations and the political systems had to work. For all its dramatic break with the late sixties and early seventies, however, recent union behaviour seems well rooted in their traditional strategic goals.

APPENDIX

Strike activity and unionisation in Italy, 1949–76

Years	Index of strike volume	Rate of unionisation		
		CGIL	CISL	CGIL+CISL
1949	13·1			
1950	6·0			
1951	3·5	43·4		
1952	2·7	41·4		
1953	4·4	38·1		
1954	3·9	38·5		
1955	4·1	38·1		
1956	3·0	28·1		
1957	3·3	27·5		
1958	2·9	22·6		
1959	6·3	22·4		
1960	3·9	21·5		
1961	6·4	20·5	11·4	31·9
1962	14·4	20·6	11·4	32·0
1963	7·1	20·4	11·7	32·1
1964	8·1	21·0	11·8	32·8
1965	4·5	20·2	11·7	31·9
1966	9·3	19·7	11·9	31·6
1967	5·4	19·0	11·9	31·0
1968	5·8	19·2	12·6	31·8
1969	23·0	20·0	12·5	32·5
1970	11·0	22·1	13·6	35·7
1971	7·7	23·4	14·7	38·1
1972	10·1	23·9	16·2	40·1
1973	12·0	25·2	16·2	41·5
1974	9·8	28·1	18·1	46·2
1975	13·0	29·6	18·8	48·4
1976	9·4			

Notes: The 'index of strike volume' is given by the number of working hours lost per employee (wage or salary earner), in all sectors of the economy.

The 'rate of unionization' shows the unionized workers as a percentage of all employees (wage or salary earners), in all sectors of the economy. Reliable data on workers organized by UIL and by other smaller unions are not available.

The official figures on employees, over which the index and the rate are built, are notoriously underestimated, as they include only regularly employed workers.

Sources: M. Benetti, M. Regini, *op. cit.*, p. 69.

I. Regalia, M. Regini, E. Reyneri, *Conflitti in Europa, cit.*, p. 71. ISTAT *Annuario di statistiche del lavoro*, Roma, 1977.

NOTES

1. On this period, a quite considerable literature is now available. The most developed interpretations are to be found in A. Pizzorno *et al., Lotte operaie e sindacato: il ciclo 1968-1972 in Italia*, Bologna, 1978, vol. VI. The research evidence on which these interpretations are based is discussed in the first five volumes of the same series.
2. Satisfactory and comprehensive analyses of this most recent period are still lacking. See the collection of unions' and PCI's documents and statements in S. Bevacqua, G. Turani, *La svolta del '78*, Milano, 1978. On union co-operation in economic policy, see M. Regini, *Changing Relations Between Labour and the State in Italy. Toward a Neo-Corporatist System?* in: G. Lehmbruch, P. Schmitter (eds.), *Corporatist Policy-Formation in Comparative Perspective*, London and Beverly Hills, (forthcoming).
3. *The Confederazione Generale Italiana dei Lavoratori* (CGIL), which remained the majority confederation, is predominantly communist, but includes socialists as well as independents. The second largest is the Catholic *Confederazione Italiana Sindacati Lavoratori* (CISL). The *Unione Italiana del Lavoro* (UIL) includes socialists, social-democrats, and republicans.
4. In the Italian union jargon, 'black' wage or labour means hidden, controlled neither by the unions nor by laws.
5. See A. Pizzorno, 'I sindacati nel sistema politico italiano: aspetti storici', *Rivista trimestrale di diritto pubblico* 1971, n. 4. This article is the best general account of the differences between the fifties and the sixties.
6. See M. Salvati, *Sviluppo economico, domanda di lavoro, e struttura dell' occupazione*, Bologna 1976, pp. 35 and 46.
7. See M. Benetti, M. Regini, *Confronti temporali e speziali sui conflitti di lavoro* in: P. Alessandrini (ed.), *Conflittualita e aspetti normativi del lavoro*, Bologna, 1978, p. 48.
8. See my account of demands and bargaining in that period in: I Regalia, M. Regini, E. Reyneri, *Conflitti di lavoro e relazioni industriali in Italia, 1986-75*, in: C. Crouch, A. Pizzorno (eds.), *Conflitti in Europa*, Milano, 1977, pp. 25-27.
9. See A. Pizzorno *et al., op. cit.* (especially the essays by Pizzorno and by Reyneri).

The concept of 'under-representation' used here (and in section 1.2) needs some explanation. Interests and demands of semi-skilled workers (as of any other group) can, theoretically, be satisfied to a degree corresponding to their market and organizational power. This power was increasing in the sixties, due to a tighter labour market and to the discovery of their central location in the organization of production (and therefore of their ability to disrupt it). Their representatives in the industrial relations system (i.e. labour unions), however, were under-exploiting this power, by signing agreements in which the specific interests of the semi-skilled were not satisfied, or by not even addressing demands related to these interests. The unions (especially the CGIL) did so partly as a consequence of their own organizational weakness, partly because their members were drawn mostly from other groups of workers; but the most important reason was that they were pursuing long-term goals which required moderation of the workers' short-term demands (see A. Pizzorno, 'Political Exchange and Collective Identity in Industrial Conflict', in: C. Crouch, A. Pizzorno (eds.), *The Resurgence of Class Conflict in Western Europe Since 1968*, vol. 2, London and New York, 1978, pp. 277-298). For these reasons, we can speak of an 'under-representation' of semi-skilled usually immigrant) workers.

10. The extension of conflict in industry—from the more to the less unionized groups of the working class (such as white collar and female workers), from big to small factories, from northern Italy to the centre and south—was due mainly to the strategy of the trade unions, which tried to use the strength they had in certain factories or industries in order to extend their power and organisation to the weakest. The diffusion of conflict in the tertiary sector, on the other hand, took place largely in imitation of what was happening in industry. Tertiary sector conflict was not mainly led by the labour unions; more often it was a spontaneous attempt by the workers to keep up with what had been obtained in industry, often against the will of the central trade unions. This was especially true for the public service employees, whose higher propensity to strike accounts for most of the increased conflict recently shown in the whole of the tertiary sector. See I. Regalia, M. Regini, E. Reyneri, 'Labour Conflicts and Industrial Relations in Italy', in: C. Crouch, A. Pizzorno (eds.), *op. cit.*, vol. 1, pp. 101–158.

11. For such a discussion, see A. Pizzorno *et al.*, *op. cit.*

12. See *La contrattazione integrativa aziendale e di gruppo nel 1971*, Roma, 1972, pp. 6–8.

13. See M. Regini, 'Come e perche cambiano la logica dell' organizzazione sindacale e i comportamenti della base', in: A. Pizzorno *et al.*, *op. cit.*, pp. 109–175.

14. Amongst the literature in English on union-parties relations in Italy, see: P. Weitz, 'Labour and Politics in a Divided Movement: The Italian Case', *Industrial and Labor Relations Review*, vol. 28 n. 2, January 1975; P. Weitz, 'The CGIL and the PCI: From Subordination to Independent Political Force', in D. Blackmer and S. Tarrow (eds.), *Communism in Italy and France*, Princeton, N.J., 1975; A. F. Greco, 'Union-Party Relations and Macroeconomic Policy: The Changing Posture of the CISL', *European Studies Newsletter*, vol. VII n. 4, March 1978; P. Farneti, 'The Troubled Partnership: Trade Unions and Working-Class Parties in Italy, 1948–78', *Government and Opposition*, vol. 13 n. 4, Autumn 1978.

15. On the relationship between Italian unions and the State in Italy see, in English: M. Regini, *Changing Relationships. . . ., cit.*; and P. Lange, 'Unions, Parties, the State and Liberal Corporatism: Some Reflections Growing out of the Italian Experience', paper given at the Conference of Europeanists, Washington, 1979.

16. See P. Ranci, 'La legge sulla riconversione come strumento di politica industriale', *Economia e politica industriale,* 1978, n. 20, 23.

17. See my *Politics of Labor Market Policy: Unions and the Labor Market*, paper given at the Conference of Europeanists, Washington, 1979.

18. See A. Pizzorno, *Political Exchange. . . ., cit.*

Organised Business and Italian Politics: Confindustria and the Christian Democrats in the Postwar Period

Alberto Martinelli*

I. THE PROBLEM

Italy's post-World War II economic development and the current international economic crisis have profoundly changed the structure of Italian social classes and status groups and the relationships of power amongst the political actors representing their interests. In particular, the Italian bourgeoisie has witnessed a decline of its power which can be traced both to the growing power of the labour unions and to growing State intervention and to party management of the economy. The aim of this essay[1] is to reconstruct this process of change. I shall focus on the relationship between Confindustria, the main political organisation representing business interests and ideology, and the Christian Democratic Party (DC) which has governed Italy since the end of the war. The relationship is a typical one between a dominant economic association and a government party. It has, however, had peculiar features in Italy, due both to the relative weakness and cultural backwardness of the Italian bourgeoisie and to the mixed character—conservative and populist—of the DC. More than in other industrialised countries, the relationship has often been triangular—business, government and labour—but in this paper the strategies of the labour unions and leftist parties will be taken into account only in so far as they directly affect the business-government relationship.

At the centre of the study are the strategy and structure of Confindustria, more specifically, the definition of the functions performed and goals aimed for by the association, the conflict and mediation amongst the interests of the major factions of the industrial bourgeoisie, the evolution of organisational patterns and the development of relationships with the government party. In addition, I shall examine the DC's policy toward organised business, its role of political representation, its mode of mediation and social control amongst different components of the dominant social bloc, and its strategy for strengthening the party's political power.

Besides the practical function of providing legal and technical services to its members, business associations, viewed as political actors, perform three major functions. The degree to which these functions are performed—or, put differently, these goals attained—is an indicator of the associations' efficacy and power in society; but, as will be indicated, these goals can rarely be maximised simultaneously. The three sets of functions are: (1) the establishment of a unified strategy toward the labour movement which is the employers'

---

*Professor of Sociology, University of Milan.

institutional counterpart; (2) the management of the relationships with government, the other major components of the dominant social bloc and the political coalition in power; (3) the fostering of business class cohesion and the management of internal conflicts and tensions, a function instrumental to the other two. Effective performance of these functions is pursued through an efficient organisation—which allows timely decisions and the channeling of members' demands to the top—and an articulated ideology—which legitimises the entrepreneurial role in the firm and in society and enhances the class consciousness of employers.

The manner and extent to which these functions are performed is influenced by a variety of factors, both structural (for example, the timing and sequence of the economic development process, the structure of the labour market, the organisation of work), and institutional (for instance, the strategy of the major political actors). These factors are linked by a complex web of inter-relations, only the most pertinent of which can be treated here. In order to assess the relative impact of these factors, I shall examine the elements of the business class and the major contradictions among them, the power of those elements to influence Confindustria's ideology, organisation and strategy in the light of the business associations' attempts to promote its own interests *qua* organisation, the network of linkages between Confindustria and Christian Democracy and between business elements and DC factions, and the role of the Christian Democrat-led governments in fostering business interests, in mediating among the components of the dominant social bloc and in controlling the opposition forces, all in the context of the DC's attempts to enhance its own power as a party.

Thus, the central theoretical issue to be addressed is the complex relationship amongst the system of interests rooted in the social relations of production, the social coalitions of classes and groups, the forms of political representation and government decision (see Figure 1). I shall examine this issue through an analysis of organised business-government-party relationships in postwar Italy and specifically in the last twenty years.

II. A WEAK BOURGEOISIE?

The starting point of my discussion is the well-known thesis of the relative weakness of the Italian bourgeoisie and of its failure to bring about a mature industrial society and to exert cultural hegemony. The roots of this relative weakness and backwardness have been traced to the dynamics of the process of industrialisation and to the lack of a completed bourgeois revolution in Italy. The Italian bourgeoisie grew in a market already dominated by other industrial powers and could not consolidate itself into an hegemonic class.[2] After the industrial take-off in the last decades of the nineteenth century and the first decade of the twentieth, Italian entrepreneurs relied heavily on an alliance with strong pre-industrial estates and asked for the protection of the State. This situation did not foster the growth of entrepreneurial skills in the business class which—with some notable exceptions—has generally been more willing to adapt foreign innovations than to introduce technological and organisational change. Traditional patterns of family and community life

FIGURE 1

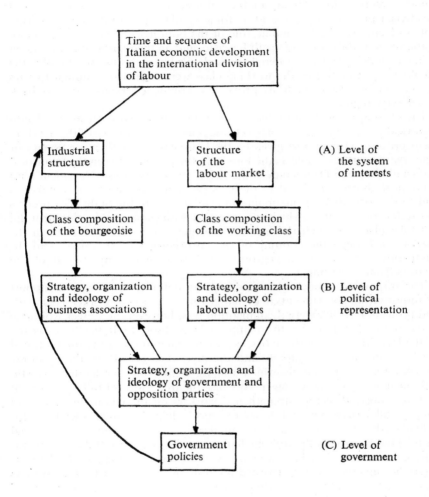

slowed down the modernisation process and have been only painfully adapted to the capitalist social relations, contrary to what happened in other late-comer countries like Japan. In the cultural realm, both Liberalism and Positivism provided men and ideas for a secular and cosmopolitan culture able to legitimise the hegemonic role of the bourgeoisie, but in their demo-cratic versions they collapsed with Fascism, and, in their authoritarian version —like Gentile's idealism—offered an ideological base to Fascism. Finally, the ideology and practice of the working class were not strong enough to gain power, but strong enough to provoke a frightened bourgeoisie to back reactionary regimes.

I tend to agree with this interpretation, but think that it must be put into historical perspective, since it neglects the timing and sequence of the develop-ment process. The support given by the bourgeoisie to either reactionary or conservative parties—such as the Fascist in the period between the two world wars and Christian Democracy in the 1950s—was no historical 'accident', but a political choice functional to the process of intense capital accumulation and to the formation of oligopolies in symbiosis with the State. The process of capital concentration which goes together with economic development did not take place so much through the growing power of major firms in the market as through the granting of special privileges by the State; and the competition amongst business groups was first of all a competition to obtain favours from government.

The traditional 'model' of business giving political and financial support to authoritarian governments in exchange for repression of worker's demands and protection from external competition was, however, no longer workable at the moment of transition to a mature industrial society. In the 'boom years' of the late fifties and early sixties, economic integration in the international market proceeded very rapidly and the diversified growth of the economy fostered the contradictions which usually stem from accelerated growth. Labour unions became stronger—because the trend toward full employment in core industrial sectors strengthened workers on the labour market—and sought full citizenship and basic reforms, while dominant social groups defended the status quo and their privileges. Thus, the political and social costs of the government party's mediation rapidly increased. Italian organised business was very slow in becoming aware of the changing social relations; the rather myopic defence of vested interests by separate sectors of business had the net effect of weakening the general position of the bourgeoisie and of helping the transformation of the Italian polity into a political regime dominated by the Christian Democrats. It took a series of major events—the explosion of labour struggles in the late 1960s and the world economic crisis of the '70s—to push organised business to change some features of its political strategy and to try to rationalise social and economic life. Renegotiating their support of the DC, businessmen sought to accomplish this without upsetting traditional power relations.

The question of the political management of the transition to a mature industrial society arose in Italy at the end of a decade of growth, when relations between organised business and the government party were at first very smooth—reflecting a maximum of business power—and then became progressively more strained due to the contradictions inherent in the development process and to internal changes in the Christian Democratic Party. In order to frame our discussion of the more recent period it is necessary to define briefly the main features of the Italian 'model' of development and its major phases.[3]

Italian post-war economic development may be divided into six major phases: (1) the reconstruction period (1945–1948), (2) the 'easy growth' period (1949–1958), (3) the 'boom years' (1959–1963), (4) the 'difficult growth' period (1964–1968), (5) the cycle of labour struggles (1969–1973), (6) the period of world economic crisis, characterised by a sequence of longer recessionary and shorter expansionary phases (1974–present). After the success of the DC in the general elections of 1948, a conservative economic policy was fully implemented. In the fifties, economic growth was stimulated, on the one hand, by increasing productivity through low wages and industrial rationalisation, and, on the other, by expanding exports of low-wage competitive Italian goods in a reconstructed international market. The oligopolistic structure of key industrial sectors favoured high rates of accumulation. Finally, the increase in private consumption of the 'middle classes' played a role, gradually increasing domestic demand. This model of development fostered basic contradictions, above all imbalances between the South and the North, between town and country, between technologically advanced and backward sectors, and between wages, profits and rents. On the whole, however, it represented a rather astute strategy of modernisation, led by a dominant social coalition which had the conservative-religious DC as its hegemonic political force and the business class as its dominant social force.

The first part of the 'easy growth' period witnessed the greatest power of Confindustria, because of trade unions' weakness and the successful confinement of leftist political parties in an oppositional role, favoured by the cold war climate. Confindustria's power at the time can also be traced, however, to the effectiveness of its policy, which was capable of unifying different factions of the business class and of developing institutional ties with the majority party.

Confindustria was at the time a centralised organisation, backed by an apparently homogeneous business class and linked by an organic relationship with the DC.[4] The objectives of the association, and the interests and values behind them, were directly incorporated into the economic policy of the government through institutional channels, such as major economic departments of government. These departments made use of Confindustria staff for 'technical' advice, information and forecasts about what the outcomes of a given course of action would be.[5] Business interests were presented as the general interest in recovery and did not need specific political representation, since employers had the discretionary power to invest. It was thus a situation, which generally tends to appear in periods of economic emergency, when employers 'disappear' from the political scene as a visible pressure group and pretend to be concerned only with business matters, but, for this very reason, claim to be considered the only economic experts.

Money was also widely used to strengthen the connection with the government. The official source of Confindustria income was an ordinary fee paid by every member firm in proportion to something less than 1 per cent of total wages paid by the firm; besides that, there were hidden contributions—mostly by large firms—to political groups, associations of various kinds, newspapers, etc. The president of Confindustria at that time, Angelo Costa, generalised the unofficial contribution to all member firms—for an amount approximately equal to the official one—and, more important than that, succeeded in channelling most financing to political parties through the association, thus strengthening its role in managing the relationship with the State.

For these reasons, the relationship between Confindustria and the DC was clearly defined as relationship between two homogeneous political organisations with separate areas of influence: the ruling party, together with its allies, was in charge of the organisation of consensus, the maintenance of law and order and foreign policy matters: Confindustria was in charge of the governance of the economy, either directly, through its own staff, or, more often, indirectly, through political leaders and government officials who were very responsive to its views (with the notable exception of some leftist Catholics).

Although an over-simplification of reality, this picture grasps the essential. In the 'easy growth' period, the bourgeoisie (i.e. private capital) was the dominant class within the dominant social bloc which held power in Italian society. But, in a country still largely rural and with traditional cultural patterns, the business class neither provided a unifying ideology nor controlled the State apparatus, as in other countries, such as France.[6] The ideological coherence of the dominant social bloc was assured by the DC, which combined within itself religious values favourable to business—such as interclassism and hierarchy—with others which were at odds with a modern industrial society—such as communal populism. The peculiar character of this party in the Italian political scene, its character as both the conservative party or the party of the bourgeoisie (like the British Tories for instance) and, at the same time, the party of all Catholics, made it the political representative of a compound social bloc.

III. ECONOMIC MATURITY AND BUSINESS IMMATURITY

The relationship between organised business and the government party did not remain smooth. After the mid-50s it suffered a series of crises for two main reasons: first, changes in Italian society strained the relationship, as Confindustria was much more reluctant than the DC to adapt to a changing environment; second, latent contradictions related to the Christian Democratic representation of a wider social grouping than the business class came to the surface and gave rise to internal struggles within the party. In the mid-50s there was a powerful convergence of objectives between the strategy of the new party secretary, Amintore Fanfani, (intended to strengthen the party's organisation by penetrating the major decision-making centres in civil society) and the plan of the President of ENI, Enrico Mattei (designed to achieve national energy self-sufficiency through a two-pronged attack on the oil cartel abroad and the electric power oligopoly at home). This convergence of strategies violated some of the unwritten rules of the game, by trying to break up a private oligopoly with a dominant position in the business association and by showing a determination to use economic resources for party goals. Moreover, it changed the relationship between the DC and Confindustria: the link between a unified party and a rather homogeneous business class became a fragmented network of influences in which different party factions were related to different centres of economic power. The confrontation ended with a compromise, a short-sighted business association succeeding in slowing down change at the price of losing part of its influence and control over the economy. But acceleration of growth and change at the end of the 1950s in a period of world economic expansion required timely and determined political responses by Italian political parties and interest organisations and rekindled the confrontation between the government party and organised business, temporarily settled in previous years.

The Italian economic boom of 1959–63 had two major implications for organised business: firstly, the strengthening of labour unions due to the development of a tight labour market in the advanced industrial sectors and to the general process of modernisation of Italian society (internal migration, urbanisation, etc.), and secondly, the weakening of the traditional centre of power in Confindustria in favour of the private oligopolies in the engineering and car industries (Fiat, Pirelli, etc.) and of the State-controlled industries' association. The Italian bourgeoisie faced problems typical of the social transition to a more mature capitalist economy, and in particular, the problem of maintaining a satisfactory rate of profit and capital accumulation in the presence of rising workers' expectations and stronger trade unions.

The end of 'easy growth' and low wages broke the superficial unity of the business class; cleavages between relatively labour-intensive and relatively capital-intensive sectors, between consumer market-oriented and industrial market-oriented firms, between technologically advanced and technologically backward firms, came to the surface. Different strategies to cope with labour demands and different political coalitions were worked out by major business components. In a simplified way, one can identify four major lines of action, one international and three domestic:

(1) the stepping up of international integration, both industrial and financial, by Italian business. This meant, amongst other things, the increase of capital investments abroad and the internationalisation of the largest Italian private firms, in order to increase productivity through a hierarchical division of labour within the international firm. It meant also promoting the illusion of being able, through continuous export growth, to postpone solving the domestic problem which would require modernisation and technological upgrading of the productive structure.

(2) the restoration of the discretionary power of employers over workers, by means of an authoritarian government implementing an overtly repressive policy.

(3) the cooling down of a heated economy, in order to restore a more favourable labour market situation and an easier command of labour, through the well-known economic policy sequence of 'controlled recession': tight money policy by the National Bank—rising cost of money—lower invest-

ments—rising unemployment—lower wage demands—higher profits—and new expansion.

(4) the introduction of elements of state planning for restructuring the industrial system and regulating the labour market, and the carrying out of some fundamental social reforms such as health, education, housing, transportation, aimed at easing the social tensions stemming from rapid economic growth (urban congestion and the like) and at controlling wage demands.

Different business groups favoured different combinations of these four strategies, which we may call the 'international', the 'reactionary', the 'short-term' (or *conjuncturelle*) and the 'long term' (or *structurelle*). The traditional power group in Confindustria was the custodian of the past. The electrical industry oligopoly feared nationalisation of strategic sectors of industry as a consequence of the Socialist entry into the government coalition. Since it did not face powerful labour unions, given the highly capital intensive character of its production, it had little incentive to accept a Centre-Left coalition capable of winning larger labour support. Furthermore, as any power group, it was afraid of any change which might diminish its power. Many small employers, often at the head of newly founded firms, were allied with this group, because they were primarily unsophisticated first-generation entrepreneurs, who employed mostly non-unionised paternalistically controlled, new industrial workers. Despite this breadth of support, however, the influence of the traditional group in Confindustria was declining. Inter-oligopolistic struggles (such as the fight between Edison, the major electric corporation, and Montecatini, the largest chemical concern, over the development of the petro-chemical industry), and the shift from neutrality to open opposition of the big engineering firms which had a different perception of the changing social climate led to a loss of power.

In those years the small firms became an important component of the Italian industrial system. To suggest, as I did, that they were the allies of the traditional group in Confindustria, oversimplifies the matter. In the boom years and in the longer 1955–65 period, there was a mushrooming of small entrepreneurs which represented a new phenomenon for Italy. This industrialisation from below absorbed large numbers of workers coming from the countryside of the South and from the less advanced regions of Italy in general. While there were frequent cases of 'improvised managers', many of the new owners had real entrepreneurial skills and played an active role in the economic boom. Whatever their differences of social and cultural background, they were on the whole unsophisticated employers, staunch supporters of the free enterprise system, tough on workers' demands and suspicious of the political game.[7] As such, they were easily mobilised by the most backward representatives of business. Once the latter had been defeated with the nationalisation of the electric power industry, however, at least a part of the new small entrepreneurs could have been persuaded to accept a more advanced industrial society had the great private entrepreneurs, who were (and are) their models of behaviour, wanted to provide the leadership. But the latter preferred to lead them to a rather backward looking line, closer to the small employers' attitudes towards workers, but rather short-sighted in view of the new needs raised by economic development and the extension and escalation of labour militancy. This new breed of entrepreneurs was then neither led by more advanced firms to a more mature political strategy, nor capable of creating their own organised forms of political representation within Confindustria. They were cornered in a backward and subordinate role, a position which was to prove very costly for them.

The business component which was at the time more distant from the position of Confindustria's traditional power groups was the 'State entrepreneurship' or 'State bourgeoisie'. While the former favoured the 'reactionary' political line of restoring law and order in the factories and in the country, the latter supported the trend toward a democratic society with elements of social planning and selected social reforms. In the boom years, the public sector of industry consolidated itself in the Italian economy and consolidated its ties with the 'left' of the DC, making overtures toward the Socialist Party as well. It was a major force behind the formation of the Centre-Left government and it supported neo-capitalist or New-Deal type strategies, through its own employers' association, Intersind, which was formed in 1957.[8] The managerial staff at the top of these State-controlled firms often shared the same values and attitudes, and often had close personal links with prominent leaders and officials of the ruling party. This new breed of manager-politicians, half way between the entrepreneurial role and the party official's role, monopolised key post in State firms, major banks, financial institutions and State agencies, accumulated posts, and passed from one post to another according to political requirements rather than business needs.[9] If one reads the writings and speeches by men such as Mattei, Saraceno, Petrilli, Cefis, Fascetti, one finds the same stress on technocratic efficiency and on the satisfaction of social needs, on pluralism and collective bargaining, on co-operation between capital, labour and government, on the maintenance of the free enterprise system, corrected by elements of State planning and anti-monopolistic devices.[10] Much of this was rhetoric and there are basic differences in the degree to which these ideas have been implemented by various State entrepreneurs; but, on the whole, they can be seen as a rather coherent strategy and ideology, i.e. an attempt to integrate the values and social relations needed by a mature industrialised society with the basic tenets of Catholic social doctrine. Whatever the subjective intentions of its proponents, however, this outlook legitimised the process through which 'party management of the economy' took place, and the public enterprise became the major instrument of this process. Government spending, special credit and endowment funds of various sorts were the technical mechanisms by which the State sector grew and transformed itself into a system of power.[11] Together with the credit system and—until the late nineteen-fifties—the Catholic trade union, the State sector of industry thus contributed to the plans of the Christian Democratic 'Left'.

The present 'degeneration' of the State-controlled sector of the Italian economy can be traced to the subordination of managerial efficiency not so much to broader social goals (as it was claimed by some of the top managers) as to narrow party objectives and corporate interests represented by diverse factions of the party. The leading firms of the private sector contributed, however, to this trend, by following a narrow-minded and backward strategy toward the labour movement and the modernising forces of the Italian political system.

In fact, the large private corporations held a key position and could play the role of arbiter between the traditional power group in Confindustria and the party-linked public sector. These firms made a rather extensive use of manpower; for many of them the growth of production meant more employment, a higher concentration of workers in the work place and a higher interdependence of the production process, all elements which reinforced workers' organised power and made their actions potentially more effective. Moreover, since they produced mostly durable consumers' goods, their growth depended on the development of a large domestic market, which in turn implied the social upgrading of workers and the modernisation of the whole society. For these reasons, their position was different from that of the traditional power group, and they were more willing to accept some political change (the Centre-Left coalition), with the hope of integrating workers into the dominant social bloc and of fostering social peace in factories through the establishment of a modern industrial relations system on the American model.

Their acceptance of the new political situation was, however, very reluctant; they were continuously tempted to go back to the previous situation. Trade union action and political pressures of various kinds led them to accept the entry of the Socialists into the government and the shift from authoritarian to contractual attitudes in labour relations as being 'the lesser of two evils'. Fiat policy in the conflict with labour over the renewal of the metal workers' contract in 1962 is a significant case in point: concessions were made to the trade unions only after a tough and long controversy, with management playing the traditional role of resisting labour demands and trying to divide workers.

The effect of this group was to weaken the thrust of reforms, and to ask for substantial compensations for accepting innovative decisions such as the nationalisation of electric power. Realism induced them to criticise the rigidity and abstractness of the backward sectors of Confindustria and the latter's declared attempt to restore bygone times. Accordingly, they did not oppose the nationalisation of electric power, but fought over the way to implement the decision. They contributed to the solution which gave the government indemnity to the corporate management and not to the mass of small shareholders in the form of State bonds. They accepted a tax on securities' income and the creation of two State commissions on monopoly power and economic planning; but they opposed structural reforms, due to their acceptance of reforms as a simple rationalisation of the industrial apparatus rather than as a pursuit of broader social objectives. Inefficient social services were criticised, and there was an attempt to socialise the costs of the process of intense growth; but there was no evaluation of the 'external diseconomies' which the firms produced in their uncontrolled expansion. This short-sightedness later backfired on employers, because workers increasingly included better social services in their demands, struck to attain them and asked for higher wages in order to compensate for the scarcity of collective services and the poor quality of urban life. Finally, economic planning was systematically boycotted. It thus became an abstract exercise because of the combined opposition of business, on the one hand, and the Communist-linked labour union, on the other.[12]

In other words, the modern private oligopolies did not lead the process, but tolerated it. The most advanced version of the neo-capitalist strategy (e.g., structural reforms, incomes policy), expounded outside Catholic circles by socialists and liberals such as Ugo LaMalfa,[13] was looked upon with scepticism. These sectors of business limited themselves, instead, to an astute but short-sighted strategy, the strategy of controlled recession, capable only of displacing contradictions and creating the conditions for more explosive conflicts in the years to come. The monetary policy of the Bank of Italy in 1963–64 aimed mostly at containing wage demands through a controlled recession. It fostered the illusion that a cooling off of the economy was sufficient to control the labour unions, and disregarded the need for a more equal income distribution and for fundamental social reforms.

Once again, business unity was forged around a rather backward position; and once again, the recovery of high profit rates was obtained at the cost of further—and this time more systematic—penetration of the Christian Democrats into the economy. In spite of the superficial unity, the deterioration of Confindustria's position as the representative of the entire business class went on, since the practice of bilateral linkages between single firms and party factions was further enhanced. The direct importance of direct linkages between economic groups and parties and factions without the mediation of Confindustria grew significantly from the fifties to the sixties. The State sector of the economy increasingly became a system of party power, while a countervailing power of private capital was slow to emerge, since, although the nationalisation of the electric power industry had weakened the traditional power group in Confindustria, vested interests in the centralised organisation were hard to displace.

IV. PARTY MANAGEMENT OF THE ECONOMY

The ineffective solution to the problem of transition to a modern economy in the boom years is at the root of the present crisis. Major contradictions were temporarily postponed at the cost of an increasing political control of the economy by the dominant party. In the span of time between the boom years and the present crisis, major changes took place in the Italian economy.

There was increasing internationalisation, both in trade terms—with growing exports and an increasing share of highly technological goods exported—and in capital terms—with the penetration of foreign capital, the multinationalisation of large Italian corporations such as IFI-Fiat and Pirelli, and integration into the international eurodollar market. To give a few figures, the percentage of foreign-controlled firms in a sample of the 150 largest manufacturing firms passed from 18 per cent to 23 per cent of total output, from 13 per cent to 15 per cent of total employment and showed rates of growth consistently higher than their Italian counterparts.[14]

There was a parallel enlargement of the State-controlled sector and of the State bourgeoisie. The percentage of the public sector in the aforementioned sample passed from 19 per cent to 24 per cent of total output, from 28 per cent to 35 per cent of invested capital and from 20 per cent to 24 per cent of total employment.[15]

The third trend, related to the other two, was the concentration of capital. It was favoured by State laws, like the March 1965 law granting fiscal facilitations which could be used for industrial mergers, and the laws for the Mezzogiorno which progressively raised the upper limit of invested capital which could benefit from State incentives. Finally, there was a significant change in the balance between self-financing of firms and financing from external sources and an increasing dependence of firms on the credit system. Between 1963 and 1973, the risk capital of firms was reduced by almost half: while in 1963 it represented 54·3 per cent of total financing, in 1973 it was down to 26·7 per cent. In the same period, the rate of indebtedness of firms rose from 51·6 per cent of total financing to 69·1 per cent and, amongst external sources, short-term credit rose to 32·8 per cent.[16]

The net effect of all these trends was an increasing polarisation of Italian industry, with private and public oligopolies together with transnational corporations, on the one side, and the multitude of small firms, on the other, and an increasing dependence of the latter on the former and on the bank system. Leaving aside international capital, which has distinctive features, the ability to influence State policy was very different for large public, large private and small firms. And, conversely, government's attitude was very different towards each of these business components: while public firms received preferential treatment, and private oligopolies defended their position, the needs of small firms were at best neglected. The policy of the credit system is an interesting case in point.

In the sixties a dual financial system came into existence; there were the 'privileged' financial circuits—one for State-controlled firms and the other for private oligopolies—and a 'regular' one for the other firms.[17] In these years, the Christian Democrats consolidated control of the bank system and made it a major element in their strategy of regime building. The alleged reform policy of the government was a major way to gain this control. Reforms were financed not through tax increases—due to the opposition of powerful privileged groups within the dominant social bloc, but through huge increases in government bonds, thus draining money available for investments. If reforms had really been made, State spending would have compensated lower investments in the private sector; but reforms were delayed because of the opposition of vested interests; and banks were interested in keeping the funds that public agencies received but did not spend and to lend them to local councils which were increasingly unable to meet people's needs for social services which went unsatisfied by the central government. Those public agencies and most local councils which lent and borrowed money from banks were controlled by the government party and became the most important customer of the credit system. Under the control of the DC, a privileged financial circuit was thus formed; it included banks, State agencies local councils and public oligopolies.

Large private industrial groups reacted by establishing another privileged financial circuit through the Special Credit Institutions (*Istituti di Credito Speciale*). They did not lack money for investments and financial speculation.

The integration of Italy into the international financial system allowed the outflow of capital from Italy; and, on the other hand, that outflow was not discouraged by the financial authorities. Large firms exported capital, substituting it with long term debts at low interest rates granted by *Istituto di Credito Speciale*.

The combined action of public and private oligopolies, together with government agencies, made it increasingly difficult for small and medium firms to find the necessary financial support for growth. These firms became very vulnerable to the monetary policy of the government in a period when State economic policy was mostly monetary policy. They did not make the necessary technological investments and tried to maintain and increase profit margins by speed-ups of production, thus contributing to the explosion of labour struggles in the late nineteen sixties.

The trends I have illustrated had clear implications for the relations of power among major components of the business class and for their linkages with government. Public enterprises became the new dominant force, taking the place of the old power group in Confindustria. Public oligopolies were, in a sense, the heirs of the old group, since control of energy sources (ENI, ENEL) and of financial means through close ties with banks controlled by the DC were again, as in the fifties, key instruments of power. The major difference with the old power group, however, was that the public oligopolies' relationship with the government was no longer a relationship between independent political organisations, but a close system of party linkages and loyalties.

Private oligopolies seemed from time to time concerned with the escalation of the Christian Democrats' control over the economy, but were on the whole more concerned with strengthening their monopoly power at the expense of small producers, and with opposing economic planning and the growth of labour unions. Their strategy was, in the best of cases, (like that of Fiat and Pirelli) one of productive growth which neglected, however, the social costs of uncontrolled expansion (e.g., the chaotic growth of Turin in the late 1960s); in the worst of cases, like Montedison, a strategy of corporate control, coupled with a paramount concern for increasing capital instead of productive growth.

One can ask why large private groups did not react to State interventionism, except by verbal attacks. The reasons are first, that they felt at ease in the re-established oligopolistic climate of Italian industry and continued to grow and to be concentrated; and, second, that they were treated with special attention by the government, due to their economic weight and their continuing linkages with certain factions of the government parties, and had access to easy money, tax incentives and the like. In other words, they took advantage of the situation by restructuring and expanding, but lost their dominant position in the business community, failing to lead the small and middle-size firms into a coalition able to control the Christian Democratic regime. Conversely, small business did not seem to be aware of the high cost they had to pay to the credit system and, in general, to the political regime; they were mostly concerned with labour costs and addressed all their frustrations towards the leftist parties and the trade unions. While expressing anti-monopoly feelings, they were, in the last resort, favourable to the DC, which ironically appeared to them as the stronghold of business values and free enterprise, while it was actually undermining them. In fact, Christian Democracy represented all major components of the dominant social bloc, from public to private business, from large to small firms, from small farmers to urban middle classes.

The values of managerial efficiency and technocratic organisation were present in the ruling coalition and in the State firms, but they were generally sacrificed to the logic of party 'aggrandisement' and to the need of compromising with traditional vested interests which were well entrenched in the party. This helps explain (much more than largely overestimated differences between private and State managers) why many State-controlled firms declined and why the State bourgeoisie was unable to remain the hegemonic force in business.

In this situation, Confindustria was no longer a major locus of power, and it no longer provided an effective representation of major business interests. Other institutions became important, above all, the bank system, which became a kind of clearing house of conflicts among business groups. Major influence on government was exerted directly by public and private oligopolies, each of them lobbying by itself and financing several parties and party factions at the same time, with the DC, of course, holding a privileged position. Besides losing the centralised management of relations with government, Confindustria was also bypassed by Intersind in collective bargaining; the public firms' association often took the lead in negotiations, and Confindustria followed.

In spite of all these shortcomings, changes in the association's strategy and structure were very slow to emerge. Traditional forces, like the remnants of the old power group and many small entrepreneurs, and vested interests in the existing structure of the frustrated 600 people working at the Rome headquarters and the many others working in the provincial branches, made any attempt to change very painful and time consuming. Confindustria thus became more and more an association providing only technical services to its members, mostly the small firms which could not afford independent technical facilities and consultants; territorial branches provided these technical services—predominantly legal assistance in the event of labour conflict—and the central office was no longer the unified political representative of the business class.

The poor performance of Confindustria in this period finally stimulated some attempts to change the organisational structure of the association. Interestingly enough, the initiative was taken by young entrepreneurs, generally heirs of family business, who were concerned with the need to legitimise their entrepreneurial role on grounds other than sheer property right. Backed by the major representatives of private capital, Agnelli and Pirelli, in 1967 they were integrated, as a group, into the structure of Confindustria. In 1969, kicking and screaming they formed a study group—financed by Confindustria—with the aim of writing a report on the 'entrepreneurial situation in contemporary Italian society and the organisational structure of Confindustria'.[19] The document contained penetrating insights into the political options of Italy and an open critique of the functioning of the association as a weak pressure group which neglected small business and was unable to bring into line major groups which negotiated directly with the parties and the government. Although it had a major limitation in the gap between the ambitious goals set for the association's political role and the scarce and scattered proposals of organisational reform, the Report raised relevant questions. But it was largely ignored.

Another study commission,[20] chaired by Pirelli and representing the major innovative and conservative components, had more impact. It focused on the organisational structure of the association and proposed a new one. The Report was given wide approval, but the joint purpose of having a more efficient and more representative association was not met, because of the potential boycotting by the central and local bureaucracy and because the social situation made it obsolete before it was implemented. In fact, the explosion of labour struggles, known as the 'Hot Autumn' (*Autunno caldo*), brought to the surface the latent contradictions among major business groups which at this time, were unable to reach an agreement on their strategy towards labour. The truce between private capital and public or semi-public capital (such as Montedison) was over and with it the smooth relations between private oligopolies and the government party.

The strength of labour unions reduced profit rates at a time when the emergence of new countries in the international market made it more difficult for Italian industry to compete. In 1970 the Italian government tried the usual way of cooling off the economy through a set of deflationary measures (tight money policy, tax increases, reduction of State spending), but almost all important business groups—ENI, IRI, Montedison, IFI-Fiat—continued to invest. Corporate strategy towards labour was, however, very different from one group to another. Relatively capital-intensive firms, both public and semi-public such as Montedison, followed a strategy aimed at reducing the trade unions' power by making the productive role of workers less important. For the managers of these firms, productive growth did not mean more employment, but rather massive financial investments. They needed a symbiotic link with the State in order to get special credit on a massive scale and in order to develop a welfare system which could take care of the increasing number of unemployed and underemployed workers. In the Senate hearings on the chemical industry, the president of Montedison, Cefis, traced an ambitious development plan for that industry; it would, in his view, develop highly technological products and enter other economic sectors, such as building, health, food processing, agri-business; then growth of the tertiary sector and of public administration should take care of excess manpower in industry.[21] And, since those developments would not be enough, an escalation in welfare would be needed. The DC, as a party pursuing a clientelistic policy in various areas of the country, mostly in the South, at the time found this strategy congenial to its interests of consesus formation.[22]

The strategy of private oligopolies like Fiat and Pirelli was different. Although they were gradually diversifying, (in sectors such as electronics and the aircraft industry for Fiat), these oligopolies were still firmly related to the car industry with its relatively labour-intensive production and need for a huge domestic market. They were, therefore, more sensitive to labour problems and, together with their allies in Confindustria, sponsored a mild line toward the trade unions and recognised their role as privileged partners in labour conflicts. They also sought to direct labour's strength toward demands for structural reforms which would reduce the cost of labour and were opposed to an undiscriminating welfare policy. In some of their declarations and writings, leaders of the private oligopoly groups envisaged a kind of 'alliance' between 'productive' forces (entrepreneurs and workers alike) against unproductive or parasitic groups, which held *rentier* positions of various kinds in Italian society.[23]

The two different strategies of the major business groups towards the labour unions and the welfare state implied as well different political coalitions and formulas. Although it is hard to identify clear-cut choices, one can risk the following interpretation: the Montedison-led group—in which the chief representative of the new 'State bourgeoisie' Cefis had as allies the remnants of the old power group in Confindustria—seemed to favour a further strengthening of the Christian Democratic party in its 'integralist' version and to back Fanfani's bid for President of Italy, which took De Gaulle's presidential Republic as a reference point. Major private groups seemed, instead, to prefer a parliamentary system less dominated by a single political force, where the government played a more traditional mediating role amongst the different components of the dominant social bloc, without subordinating the economy and society to party needs. This view implied a temporary withdrawal of the support given to the dominant party in favour of the smaller centre parties.

After Fanfani's defeat in the presidential elections of 1971, a government headed by Andreotti was formed which, among other things, supported the proposal of forming a control group over Montedison, thus reducing the party's control over the economy and weakening the 'State bourgeoisie'. The lack of support by the parties of the left, together with the reaction of most Christian Democratic leaders caused the fall of Andreotti's government. A subsequent agreement between Fanfani and Aldo Moro led to a new government headed by Fanfani who stressed once again the party's penetration into civil society and the expansion of welfarism as a source of consensus. This party strategy eventually led to two electoral defeats in the referendum for divorce in 1974 and in the elections of 1975 and to a change of power relations within the DC: the naming of new party Secretary (Benigno Zaccanini) and the return of Andreotti as head of a new government. This time the government had much wider political support, including that of the Communist Party; at the same time, it was more sensitive to the strategy supported by the major private industrial groups than the one which had been headed by Fanfani. Both Christian Democratic strategies—the 'integralist' one and the 'mediating' one—sought to manage the crisis and to accomplish a new stabilisation, but with different means: the former by a further rooting of the party into all major centres of power in the country and by stressing confessionalism, inter-classism and the patronage system; the latter by forming the dominant social bloc and by mediating amongst its major components and between them and the emerging social forces represented by the leftist parties. Of the two strategies—which are analytically distinct but actually co-exist in several factions and even in single DC leaders—

the latter prevailed. This was primarily due to the strength of the left. It was also, however, due to the fact that the 'modern' component of private business, after much delay, had reacted to the changing social and political climate and had become the new hegemonic force in the business class. This was reflected in the changing strategy of the employers' association, most significantly displayed in the confrontation over the presidency of Confindustria in 1973–1974.

V. TOWARD A NEW BUSINESS STRATEGY

The performance of the business organisation in the four years after the 'Hot Autumn' was unsatisfactory. Internal changes were very slow to appear, the 'dialogue strategy' toward organised labour had encountered widespread suspicion, and the association's political role was not performed with enough determination and autonomy from the government party. Moreover, Confindustria was a major testing ground for the capability of the large private groups to return to a more central position in Italian business and in the dominant social bloc. Bruno Visentini, the candidate for Confindustria president of the private capital coalition, was the general manager of Olivetti, had previous experience in government and was a member of the Republican Party, considered by most 'progressive' employers as the best political representative of business interests. As a finance expert, he had often attacked bureaucratic inefficiency and State deficits, and implicitly, the welfarism of the DC. His choice represented a challenge to the ruling party and he was not elected due to the veto of Cefis, the general manager of Montedison, who was backed by Fanfani, at that time head of the government. Agnelli was forced to enter the field directly in order to defend the positions of private capital and his bid could not be opposed, since it would have meant open war between major components of the dominant social bloc, at a time when labour unions and leftist parties were very strong.

   With Agnelli (and Guido Carli, the former head of the Bank of Italy who succeeded him), Confindustria tried to perform the three basic sets of functions outlined earlier. The association sought to form a solid bloc behind its policy, to become again a key political actor and a privileged but autonomous partner of government and a skilled negotiator with organised labour; Confindustria also tried to rebuild its image and to wage an ideological offensive in favour of the 'centrality of the firm' and against State interventionism and managerial inefficiency. The writings and speeches of Agnelli, first, and later Carli, clearly articulated these goals. Perhaps the most coherent version of the new strategy of Confindustria, however, was expressed by Visentini.[24] In his article, the role of Confindustria as a political actor is strongly reaffirmed, while its service role is delegated to the territorial and industrial associations. Employers are asked to increase their political awareness and independence from political parties and to substitute strategy to astute political manoeuvring. They are also asked to defend the principles of efficiency and competition against the centralisation and bureaucratisation of the economy, and, at the same time, to respect the law and to show a modern attitude toward industrial relations. Finally, in order to foster such a strategy, the article asks for more collegiality in decisions at the top of the association and for a fight against the vested interests of the internal structure and of all those who use the association for their particular interests.

The main elements of the suggested strategy, i.e. centrality of the firm and private capital, employers' education to respond creatively to the new times, autonomous political role in a long-term perspective, dialogue with trade unions, modernisation of the internal structures, have been often reaffirmed in the last few years by Confindustria's leaders.[25] But the question remains whether they can be and have been implemented or are mere ideological legitimations of a much less autonomous and innovative strategy.

Various factors have contributed to create favourable conditions for the re-emergence of Confindustria as a major political actor and for the reinforcement of the position of private capital within it. The economic crisis and the Communist Party's approach to the arena of government, have to some extent, reduced trade unions' pressure. The crisis of public firms, manifested through a series of political scandals and disastrous economic performances of many of them, have reversed the situation of the late fifties and early sixties, when public firms represented innovation and industrial democracy. Moreover, the electoral defeats of the Christian Democrats, the defeat of Fanfani in the party and that of Cefis in Montedison have weakened the alternative strategy we have described.

The way in which Confindustria's strategy is implemented shows, however, the existence of contradictions in the business class—mostly the contradiction between oligopolies and small firms, and the tension inherent in the linkage with the DC.

The confrontation between 'modern' private oligopolies and the Montedison-led coalition ended with the victory of the former, who are the new hegemonic force of business. But, behind this re-adjustment of power and influence, there is the usual compromise between large private and State-controlled oligopolies at the expense of the more competitive small and medium-sized enterprises. The debates on the best way to cope with the growing rate of indebtedness of firms—such as the proposal to consolidate firms' debts through shares owned by banks—show the privileged position of large groups, despite the free enterprise rhetoric. And the present law for industrial restructuring tends to favour large corporations as well, as was the case with the laws for the development of the Mezzogiorno. This policy of discrimination against small and middle employers cannot be pushed too far, since Confindustria aims at the cohesion of the business class, but the relationship of strength is such that the costs and benefits of the crisis and of government policy are distributed unequally.

The cohesion of the business class is, therefore, pursued through an 'ideological offensive'—which has escalated with Carli's presidency—that is intended not only to reassure employers about the legitimacy of the entrepreneurial role vis-à-vis workers, but also to obscure conflicts of interest between oligopolies and small firms. Grass-roots participation in the local associations is also encouraged as a safety valve for small employers' discontent, but proposals from below seldom reach the central organisation and affect basic decisions. On the other hand, there are clear signs of a willingness to compromise with public firms, to define areas of influence with them and to encourage within them the managerial component against the bureaucratic one.

The second key area of tension in the new strategy of organised business is the relationship between Confindustria and the DC. The most coherent supporters of the autonomy from the government party have fluctuated between the attempt to reach direct agreements with the trade unions— bypassing the government—and the attempt to develop a third political force of liberal character between the two major Italian parties. The former attempt can lead to single agreements—like the one on the cost of living escalator (*contingenza*)—but cannot systematically replace party activity, unless it wants to risk the institutionalisation of a neo-corporatist state. The latter attempt was defeated at the last political elections and does not seem a feasible out-come in the near future. Besides, the most prominent representatives of the new business strategy do not seem to think that they can make do without the Christian Democrats. This withdrawal of support must be seen as an alarm signal for the government party, aimed at reducing to some extent Christian Democratic power to the benefit of the smaller centre-left parties, at provoking changes within the DC and at modifying its relations with the other political parties. As we have seen, the two electoral defeats in 1974 and '75 have actually modified the internal balance of strength in the party with the supremacy of the 'mediating' line over the 'integralist' one. These changes, however, have gone along with the strengthening of the Communist Party. The joint effect of internal changes in a direction more favourable to modern private business and of the preoccupations raised by the strengthening of the Communist Party have weakened Confindustria's opposition to the Christian Democratic Party.

In conclusion, the political representation of organised business is still primarily provided by the Christian Democrats, despite recurrent conflicts of interests and periodic disappointments on both sides. The present sharpening of the confrontation between major political forces in Italy further reduces the autonomy of business and the government party from one another. The prevailing strategy of Confindustria is to try to influence the government party from within—by backing the 'mediating' component and affirming business values and attitudes—rather than by making a clear choice to support other political parties. A certain weakening of the party's pervasive role is favoured, but the criticism does not go far because of the fear of the powerful leftist unions and parties.

The impact of labour unions' and of the Communist and Socialist parties on the strategy of organised business is clearly much more complex than that of limiting the drive to criticise the ruling party. Very briefly, one may note that unions have increasingly affected the range of choices and the degree of discretionary power held by business and have reduced overt attitudes of support for business by government and political parties. On the other hand, the very growth of trade unions' political strength contributed in recent years to revitalise private capital and to bring Confindustria back to a central political role. The relationship of organised business with the Communist Party is also not univocal. Traditionally an anti-bourgeois party, the Communist Party is becoming more and more a 'catch-all party' with a wide social base and a reformist strategy, and has started a dialogue with business-men. The response of the latter is often a mixture of 'rational' acceptance of the Communist Party as a modernising force in government and an 'emotional' opposition to Communism. The positive evaluation of the benefits stemming from the entry of the Communist Party into government—i.e., the stabil-isation of the political scene and reduced freedom of action for the Com-munist-linked trade union—is mixed with fears of 'working class hegemony'. Both the refusal and the acceptance of the Communists' governmental role foster, however, the notion of a strong Christian Democratic Party as a counterweight, and pave the way for further compromises between business interests and the Christian Democratic Party's logic of consensus formation through the patronage and welfarism. How that policy can be consistent with the needs of business for capital accumulation is a major unsolved question.

NOTES

1. This essay is based essentially on the analysis of relevant government, party and business association documents and on the critical appraisal of the rare contributions on the subject. It is part of a larger research project on the Italian business class in comparative perspective financed by the Italian National Research Council undertaken by a group which I co-ordinate at the University of Milan.
2. This failure was due to a delayed nation-building process, which in turn can be traced to a variety of factors, amongst which the fact that Italian feudalism was not able to create a solid hierarchical organisation of society, the subordination of the countryside to the city, the separation between peasants and absentee-landowners and the presence of the temporal power of the church.
3. The interpretations of Italian economic development are numerous. See, amongst others, G. Fuá ed., *Lo sviluppo economico in Italia*, Milan, 1969, 1978; A Graziani ed., *L'economia italiana 1945–70*, Bologna, 1972; M. D'Antonio, *Sviluppo e crisi del capitalismo italiano*, 1951–72, Bari, 1973; M. Salvati, *Il sistema economico italiano, analisi di una crisi*, Bologna 1975.
4. There are only a few accounts of the business association history. See J. La Palombara, *Interest Groups in Italian Politics*, Princeton, 1964; D. Speroni, *Il romanzo della Confindustria*, Milano, 1975; G. Pirzio Ammassari, *La politica della Confindustria*, Rome, 1976.
5. Typical in this respect was the link with the Department of Industry, which La Palombara defined as an example of *clientela*.
6. For a business criticism of these phenomena, see G. Carli, *Intervista sul capitalismo italiano*, Bari, 1977: 'the State in Italy, at least since 1875, is the State of the petty bourgeoisie . . . the political personnel, but mostly the ideals, the type of culture, the concrete interests of the Italian State have been those of the petty bourgeoisie' (p. 75).
7. For an analysis of the social background, managerial skills, political values and attitudes towards the crisis of a selected sample of small Italian entrepreneurs, see A. Martinelli, D. Bratina, *Gli imprenditori e la crisi*, Il Mulino, Bologna, '78.
8. Intersind played at first an autonomous role from Confindustria, by introducing new types of work organisation in the factories (job evaluation) and 'plant-level collective bargaining' in industrial relations—in agreement with CISL (the Catholic trade union). But this autonomous role progressively faded away. See A. Collidi, 'L'Intersind, in *La Politica del padronato italiano*, De Donato, Bari, '72 e G. Sasso, 'Partecipazioni statali e politica del lavoro', in G. Cottino ed., *Ricerca Sulle Partecipazioni statali*, Einaudi, Turin, 1978.
9. On the so-called 'State bourgeoisie' see E. Scalfari, G. Turani, *Razza padrona*, Feltri nelli, Milano, 1974: G. Galli, A. Nannei, *Il capitalismo assistenziale*, Sugar, Milano,

1976: F. Alberoni, 'La nuova classe imprenditoriale italiana', in *Sociologia*, VI, 3 Sept. 1972: A. Nannei, *La nuovissima classe*, Milano, 1978.

10. See among others, the report by P. Saraceno at the S. Pellegrino Congress of the Christian Democratic Party, in September 1971; G. Petrilli, *Lo Stato imprenditore*, Bologna, 1967; and the articles by Mattei, in the ENI magazine, *La scuola in azione*, and by Fascetti in the IRI magazine, *Notizie IRI*.

11. See G. Amato, ed. *Il governo dell'industria in Italia*, Bologna, 1972; F. Cavazzuti, *Capitale monopolistico, impresa, istituzioni*, Bologna, 1974.

12. The best accounts of the difficulties met by the planning agencies of the Italian government are those of the policymakers involved. See G. Ruffolo ed., *Rapporto sulla programmazione*, Bari 1973; M. Colitti, *Un ventennio di programmazione, 1954–1974*, Bari, 1977.

13. See U. La Malfa, *Problemi e prospettive dello sviluppo economico italiano*, nota del Ministro del Bilancio presentata al Parlamento il 22 maggio 1962, Istituto Poligrafico di Stato, Rome, 1962.

14. See G. L. Alzona, 'Grande industria: sviluppo e strutture di controllo, 1963–1972', A. Graziani, 'Aspetti strutturali dell'economia italiana nell "ultimo decennio" ' e M. D'Antonio-U. Marani, "Sul commercio estero italiano negli anni sessanta', in A. Graziani ed. *Crisi e ristrutturazione dell'economia italiana*, Turin, 1975.

15. See E. Filippi, 'Un contributo al dibattito sull' impresa pubblica in Italia' in *Rivista di economia e politica industriale*, n. I; 1975. And A. Martinelli 'The Italian experience with state-owned enterprises' paper presented at the Harvard Business School Conference, March '79.

16. See L. Barca, G. Manghetti, *L'Italia delle banche*, Rome, 1976.

17. M. De Cecco, 'Banca d'Italia e conquista politica del sistema del credito' in *Il governo democratico dell'economia*, Bari, 1976.

18. Our research on the Italian business class shows that mobility from private to public firms and vice versa concern 25 per cent of top management. See A. Chiesi, A. Martinelli, 'Primi risultati della indagine sulla classe dirigente economica', *Rassegna italiana di Sociologia*, Autumn 1978.

19. See, *Una politica per l'industria. Rapporto sulla figura dell'imprenditore e sulla organizzazione industriale nella societa italiana*, a cura della commissione organizzativa del Comitato centrale dei giovani industriali, May 1969.

20. See CGII, *Revisione Dello Statuto confederale*, Relazione della Commissione, February 1970.

21. See E. Cefis, L'industria chimica italiana e la crisi Montedison, *Indagini conoscitive del Parlamento sull' industria chimica*, Rome, 1972.

22. The two strategies we have exposed have been thoroughly analysed by A. Graziani, in V. Castronovo (ed.), *L'Italia contemporanea*, Turin, 1976.

23. See the interview by G. Agnelli in L'Espresso, 19 November 1972 and the speech by G. Amendola at the Symposium organized by Il Mulino in April 1973 among businessmen, political leaders and experts of major parties.

24. See B. Visentini, 'Sulla presidenza della Confindustria', in *Corriere della Sera*, 12 December, 1973.

25. Amongst other documents see the General Reports by G. Agnelli at the XXXI and XXXII Assembly of Confindustria, his farewell speech at the XXXIII Assembly and the speeches by G. Carli at the Assemblies of the following years. See also CGII, 'Vincoli ed oneri gravanti permanentemente sulle imprese italiane industriali', 'L'impresa industriale nella societa italiana', October 1977, and 'Operazione sviluppo', January 1978.

Italian Christian Democracy: A Party for all Seasons?

Gianfranco Pasquino*

The Italian Christian Democratic party represents an almost unique case among Western competitive multiparty systems. Since December 1945, the DC has supplied all the Prime Ministers and most of the ministers in the various Italian governments. It has done so by dominating all the different phases of the evolution of the Italian political system and by adjusting to them. The DC has governed first in coalitions including the minor centrist parties—the Liberals, PLI; the Republicans, PRI; and the Social Democrats, PSDI—from 1948 to 1960: the *centrismo* period. Then it was able to co-opt the Socialists, PSI, ousting the Liberals, in the period from 1962 to 1972: the *centro-sinistra*. After a turbulent period in which various coalition formulas were tried, including a return to the past with a centre-right government geared around Andreotti (DC) and Malagodi (PLI) and in which the party suffered some electoral defeats, a new phase opened. After 1976, the DC has been obliged to bargain for the support of the Communists, PCI, and has succeeded in obtaining the confidence of Parliament for *monocolore* governments, which are made up of Christian Democratic ministers only.

From many points of view, Italian Christian Democracy represents the case of a continuous and successful adaptation of a complex organisational structure to environmental changes and political challenges. It needs to be stressed immediately, however, that the success of the party in remaining in power and in polling the relative majority of votes throughout the entire post-war period has not been matched by a satisfactory governmental performance. This has, if anything, sharply declined after the first stage of the centre-left experiment, at the end of the sixties. The relationship between the party as a political structure and the party as the dominant element in any governmental coalition is naturally very close. It is, nonetheless, necessary and useful to disentangle the various components for analytical purposes. After a brief look at the structure of the party as such attention will be devoted to the constitutive elements of the political consent enjoyed by the DC. The quality of this consent and its transformations through time will be analysed. The article will then deal with ongoing changes and will provide some guidelines for the understanding of forthcoming adaptations and emerging problems.

* Department of Political Science, University of Bologna

Written while the author was a fellow of the Woodrow Wilson International Center for Scholars, Washington, D.C. I should like to thank Arturo Parisi, to whom I owe much of my understanding of the DC, and Peter Lange and Sidney Tarrow for their helpful comments and suggestions on the first draft.

THE NATURE OF THE PARTY

For various reasons, the Christian Democratic Party as an organisation has always been weak.[1] From the beginning, the DC was dependent on outside support—particularly, that coming from and produced by Catholic organisations. Attempts at creating a strong and autonomous party structure, especially by Fanfani in the mid-fifties, resulted instead in the fragmentation of the party into competing factions with outside bases of support. As for other features of the DC, this fragmentation was both an element of weakness and of strength. While drastically reducing the decisional effectiveness of the DC as a government, it allowed the party as an electoral organisation to branch out to different, and sometimes not easily reconcilable sectors of Italian society. The basis of electoral support was widened and remained so for a long time, while the excesses of factionalism plagued governments.

Needless to say, the various factions also constituted the major channels of career and influence for party members. The dominance of party leaders who emerged from Catholic organisations remained, nevertheless, the single most important phenomenon until the early seventies. Even today, while a transformation has taken place in parliamentary personnel, which experienced an unprecedented turnover in the 1976 elections, power still lies in the hands of few established leaders. Their leadership, however, is no longer taken for granted. A different relationship exists between party leaders and the parliamentary group, while the problem of the change in party leadership is still very thorny. In fact, due to a variety of circumstances (and especially to the stifling power of the old generation), the younger generation of DC leaders has not acquired comparable visibility and prestige within or outside the party, not shown leadership qualities, and has not produced a single charismatic, reliable, unifying personality.

Both as a cause and an effect of the structural organisation of the party, power has always been centralised in a small oligarchy, never unchallenged, but always strong enough to deflect, if not defeat, challenges and clever enough to absorb incoming members who show special qualities. Of course, it is possible to single out some major figures and their respective periods (De Gasperi 1945–1953; Fanfani 1954–1959; Moro 1963–1968). But Fanfani and Moro always had to make room for other power contenders and consistently retained positions of power either in the government or in the party throughout the entire post-war period. De Gasperi, the towering figure of reconstruction, was openly challenged and then defeated in 1953. The sixties can be characterised more satisfactorily as the decade of the powerful Dorotei faction, while Moro devoted his attention more to inter-party coalition-building—his fundamental concern in the second half of the seventies as well—than to purely partisan matters. Recently, two old-time party leaders have emerged as dominant figures in the party: Benigno Zaccagnini as Secretary General and Giulio Andreotti as Prime Minister. While by no means without challenges, they represent the image of the party at the end of the seventies: honestly the first, (alleged) technical competence the second. Interestingly enough, while both have been important factional representatives, their factional identification has been considerably diluted.

As a matter of fact, poularity, prestige, a strong and active personality have never completely obliterated the need for a Christian Democrat to be a member of a faction in order to become powerful and to acquire control over ministerial patronage for the purpose of strengthening his own and his faction's influence.[2] It is true that the phenomenon of party fragmentation into competing factions is less visible and less devastating than in the past. Although undergoing a process of change and realignment, factions do exist within the Christian Democratic party today. In a multifaceted, diversified, large party, the existence of differences of opinion is not only legitimate, but are to be expected. In a party combining the support of many groups and wielding governmental power, it is understandable that groups will try to find (and even create) channels of access to decision-making arenas. Again, differences of preferences over policies to be enacted might be quite natural. What has been pathological about the Christian Democratic Party has been the sheer number of the factions. What was peculiarly disruptive was that acceptable differences of opinions became sharper and sharper over time and, above all, became institutionalised in a system geared to the acquisition of consensus and distribution of resources —not to implementation of policy.

Strictly hierarchically structured, rotating around a leader of national visibility, usually geographically-based (that is, emerging from some specific region, the sole exception being the Dorotei with an even distribution nation-wide, despite predominant support in two strongholds: Veneto and Sicily), each faction has individual headquarters, owns a news agency, is able to draw resources from outside party channels through privileged connections with flanking organisations. It is symptomatic of the factions' strength and resilience that they have, in fact, changed very little in the past twenty years, even though their political alignments might have changed. Labels, in a few cases, have changed, but the relationships of factions with outside flanking organizations have largely remained stable. From the left to the right, the DC factional spectrum between 1959 and 1974 can be described as follows in Table 1.

THE COMPONENTS OF DC POLITICAL CONSENT

Various DC factions rely on patronage for their organisational maintenance, and some of them emerged out of an unscrupulous exploitation of State patronage. DC electoral support, however, cannot and should not be explained exclusively in terms of patronage and clientelism. By a way of response to recent unilateral interpretations, the following analysis will start from an assessment of the nature of consent coming from the Catholic subculture, will then proceed to an evaluation of State clientelism and conclude with some reflections on the enlarging electorate of non-Catholic urban, moderate voters.

There is no doubt that the major component of Christian Democratic strength has always been and still is the large, stable support of Catholics.

TABLE 1

FACTIONS IN THE CHRISTIAN DEMOCRATIC PARTY

FACTION	Forze Nuove	Base	Morotei	Nuove Cronache	Iniziativa popolare (Dorotei)	Impegno democratico	Forze libere
LEADERS	Donat-Cattin Bodrato	De Mita Marcora	Moro Zaccagnini	Fanfani Forlani	Rumor-Piccoli Bisaglia	Colombo Andreotti	Scalfaro
FLANKING ORGANIZATION	CISL	ENI		RAI-TV and IRI	Coldiretti State Participations	Vatican Banking	

(Left)   (Right)

The party itself, as an organisation, successfully relied on the Catholic organisations for access to these voters. It is a well-known fact that religious attitudes and practices sharply distinguish Christian Democratic voters from non-DC voters and to a large extent characterise its following. But the party has always been more than simply a confessional party (and, at the same time, Catholics have always voted for other parties as well, even though in lower percentages for the parties of the left than of the centre-right).

This said, a major component of DC success in getting established and competing successfully with leftist parties was the support it obtained from the Church and Church-sponsored Catholic associations. And the DC remains considerably dependent on the support—for activists, funds, and networks of communication—of the Vatican and Catholic associations, and on more or less practising Catholics for votes.

Thanks to the early commitment of Catholic Action and the unrelenting efforts of the Civic Committees (created by Luigi Gedda, President of the Catholic Action members), the DC was able to achieve a resounding victory over the Popular Front in 1948. This victory and that organisational support allowed the DC to establish itself as the dominant party of the Republican era. Moreover, it is in this period that the great majority of present DC leaders entered the political scene. Almost all of them came from various, more or less specialised Catholic associations—the already mentioned Catholic Action provided the bulk of the members and cadres; smaller associations, such as those for University students and graduates (Federazione Universitaria Cattolici Italiani [FUCI] and Movimento Laureati), supplied the leaders.[3]

The strength of these associations and their appeal to Catholics obviously have been influenced by major social changes and have largely declined with the passage of time. One has only to recall mass migration from the South to the North and from the countryside to the cities; an industrialisation process that reduced the percentage of the population working in the agricultural sector from about 60 per cent in 1945 to less than 18 per cent in 1976; the spread of literacy and the expansion of the mass media; and finally, the growth of per capital income and the development of a consumer society. All these processes had an impact on the secularisation of Italian society and consequently appeared to affect the strength of the DC.

A major process of secularisation, the product of different factors, has, of course, taken place but its impact on the strength of the party has been largely, and so far successfully, checked. The two major aspects of the secularisation process, insofar as they can affect political behaviour, are: first, a decline in the number of Italians who consider themselves religious; second, a decline of religious practice even amongst those who still consider themselves to be practising Catholics. There are fewer Italians attending Church, and those who still attend do so less frequently than in the past. Therefore, they are in all likelihood less exposed to political messages transmitted from the pulpit (also, fewer of these messages are transmitted in the late 1970s).

This process of secularisation of attitudes, particularly dramatic and certainly growing in the aftermath of the Vatican Council, has been accompanied by the organisational decline in the various Catholic associations. For instance, Catholic Action had almost 3 million members in the early 1950s, it has now 600,000; the Italian Christian Workers' Association (ACLI) had over one million members in the same period, it has now 400,000, and is less inclined than ever before to campaign for the DC. As a matter of fact, after having left its members free to vote for parties other than the DC in the late 1960s, ACLI gave birth to a splinter group, the Workers' Political Movement (MPL), led by former ACLI president Livio Labor (now a senator for the PSI). The MPL candidates' list for the 1972 elections polled a disappointing 120,220 votes (0.36 per cent), well below the threshold of parliamentary representation, and soon after was dissolved.

The overall organisational decline of Catholicism was dramatically signalled by the defeat in the divorce referendum.[4] To put it in oversimplified terms, it was then that the Catholic subculture discovered itself to be a minority. Any project of societal re-confessionalisation was buried forever in 1974 and can find only very temporary remedies and certainly no hope of reversal. Thus, the emergence and strengthening of the militant, aggressive, predominantly student movement called *Comunione e Liberazione* (80,000 members) fundamentally located in Northern urban areas, although disciplined and committed, cannot revive the Catholic subculture to its past peaks. Nor, for that matter, can it be expected to launch a drive for the re-Catholicisation of Italian society, At best, it can provide an avenue through which the DC might re-acquire or hold votes, channel preferences to specific candidates, and maintain an organised presence among students. These efforts may delay the process of secularisation and, perhaps, deflect some of its political consequences. Still, in terms of the size of the pool of committed Catholic voters the DC will have to appeal to, the future does not look bright (as Table 2 suggests).

TABLE 2

ATTITUDES TOWARD RELIGION IN DIFFERENT AGE GROUPS, 1975
(IN PERCENTAGES, REAL FIGURES IN PARENTHESES)

Indicators of Religiosity	Young Voters	Intermediate group	Older group
Do not consider themselves Catholics	23.2 (939)	11.4 (481)	6.2 (869)
Never attended Church	27.2 (995)	18.9 (492)	11.0 (876)
Attended Church in 1975 less often than five years before	51.2 (989)	30.6 (485)	25.1 (879)
Consider themselves not religious	43.7 (979)	33.8 (483)	21.9 (874)

Note: "Young voters" include respondents who obtained the right to vote in 1972 or in 1976; "older group" include voters who voted for the first time in 1946, 1948, or 1953. Other respondents were included in the "intermediate group."

Source: G. Sani, "The Italian Electorate in the Mid-1970s: Beyond Tradition?," in H. R. Penniman, ed., *Italy at the Polls* (Washington, D.C.: American Enterprise Institute, 1977), p. 118.

As we have speculated elsewhere,[5] the weakening intensity of the ties binding the voters to their Catholic subculture does not automatically imply a shift in their voting patterns and orientations away from the DC, but it may represent a prerequisite for this kind of shift. There are reasons to believe that this has indeed been the case. On the other hand, had the Catholic component been the only one in determining a support for the DC, the strength of the party should have been severely curtailed in the wake of spreading secularisation. Indeed, some authors openly hypothesised, even predicted, the collapse of the "Catholic party" on the basis of a reasoning attributing exaggerated importance to the role of the Catholic organisations, to the shrinking of the Catholic subculture and to the weight of Catholic voters in the overall electorate of the DC.

The most articulate statement in support of this thesis puts the emphasis on the ideological-organisational cohesion as well as on the diffusion of the Catholic system in producing high percentages of electoral consent, and ends up by stressing that "the party was, in essence. the expression of the Catholic world and its institutions . . . a mass party of believers with an internal and external apparatus of activists by far superior to that of any other party, even the Communist party."[6]

This interpretation largely under-rates the importance of other factors in producing the DC vote: above all, the close connection between the party and the State apparatus, as well as the privileged position the DC has always enjoyed in the multiparty competition taking place in Italy. Thus, while it is certainly true that the Catholic element of the DC vote and the support of Catholic associations were instrumental in establishing the party and maintaining its dominance on the Italian political scene, at no time were they the only components of success. A satisfactory explanation of the nature of the party and of its transformation requires, therefore, that careful consideration be given to other components and different, oft-neglected (but sometimes over-emphasised) factors.

In recent periods particularly, there have been repeated attempts to characterise the DC as a party machine, similar to American party machines (or to Third World populist parties), thriving solely on clientelism. While clientelism is undoubtedly an element in the configuration of DC electoral support and governing power, any attempt to make it the dominant factor misses the point and condemns the analysis to sterility. It is true that in many local cases the party has functioned according to clientelistic practices,[7] but in no case can the strength of the party be explained solely by pointing to clientelism. The degrees to which the party and the various local organisations and factions have been willing and able to resort to clientelism varies from one place to another and from one geographical area to another, but nowhere is clientelism alone the basis of the strength of the party. It has to be noted, for instance, that the party won its major electoral success in 1948 when the clientelistic system, if it had been shaped already, was a fragile element. True, the DC was able to count on the support of Southern notables and some sectors of the bureaucracy from the beginning, but its control of local administrations up to 1951–52 was limited, especially in Northern and Central areas. However, there is no doubt that clientelism constituted later on one of the pillars of DC support.

The major step toward the creation of a clientelistic system was made with the establishment and subsequent enlargement of the public sector of the economy (1953–1956). This measure, widely supported by the left as a blow against private, monopoly capitalism and a step toward a mixed economic system, produced the prerequisites for the inauguration of a modern, managerial system of clientelism. But there was nothing inevitable in its subsequent development. What made this development possible was the privileged political position the DC continued to enjoy. Always present, and in a dominant role, in all the various national governmental coalitions, often leading exclusively DC cabinets *(monocolori)*, the party and its leaders were able to strengthen and consolidate their ties with the bureaucracy, the public managers, the Cassa per il Mezzogiorno (Southern Development Agency), the banking system. Unfettered by any control, DC hegemony over these sectors was taken for granted by the "controlled" as well as by the party.

As long as the economic system produced resources, the (selectively) distributive policies associated with the successful maintenance of the clientelistic network could be satisfactorily implemented. With the appearance of inflation, excessive government spending came under attack and the deficits of local administrations—the product of long-term policies of yielding to powerful local groups, which gave birth to the so-called "wage jungle"—had to be curbed. At this point the first cracks in the Christian Democratic clientelistic system were manifested. They acquired particular visibility in the 1975 local and regional elections when Christian Democratic local administrations were defeated in large numbers. Had clientelism been the decisive component of the DC-vote, loss of power at the local level should have deprived the party of the resources and grass-roots organisers necessary to carry out a meaningful electoral campaign in 1976. This was not the case, precisely because clientelistic rewards and motivations are but one element of DC strength.

The electoral defeat of 1975 was particularly sharp and resounding (the party slumped to its all-time lowest point: 35 per cent), because it was the simultaneous product of the movement of progressive Catholic voters towards leftist parties, the abandonment of the party by groups of clientelistic voters and the winning of a disproportionately small share of the recently expanded youth vote. The electoral recovery of 1976, on the other hand, cannot be explained only by the revival of the Catholic subculture or, even less, by the return to the fold of clientelistic voters. Its explanation must be sought in the third major component of the Christian Democratic vote. For many reasons, this component is the most difficult to pinpoint because it is multifaceted and changing over time. To say that the DC is an inter-classist party is almost a truism, since it is quite obvious that no purely class-based party would attain, consistently, around 40 per cent of the vote in a multiparty system without having a broad poly-class or inter-class appeal.

It is important to underline that the appeal of the DC always had a populist component. This fact explains something of the Christian Democratic ideology as well as the response of some sectors of Italian society, particularly the petty bourgeoisie and the small farmers, who constituted the real backbone of the DC vote. And it is relevant to add that the Confederation of Small Farmers *(Coldiretti),* with its three million members and with enormous funds at its disposal for social security purposes, represented the single most powerful satellite organisation of the DC from the mid-fifties up to the early seventies (when the importance of the agricultural sector declined and so did *Coldiretti* membership and political power).

To stress that the cohesive factor of all these appeals—Catholicism, clientelism, populism, interclassism—was a rigid anti-communism is but to identify the final component of DC electoral strength. While there are various forms of anti-communism, all at one stage or another held, manifested, and manipulated by the party leaders and all in different ways and in varying degrees shared by members and voters of the party, it is likely that the major unifying element today is represented more by shared hostility to the policies the PCI would like to implement once in power, and less to its ideological positions. If the two major components of the PCI's historic compromise strategy are identified as austerity and rejection of corporatist demands, then their implementation would certainly strike at the heart of some important and influential groups supporting the DC, specifically those advocating the continuation of a mass consumer society and of large scale "unrationalised" distributive policies.

To be sure, the success of the DC has been based as much on a policy of selective rewards for followers and interest groups in a quasi-corporatist way as on its support for industrial development and especially the production of consumer goods. It is on this ground that a socio-political coalition could be built and maintained through time, essentially unchanged. Since the time when the DC leader De Gasperi made the fateful decision to request the government collaboration of the minor parties of the moderate right and centre, representing a non-confessional tradition and electorate, the flow of voters from these parties to the DC and vice versa has constituted a constant phenomenon on the Italian political scene. Thus, it was no surprise when many voters of these parties gave their support for the DC in the fateful elections of 1976. Faced with a momentous choice, epitomised by the likelihood that the PCI might overtake the DC in electoral strength, moderate non-confessional voters threw their decisive support behind the strongest anti-communist party. While it is certainly true that the quality and the intensity of DC anti-communism have changed with the passage of time, there is little doubt that this feature of the party's position is still the most appealing one for many voters (and this realization puts, of course, numerous constraints on its leaders' behaviour).

At the end of this brief discussion on the sources of the DC's strength and in the light of the weakness of the party structure, some legitimate questions have to be posed. All revolve around one single point. How did the party overcome the 1974–76 crisis and how solid is its recovery?

CRISIS, CHANGE, ADAPTATION IN THE 1970s

The crisis of 1974–76 was essentially the product of the cumulation of issues and the climax of some transformations. Dissatisfied progressive Catholics left the party in 1974. Urban dwellers took the opportunity of the local elections of 1975 to "punish" the DC for its very poor governmental performance. The lowering of the voting age produced a disproportionately high percentage of votes for the left in the eighteen to twenty-one year old group. Fear was the predominant feeling among Christian Democratic politicians before the 1976 political elections. The results, which allowed the DC to poll the same percentage of votes as in 1972, were perceived and interpreted as an electoral victory. But the problems for the party and for the government have not vanished. Flaminio Piccoli (long a leader and currently president of the party) was right when he remarked that the DC "broke the siege," but Arnaldo Forlani, too, was correct in stressing that the DC had devoured its children—the minor parties, the faithful coalition partners.

One has to be impressed by the recovery of the DC after the profound crisis of 1974–1976. At the same time, one should not forget that the party still faces many problems—on the one hand, in terms of finding an adequate organisational formula for acquiring political consent and extricating itself from the embarrassing connections with the State apparatus, and, on the other hand, for strengthening the party and for creating viable government coalitions, possibly excluding the Communist party. Let us turn our attention toward what has been done so far.[8]

Benigno Zaccagnini was elected to the office of Party Secretary in July 1975, in large part due to pressures for a *rifondazione* of the party, that is, as a response to demands for an end to political corruption, for renewal of the party leadership, for the creation of an open and flexible party structure not based on factions. What has been accomplished since then, and what remains to be done?

Recognising that the Italian electorate has changed, that the party might not be able to rely on the State apparatus and its agencies in the near future, and that traditional organisational techniques might not be appropriate in dealing with their voters and sympathisers, the Christian Democrats have launched a two-pronged effort. For the first time since the end of the nineteen fifties, they held, in March 1977, a Conference on Organisation with the specific purpose of identifying weaknesses and suggesting solutions. The overall thrust of this effort consists of reaching the many voters who are not members of Catholic and DC flanking organisations and are not connected with the Catholic subculture in any systematic way. This has been implemented through the *Feste dell'Amicizia* (Feasts of Friendship), widely publicised and well attended mass rallies, rivalling the Communist *Festivals dell 'Unita'*. These fêtes have rather successfully spread the image of the DC as an open mass party and possibly have mobilised new energies.

Secondly, in the wake of an emerging difficulty in recruiting new card-bearing members, and taking into account the peculiar nature of its urban support among private and public employees, the DC has moved to endow itself with a new organizational instrument. The Gruppi di Impegno Politico (GIP, Groups of Political Commitment) introduced a fundamental innovation into party life. They make it possible for sympathisers to play an active role in their working place, without becoming formal party members, provided that at least a fifth of the GIP units are formal DC members.

It is too early to assess the impact of these changes on the party structure, to evaluate the success of the Christian Democrats in establishing GIPs and to measure their vitality. Party members have already expressed their scepticism about the renewal of the party. (See Table 3). The forthcoming National Congress (January 1980) will have to devote some time to this task. What can be said is that, somewhat paradoxically, the organizational weakness of the DC in the late 1970s in spite of renewed electoral mobility and political competition, may be less of a problem than at any previous time.

TABLE 3

CHANGES IN PARTY LIFE ACCORDING TO A
REPRESENTATIVE SAMPLE OF DC MEMBERS*

		Positive	Negative
Have noticed changes	56.7	31.5	25.2
Have not noticed changes	32.3		
Don't Know	11.0		
N	1,001		

Question: "In the last year have you noticed changes in DC party life? For better or for worse?"

*Source: Doxa survey, March 1977 published by AREL, *Risultati di un sondaggio tra gli iscritti alla D.C.* (Rome: August 1977), p. 29.

This is a consequence of the fact that many Italian voters appear to be more readily mobilisable on concrete issues than on purely partisan appeals. They receive their political information more from peer groups (friends, colleagues, trade union delegates) than from party sources and militants, are more directly exposed to the mass media (and less influenced by opinion leaders), and more willing and capable of shaping their own opinions. (See above, 'Changes in Italian Electoral Behaviour' for an evaluation). If this is the present situation or, more precisely, the ongoing trend, then it becomes understandable why the party organisation is of less importance today than in the past, even though, certainly not irrelevant, particularly for still large sectors of the electorate. On the whole, however, the problems Christian Democratic leaders would have had to face some years ago in mobilising their potential voters and in competing with Communist organisers are becoming less severe and less acute.

Thus, while the problem of recruiting capable militants remains, the problem of creating a mass party in terms of a large membership is no longer of primary relevance. If anything, the real issue is represented by the establishment of sound criteria for recruiting and counting new members. This issue is tied to the attempt to limit the power of clientelistic factions. The most important step taken along the now forgotten road to the *rifondazione* of the party was the enforcement of strict recruitment rules and criteria. This produced a reduction in size of many local organisations, in some cases a mutually bargained reduction for all factions.[9]

There is no doubt that the factions have lost some of their grip on the party and some of their legitimacy in the eyes of party members and DC voters. However, they survive and still play a role, though a less important one than in the past. Moreover, there has been a process of factional realignment which is still going on. Essentially, one can identify a major dividing line between those who support the 1976–9 political strategy followed by Zaccagnini and Andreotti and those who oppose it, particularly Bisaglia, Donat Cattin and Forlani. During the long and tormented crisis of January–March 1978, which led to the creation of a *monocolore* government supported by the PCI, a new dividing line emerged. This cleavage cuts across various factions, especially Forze Nuove, Base, and Dorotei, separating those who are apparently inclined to work in the long-term direction of an agreement with the PCI (above all Zaccagnini's and Andreotti's supporters, perhaps joined by Piccoli) and those who work in the direction of re-establishing a privileged relationship with the PSI, isolating the Communists (a less homogeneous group including the self-labelled liberal-democrats such as Segni, Mazzotta, De Carolis, the Dorotei led by Bisaglia, Forlani and his supporters, Donat Cattin).

Fluidity, however, is still the predominant characteristic of factional alignments. Under the present circumstances, in structural terms the party remains sharply divided and no less fragmented than in the near past, unwilling and incapable of formulating a long-term strategy (as the one to which Moro devoted his attention). On the other hand, while it is unclear how much power the factions still have in the allocation of major chunks of resources and offices (ministerial, undersecretarial, and managerial positions), their legitimacy seems to be declining. In the eyes of the DC membership and above all of DC electorate, the prestige and popularity of Zaccagnini clearly outshines them, at least for the time being. But, weak and structurally fragile, the party exists only as a conglomerate of factions: it has to rely on them, and on their local organisations and flanking groups in order to mobilise resources, energies, and votes in electoral competitions.

Once more, the DC presents the analysts with a paradox. The fragmentation of the party into factions is an element of weakness, makes for excessive bargaining and incoherent decision-making when it comes to governing. Patronage-oriented factions still provoke incessant struggles over resource allocation, slow down the decision-making process, allow for the introduction of contradictory measures, support the approval of piecemeal legislation instead of structural reforms, encourage the satisfaction of corporatist demands. Seen from the point of view of the party, however, the existence of factions is up to a certain level a positive and indispensable element. The sheer organisational vitality of the various factions, "condemned" to be present and well-rooted and well-staffed at the local level, their diversified electoral appeal, and even their interfactional struggles are useful factors when it comes to turning out the vote for Christian Democratic candidates, and consequently for the party as such. A cohesive and centralised party probably would not prove as effective in maintaining a flexible relationship with a very diversified electorate. In any case, the price of enforcing central-isation and cohesion is certainly too high for the DC to pay—if it is worth-while at all. Of course, lack of centralisation neither implies nor produces internal democracy. Decision making-power remains firmly in the hands of a small oligarchy of faction leaders. After the 1976 elections, the renewed parliamentary party has shown some signs of insubordination to the decisions "communicated" to it by the National Council where only top party members are represented.

TIES WITH THE STATE APPARATUS

The difficulty of analysing the DC derives fundamentally from the fact that it is necessary to focus on the party and the factions, and on the relationship between the party and the government at the same time. Nowhere is this more evident than in accounting for the resources available to the party. The bulk of financing, particularly in order to finance electoral campaigns, came from the patronage system created over a long period of time—and there are reasons to think that not even the enactment of a law providing for the public financing of political parties has completely stopped this flow, at least insofar as some powerful potential ministers are concerned. Nevertheless, securing enough money to make its organisation work has always been a problem related to the lack of a reliable and fully committed membership (in many frequent cases the dues were paid by the faction machines). While not automatically decisive, a large number of dues-paying members is a prerequisite of an autonomous organisation. And because of their absence during certain periods, the party had to rely on donations and also on funds channeled by the Catholic organisations, the Vatican, Confindustria and, as has been confirmed, by the CIA.

Two aspects of the reliance on external sources of financing must be emphasised. The first is that, of course, there were strings attached to the funds provided to the DC; the second aspect is that, very often, these funds were channeled more to specific factions than to the party as a whole. Realising that financial independence is an important prerequisite of an independent policy, Fanfani, in the late 1950s, decided it was preferable to disengage the party from an excessive reliance on the Confindustria and organised Catholicism through access to funds to be provided by the public sector of the economy. As a matter of fact, the Ministry of State Participation, whose control has always remained in the hands of powerful Christian Democratic personalities, has functioned not only as a source of funds but also of vital patronage through which party supporters were rewarded and party militants given jobs (procedures that were openly acknowledged by no less than a DC Minister of State Participation, Ciriaco De Mita).[10]

Obviously, this close relationship between the party and powerful public agencies has entailed a price for the decision-making process. The contrasts among external flanking organisations often led to stalemate and forced acceptance of the *status quo* or produced the allocation of rewards on the basis of the strength of the various groups (and in their functional areas the Vatican and Confindustria were always able to make their voices heard). The ties between the DC and the various State agencies and specialised bodies not only remained very close, but even became more intense with the passing of time. The sheer prolonged control of some important ministries created a symbiotic relationship between their bureaucracies and the representatives of the sector under their jurisdiction. Powerful external organizations always had a very influential say in the selection of top personnel of various ministries, prominent among them *Coldiretti,* which never loosened its grip on the Ministry of Agriculture.

In addition, the combination of power at the national level and power at the local level allowed the Christian Democrats thoroughly to penetrate some sectors, specifically the banking and credit system—so much so that only few changes have taken place even after the 1976 shift in the balance of power in the party system. The overstaffed, politically recruited and corporatively run bureaucracy constitutes one additional element in the pervasive penetration of the State apparatus by the Christian Democrats. This relationship has not made for a more effective and incisive decision-making process. On the contrary, in many cases, it appears that the bureaucrats have enough power squarely to oppose some decisions, to delay the implementation of other decisions, to bring the functioning of some ministries to a standstill. The very power of the CISL branch organising public employees has been more often used to stifle any reform effort than to streamline the bureaucracy and to achieve a more rational and more responsive performance of indispensable tasks.

Finally, control of the Ministry of Defence, particularly during the long tenure of Andreotti (fifty-eight months between July 1958 and December 1968 and thirty-two continuous months at the beginning of the 1960s) laid the foundations for an exchange relationship between the Armed Forces, especially the Army, and the DC. This kind of relationship, which has improved the financial condition of the officers, but not modernised the equipment of the Armed Forces nor modified its obsolete structure, was epitomised by the creation of so-called electoral barracks in the area surrounding Rome, where votes could be turned out from large barracks in support of the Christian Democrats and above all in support of Andreotti himself (who always enjoyed a very high number of preference votes).

This impressive network of connections, ties, exchange relationships, while producing resources, support and votes for the party also meant that reforms had to overcome the resistance of entrenched groups and vested interests. The dismal failure of the Ministry of Bureaucratic Reform and the recently encountered difficulties in the devolution of law-making powers to regional governments and in the elimination of so-called useless agencies (catering to needs and groups no longer existing) are suggestive of this state of affairs, and are indicative of the existence of powerful forces within and outside the DC pressing for the maintenance of the *status quo.*

Thus, it is certainly correct to state that there are "inextricable links between the existing character of the Italian State and the DC's coalition for patronage." In the light of the origin and nature of DC implantation and consent, however, it is less plausible to argue that "reform the former [the State] and the latter [the DC's coalition] is certain to collapse; preserve it unchanged and the DC—perhaps in some suitably modernised form—will maintain a share of power. The problem with maintaining such a coalition, however, is that it is geared to solving distributional problems at the cost of the legitimacy of the regime, especially among the lower classes."[11] Aware of the elements of weakness inherent in its position as well as of the assets deriving from the continuation of its privileged relationship with the State apparatus, the DC has tried to buy time, accepting the implementation of those reforms and changes which cannot be resisted (for instance, allotting a share of power within the banking system to the PSI and the PCI, while maintaining essentially intact the overall structure and control in the hands of DC ministers; approving a new code for the Armed Forces and speeding up the process of retirement of the too numerous top personnel, but making sure that trade unions will not be allowed to politicise the rank and file conscripts and the NCOs).

By preventing a sharp break with the past and by making it impossible for the parties of the left to claim credit for it, the DC has been able to soften substantially the impact of inevitable changes on its sources of support and votes. At the same time, it has delayed the emergence of a reformist coalition dominated by the left. In addition, the DC has made some steps albeit haltingly, away from too close a relationship with various State agencies. The relationship still exists, but it is more flexible: the public financing of political parties also makes it less vital for the DC. Based on shared opinions and preferences as well as on ties of loyalty, the close relationship between public managers, top bureaucrats and DC leaders still constitutes one of the pillars of Christian Democratic power. It allows the Christian Democrats to buy additional time in their long-term strategy of "wearing out" potential partners and opponents. It affords the luxury of filtering gradual transformations through to many agencies still under the control of DC members, supporters, and sympathisers.

POLITICAL COMPETITION IN ITALY AND CONTINUING DC STRENGTH

The electoral strength of the DC, as we have seen, is neither fully nor satisfactorily explained by its connection with the State apparatus. The sub-cultural presence and the network of Catholic organisations provide the indispensable background to the intensity and extent of this political support. Moreover, the apparent revival of the DC in the period after 1976 can be explained only with reference to another oft-neglected factor: the nature of political competition in Italy. Such an explanation is provided by looking at the voters' motivations as well as to the strategies of the leftist parties.

Of particular importance is the image Italian voters have of the DC, especially when compared with the positive and negative features attributed to other parties. Table 4 shows that Italian voters do find many serious

TABLE 4

PARTY EVALUATIONS BY A REPRESENTATIVE
SAMPLE OF VOTERS (APRIL 1978)

	MSI	PLI	DC	PSDI	PRI	PSI	PCI	Don't Know
The best organized	4	1	9	1	1	3	54	27
Contributed more to the defense of democracy in Italy	1	1	32	2	3	12	18	31
Linked with foreign interests	2	2	44	3	—	1	13	35
Most involved in scandals and corruption	5	2	58	4	—	5	3	23
Most honest and best trained leaders	5	2	8	1	7	5	26	46
Most linked with economic power	3	8	36	1	2	4	7	39
Most divided and fragmented	3	1	58	2	—	6	4	30
Full of opportunistic, greedy people	6	3	34	5	1	9	7	35
Could do more for the country	2	1	40	2	3	15	14	23
More young and enthusiastic party members	6	1	6	1	2	5	41	38
Tied with non-productive parasitic groups	18	9	19	2	1	3	4	44
Less reliable	20	1	22	2	1	4	19	31

Source: Adapted from G. Fabris, *Il comportamento politico degli italiani* (Milan: Angeli, 1976), pp. 91–92.

drawbacks in the DC: subservience to foreign interests and to domestic economic power, corruption, fragmentation into factions, unreliability, ties with parasitic groups. On the positive side, the DC receives credit because :"it has made the greatest contribution to the defence of democracy in Italy" and "it is the party which could do the most for the country." Note that there are two equally acceptable interpretations of this answer. The first is that the party does not do enough and ought to do more. This interpretation still implies confidence in the capabilities of the party, even while perhaps passing a negative judgment on its actual performance. The second interpretation is that, of all Italian parties, the DC is one potentially better equiped to do more for the country. In the same vein, DC politicians enjoy two positive evaluations. They are seen as defenders of freedom and are considered to be against violence. If one recalls the four major objections held against the PCI—the party is a threat to democracy, it is anticlerical, it protects the interests of the Soviet Union, it is involved in episodes of political violence—then, the opinions expressed by large sectors of the Italian population can be better understood and appreciated.

The DC is generally considered, and rightly so, a counter-balancing force to the feared antidemocratic behaviour of the PCI—an opinion which is not rendered less meaningful by the guarantees offered by the historic compromise. On the contrary, not the promises of the PCI but only the strength and the willingness of the DC to defend the democratic framework can reassure these voters.

The second factor to be taken into consideration in order to understand the still dominant position of the DC, derives from the configuration of the Italian party system. Defining itself as a centre party and being so perceived by most voters, the DC succeeded in pushing to the margins of the political spectrum the MSI (Fascism) and the PCI (Communism): the so-called opposed extremisms. The DC exploited its position in order to reap all the benefits deriving from its coalition indispensability. Because of the results of the 1979 elections, the problem for the DC of creating politically stable and effective governmental coalitions remains a very difficult one. Nevertheless, the DC has not lost its pivotal role: no parliamentary majority is feasible if it excludes the DC with the exception of a very heterogeneous secular front (PR+DP+PCI+PSI+PSDI+PRI+PLI), which has no political plausibility.

The third factor which highlights the privileged position and the essential role the DC plays, one way or another, is represented by the very strategies of the two major leftist parties. The Communists' historic compromise would be simply unthinkable were not the Christian Democrats the dominant party representing the interests of large and diversified sectors of the Italian electorate, encompassing not only the middle strata, but sectors of the working class. Only insofar as the DC retains this role is the historic compromise conceivable. The simple formulation of this strategy, not to speak of its implementation, provides the DC with a fundamental asset: the recognition of its indispensability. On the other hand, the strategy pursued by the Socialists is inconceivable without the existence of a strong moderate-conservative pole. A government of the left and the very process of rotation in power (the *alternativa* as well as the *alternanza,* which the Socialists maintain to be their goal and the feature of modern constitutional governments) are based on the presence and continued existence of an effective opposition, capable of playing democratically the role of credible check on the behaviour of a Socialist-Communist government.

Thus, in both instances of such different strategies, ample room is left for the DC to fill a pivotal task in the Italian political system. On this very basis, electoral support for the DC can easily be mustered from many sectors of the Italian population. The very nature of political competition in Italy has allowed the DC to appeal to many moderate, non-Catholic voters as well and makes its existence and strength a fundamental feature of the Italian political system, as we know it.

Thus in spite of the electoral growth of the left, the DC has not only been able to retain its position in the centre of the Italian political continuum, but to have other parties repeatedly recognise it as indispensable. This said, however, it must be immediately stressed that the DC itself also does not have many options. In the obscure language used by DC politicians more frequently than other Italian politicians, the phase characterised by the abstention first and the parliamentary support by the Communist party of Andreotti's *monocolore* governments later is defined as *confronto*. This presumably means not confrontation, but comparison, competition of strategies, programmes, proposals, capabilities, and policy outcomes essentially between the DC and the PCI.

STRATEGIES FOR THE FUTURE OF THE PARTY AND THE GOVERNING COALITIONS

It would be hard to identify a coherent, well-defined strategy for the future of the DC as a party and for the creation of stable governing coalitions. No doubt the parliamentary arithmetic makes the latter rather difficult. As to the former, rarely have DC leaders engaged in strategic speculations. After all, the very strength of the party lies in its diversified composition, in the presence of seemingly irreconcilable interests, in its ambiguity. However, a debate is going on concerning both problems and some attention deserves to be devoted to it.

Among the differing interpretations of the strategy of the *confronto,* there is no doubt that the most widespread is that which is intended to strain the relationship between the PCI and its voters, between PCI leaders and the rank-and-file, between the PCI and the trade union movement. Moreover, this strategy attempts to show that governing with the PCI does not solve any problems and therefore, to sap the international confidence the PCI might enjoy or acquire. The PCI is then treated as was the PSI in the 1960s in the hope of breaking its reformist inclinations. Other DC leaders appear resigned to an agreement of collaboration with the PCI, are more inclined to accept the prospect of having to share power with them. They take their time largely to minimise the electoral losses and in order to obtain a better bargaining position. Still others consider it possible to create a governmental coalition with the PSI—once called "preferential axis"—relegating the PCI again into the opposition. Finally, others even think of the possibility of a new DC electoral breakthrough and, perhaps, the rebuilding of a coalition of "democratic solidarity."[12]

The first position which is probably the most widely held cannot be, for obvious reasons, openly advocated. The second position is attributed, often in order to discredit them, to Secretary General Zaccagnini and his closest collaborators. The third position is shared by the still powerful Dorotei faction and is articulated by its leader, Bisaglia. The fourth position has been put forward by recently elected Deputy De Carolis and has much support, albeit not explicit, within the parliamentary groups, particularly of the lower House.

On the basis of what is known, some tentative speculations on DC future strategy can be formulated, taking into account its special problem of dealing with electoral realignments. In trying to identify the options open to the Christian Democrats several variables deserve attention. The most important one is the fact that the party is not a cohesive, homogeneous organisation either in its leadership and parliamentary representation or, even less, in its electoral supporters. This fact, however, as the overall experience of the party clearly demonstrates, is as much an element of strength as of weakness. Even if with difficulty, the party has been able to retain its dominant role thanks to its capability of combining different groups and different demands, albeit often in "negative" coalitions. Social and political ambiguity and ambivalence have always represented the foundation, the mainstay of Christian Democratic power. It can be argued that any attempt to solve some of these ambiguities might easily provoke a reduction in the appeal of the party, a limitation of its strength, and, perhaps, even a split. De Carolis has correctly described the present configuration of the DC. It is worthwhile quoting him at length:

> Four new political movements may be recognised within the party. Two of them are characterized by their reference to the Italian socio-economic situation and could be defined as nonconfessional. The other two are characterised by their reference to Catholic traditions, and are thus at odds with the former ones.
>
> The two political trends with confessional intent are: 1) the "Democratic Catholics" gathered around party secretary Zaccagnini; 2) the group called "Communion and Liberation." The Democratic Catholics aim at an impossible reconciliation between an "integral" Christian identity and the management of power; the second group recognizes the impossibility of that, chooses fidelity to Catholicism, and moves toward the formation of a party sect whose clear, if perhaps unconscious, vocation is to be a minority group.
>
> Of the two nonconfessional trends, one is typified by the technocratically oriented group gathered around Senator Umberto Agnelli,[13] and the other, by the group that aims at restructuring the "Democratic Alternative." The former is vitiated by its limited objective, namely, to salvage the economic system, and above all the management of industry, by setting aside the solution of the political problem (in other words by dodging the Communist issue). By contrast, the Democratic Alternative recognizes that in Italy the fundamental issues are the Communist issue and democratic solidarity—and that they are strictly interconnected.[14]

It is interesting to remark that De Carolis does not attribute a policy content or a societal project to the two confessional trends. Understandably enough, he assumes that both trends would attempt the creation of a Catholic society—which might be true of "Communion and Liberation" along, and is an unrealistic policy aim, not influencing the choices of either group. On the other hand, the combination of political and economic objectives in the definition of the two nonconfessional trends works satis-factorily only in the case of the technocratic wing, far less so for De Carolis' own "Democratic Alternative" whose component appears to be an exclusively political emphasis on the containment and the roll back of Communist influence and power through democratic solidarity.

Having sharply contrasted the four movements and having suggested that their support comes from outside the party (which he stresses an a novelty, rather surprisingly in the light of Christian Democratic experience with flanking groups and Catholic associations), De Carolis goes on to state that "it is difficult to foresee which one of these four trends will impose its identity upon the party, and it is not clear whether any of them will jeopardise the party's unity."[14] If the analysis we have carried out so far has identified the major reasons of DC strength correctly, then it would be quite clear and obvious that the ascendancy of one trend over the others will easily produce centrifugal tensions—and the dominance of one of them will lead to likely splits. But it would be rather unrealistic to expect one of the two confessional trends to achieve full control of the party (and this is certainly not in Zaccagnini's mind). At the same time, it is premature to believe that the technocratically-oriented group has enough power to present itself as a cohesive and encompassing force. De Carolis' own characterisation of the "Democratic Alternative" trend might make it more appealing than the other groups. Nevertheless, this trend is today a minority current within the DC somewhat over-lapping with the technocratic group (in terms of membership, actual and potential, and of values). And while it certainly enjoys the support of the moderate nonconfessional bourgeoisie, it remains to be seen whether this social group is inclined to accept or provoke a showdown with the PCI.

In addition to the heterogeneity of the party, a second important factor which makes any speculation on the future of the DC rather hazardous is the apparent lack of any political project for the restructuring of Italian society. At a time when the Communists published their much-criticised and quickly shelved *Piano a Medio Termine* and the Socialists produced and marketed their ambitious *Progetto Socialista,* the Christian Democrats kept on relying on the old quotations by De Gasperi, speeches by Moro and Zaccagnini, and perhaps some reform measures advocated by the technocrats grouped around AREL (Agenzia Ricerche e Legislazione). It is fair to recall that not even in the past did the DC distinguish itself for its blueprints for change. Some elements can be found in the famous journal of the DC left wing of the forties and early fifties, *Cronache Sociali,* others in Dossetti's *Libro Bianco* prepared for his unsuccessful bid for Mayor of Bologna in 1956, others still in Moro's celebrated speech launching the opening to the left at the Naples Congress of 1962. On the whole, however, the Christian Democrats have shied away from ambitious long-term projects, not so much because they are non-ideological and pragmatic, but because they are content with their governing tasks and immersed in them. The same reasons that prevent a fundamental restructuring of the party from taking place, would make it ill-advised and almost impossible for any party current to be able to mobilise majority support to proceed to the formulation of a Christian Democratic project for Italian society. Furthermore, an unsuccessful attempt of this sort might prove a boomerang, and not simply for the groups that dared launch it but for the party as a whole as well as for its relationships with the other parties (which would resent any rebirth of clericalism).

Most important of all, of course, is the fact that the party's implicit, and widespread philosophy seems to be adaptation to circumstances and adjustment to unavoidable changes. And it is largely because the party or, more precisely, the Catholic subculture is well-rooted and widely diffused and also because of the many Christian Democrats in elected assemblies and in positions of responsibility and power, that the DC has been able to remain in touch, sometimes trailing behind, never innovating or anticipating changes, with large sectors of Italian society, and has performed a successful effort of adaptation after the defeats of 1974 and 1975.

CONCLUSION

Building on its adaptive ability and on the recognised political capabilities of many Christian Democratic administrators as well as on their deep inside knowledge of the workings of the governmental apparatus, it is easy to predict more of the same in the future. The major risk and challenge to the DC come from the great instability of present political arrangements and from the socio-economic crisis.

For the time being and perhaps for the conceivable future, the power of the Christian Democrats will continue to lie in their ambivalent policies, multifaceted, diversified, sometimes conflicting, sources of support, their capability to absorb diverging demands, to adjust to varied circumstances, to avoid frontal challenges. The solution of the Italian crisis will be as difficult with a fragmented DC party strictly interwoven with the State apparatus as with a "coherent" DC representing exclusively moderate and conservative forces and demands. The decline of a dominant party can be very painful for the political system in which and on which it once thrived.

NOTES

1. Standard references are: *L'organizzazione partitica del PCI e della DC* (Bologna: Il Mulino, 1968); and G. Galli and A. Prandi, *Patterns of Political Participation in Italy* (New Haven: Yale University Press, 1970).
2. On this subject see A. Zuckerman, *The Politics of Faction: Christian Democratic Rule in Italy* (New Haven: Yale University Press, 1979).
3. For the post-war period up to 1963, see *La presenza sociale del PCI e della DC* (Bologna: Il Mulino, 1968).
4. See A. Parisi, *Referendum e questione cattolica. L'inizio di una fine* (Bologna: Il Mulino, 1974).
5. See the above contribution by A. Parisi and G. Pasquino, "Changes in Italian Electoral Behaviour: The Relationships between Parties and Voters," and the bibliographical references for additional details on electoral trends and results.
6. F. Alberoni, "Il partito cattolico deve temere il pericolo del collasso," originally published in *Il Corriere della Sera*, 29 November 1974, now in *Italia in trasformazione* (Bologna: Il Mulino, 1976), pp. 33–39.

7. The best documented analyses are P. Allum, *Politics and Society in Post-War Naples* (Cambridge University Press, 1973), and M. Caciagli *et al.*, *Democrazia Cristiana e potere nel Mezzogiorno, Il sistema democristiano a Catania* (Rimini-Florence, Guaraldi, 1977).
8. For a more extended discussion, see my piece 'La Democrazia cristiana: trasformazioni partitiche e mediazione politica,' in A. Martinelli and G. Pasquino (eds.), *La politica nell'Italia che cambia* (Milan: Feltrinelli, 1978), pp. 124–143.
9. See the thorough analysis by M. Rossi, 'Le caratteristiche sociodemografiche degli iscritti,' in A. Parisi (ed.), *I democristiani* (Bologna: Il Mulino, 1979).
10. Most recently by a top DC manager of the public sector, Marcello Colitti, in his forthcoming book on ENI: *Enrico Mattei: storia di un condottiero moderno.* ENI 'was a powerful clientelistic structure because it was endowed with great wealth and dynamic capabilities, which could serve as a source of financing and training ground for party men.' Quoted in 'Questo partito fara' strada: ha sei zampe,' *L'Espresso*, 10 Dec. 1978, p. 255.
11. Both quotations are from S. Tarrow, 'The Italian Party System Between Crisis and Transition,' *American Journal of Political Science* (May 1977), p. 220. I made a similar, more detailed argument in 'Crisi della DC e evoluzione del sistema politico,' *Rivista Italiana di Scienza Politica* (December 1975), pp. 443–472.
12. Contrast these positions with the preference and the expectations of a sample of DC members in March 1977 as analyzed by G. Pasquino, 'Gli atteggiamenti verso la congiuntura politica,' in *I democristiani*.
13. Umberto Agnelli declined to run in the June 1979 elections, but the 'technocratic' group is still vital, and is represented by amongst others Senator Beniamino Andreatta, former economic advisor to Aldo Moro.
14. M. De Carolis, 'The Christian Democratic Party Today,' in A. Ranney and G. Sartori (eds.), *Eurocommunism: The Italian Case* (Washington, D.C.: American Enteprise Institute, 1978), pp. 153–154.
15. *Ibid.*, p. 154. Useful information on DC members' beliefs and ideology is provided by P. Ignazi and A. Panebianco, 'Il sistema di valori politici,' in *I democristiani*.

H

Crisis and Consent, Change and Compromise:
Dilemmas of Italian Communism in the 1970s

Peter Lange*

On 16 March 1978 the Italian Communist Party (PCI) became a formal member of the Parliamentary coalition supporting the Italian government for the first time since 1947. On that same day, Aldo Moro, President of the Christian Democratic Party (DC) was kidnapped by leftist terrorists as he was on his way to the Chamber of Deputies to speak in favour of the new coalition. The conjunction of the two events was neither accidental nor without its ironies. The entrance of the PCI into the majority was the apogee of success for the policy of accommodation and national unity which the PCI had been pursuing for a number of years. That policy had been most dramatically expressed in Enrico Berlinguer's 1973 call for an "historic compromise" between the major historical and political traditions of Italian life, including the PCI and the DC. Aldo Moro had been the chief advocate among Christian Democrats in favour of at least a short-run version of that compromise.

There was a deeper significance to the events of that day. The new majority, tortuously arrived at after months of negotiation, represented the response of the leadership of Italy's major political parties to the economic, social and political crisis which had gripped the country for almost a decade. Whatever the continuing differences within the new majority, it symbolised a drawing together in defence of Italy's institutions and an at least avowed search for the broad consensus deemed necessary to undertake the policies which might begin to resolve the crisis. The terrorism, in contrast, represented the most extreme form of discontent with the politics of unity and with the compromises and the at best half measure of reform which could be expected to result.

For no party were the contrasts and ironies of that day more telling than for the PCI. Its arrival on the brink of power had been no mean accomplishment. Only a decade before the PCI had seemed at a strategic impasse: organisationally embedded and secure in its better than one quarter of the electorate, but apparently destined to remain in relatively permanent opposition. Now the Communists had dramatically extended their social and political alliances, their institutional power in subnational governments and their organisational strength. Due to their expanded following and growing social presence, they had become a seemingly indispensable part

* Associate Professor of Government and Research Fellow, Center for European Studies, Harvard University. My special thanks to Roberto D'Alimonte and Sidney Tarrow who gave me extended comments on an earlier draft of this paper.

of the solution, whatever some might argue had been their contribution to the country's problems.

Yet the success of the PCI, inseparable from the policy pursued by the party leadership, had brought new tensions and challenges not only from outside but also from within the party's traditional constituencies and membership and from those newly recruited to its ranks. Trade union leaders and rank-and-file were diffident at best toward PCI recommended political-economic policies, advocating economic austerity in exchange for structural reform of the economy and economic decision-making. Debate grew within the party about the advisability of compromises and accommodation with other political parties in exchange for putative influence over government policy. It seemed to many that the PCI was in danger of sacrificing too much of its traditional identity and policy goals for what, they argued, was proving to be ephemeral compromise. This scepticism and diffidence were expressed not only in party debate but also through a decline in party activism and mobilisation and, in 1978, a fall in membership for the first time in a decade.

The successes of the Communists and the growing tensions and problems which they faced were, at one level, easily explicable. The former could be counted as the benefits of long-term opposition. The PCI was reaping the benefits of the failure of the Centre-Left and of the disillusionment which that failure, in the context of Italian and international economic cirsis, had sown among traditionally anti-communist segments of the population.[1] The party's difficulties were simply the other side of the coin. Diffidence and disillusionment among old and new supporters were only to be expected, as the Communists increasingly assumed governmental responsibilities and had past (inflated) promises compromised by contemporary political and economic constraints.

These explanations certainly bear on the truth. Yet in their simplicity they fail to take sufficient account of the degree to which the successes and problems of the PCI in the last decade have derived from choices made by the party itself. Further, they tend to ignore the roots of those choices in the strategy to which the Communists have been committed for most of the postwar period. This strategy represents a major departure from the classical tenets of Leninism, for it seeks to promote fundamental transformation of the political economy not through rapid, traumatic change but rather through gradual structural reform within and through the democratic process. In the context of the Italian crisis of the 1970s, this strategy required the PCI to take decisions which it had long avoided and which involved significant risks for possibly great advantage.

In the pages which follow, we will explore these decisions, their links with some characteristics of the Italian political-economic system and with the evolution of the Italian crisis of the 1970s. This will allow us better to understand the reasons for and constraints on the PCI's movement from party of permanent opposition toward potential (but as yet unrealised) party of governance.

I. STRATEGIC THEMES AND AMBIGUITIES

Postwar PCI strategy has rather consistently stressed a series of themes and principles for party action. Each of these themes, however, has contained significant ambiguities with regard to the stress to be placed on various arguments and activities in day-to-day strategic implementation. This permitted tactical interpretation in the light of the ebb and flow of developments inside and outside the party and in response to changing conditions at the national or grass roots levels. It was unquestionably a source of strength during the party's long political opposition, enabling it to maintain strategic coherence while seeking to capture newly available constituencies or to build new alliances. Maintenance of these ambiguities, however, became more difficult, as the party increased in power and had to assume national responsibilities.

The basic strategic themes and their unresolved elements may be summarised as follows:[2]

1. The PCI very early determined that democracy was the only (and perhaps the best) terrain on which it could hope to come to power in postwar Italy. However, the party only gradually addressed itself to the issue of the compatibility of democratic institutions with socialism once achieved. In addition, it continued to argue for the need to add other, more participatory, forms and institutions of democratic practice to those of parliamentary democracy. The balance between traditional and new forms of democratic life remained a subject of debate.

2. The exercise of the democratic option meant that victory would require a "long march through the democratic institutions." If this were the case, and with the Fascist experience still embedded in the leadership's collective mind, those institutions must themselves be defended, for an attack on democracy would be one of the principal arms of those threatened by PCI advances. The primary requirement of democratic defence was the effort to impede the growth of a mass anti-democratic coalition of the right. The inherent tension between democratic defence and party success, however was rarely considered: what course of action was appropriate if party gains or political and economic reform threatened to expand and mobilise the right?

3. The party recognised that the character of Italy's historical development had created a highly fragmented economic and social structure unlikely to produce a politically unified and majoritarian working class. Thus, formation of a rather heterogeneous set of social alliances would be required, extending beyond the marxist subculture to Catholics, outside the industrial north to the peasantry of the South, and beyond the working class to segments of the traditional and modern middle strata *(ceti medi)*. Priorities among social alliance targets and the appeals by which they were to be attracted remained unclear. So, too, did the possible responses to the conflicts of interest which such a heterogeneous set of allies would encompass. Finally, the goals for which social allies were sought were also unspecified: were they to be mobilised in pursuit of specific programmes, and/or to build an electoral base and/or merely to neutralise potential opposition?

4. The PCI also recognised that the party system reflected the historically rooted fragmentation of society. The working and middle class divided their political allegiances among diverse political parties and often on the basis of

loyalties only indirectly related to the substantive issues of class conflict. Thus an articulated set of political alliances was also required.

The Christian Democratic Party was of central concern. The DC was viewed by the PCI as an interclassist party, binding together a significant popular and progressive mass constituency with big monopoly capital and reactionary and "parasitic" sectors of the middle classes. Functionally, the DC was the instrument for a peculiar form of monopoly and clientelistic capitalism but, at the same time, also a force which, through its commitment to democratic institutions, secured the democratic loyalty of social strata which might otherwise provide a mass reactionary base.

What approach was to be taken with respect to the pursuit of political alliances in the Catholic world? Several lines of attack were permitted to co-exist. At various times party leaders specified its target to be a new "progressive" Catholic party formed by the left of the DC, a coalition with the bulk of the DC, a transformed DC in which political alignments had been altered by the construction of social alliances with progressive Catholics which would force the Christian Democratic leadership to the left. Accommodation with Catholicism as a cultural and political force was indispensable to a socialist project in Italy, but the exact targets and means of that accommodation were loosely defined.

5. The strategy thus far delineated was premised on the PCI's acceptance of a series of "stabilities" of Italian economic, social and political life. This historicist realism, however, posed for the party the critical question of how to introduce dynamism into the system in order to advance toward its socialist goals. This issue once more introduced ambiguities into the party's strategic line along several dimensions.

First, the party proclaimed the need to create a dynamic interaction between activity in society and activity in the institutions of State, between social alliances and mobilisation and political alliances and policy making. But what balance was to be struck between the two? Second, on what basis was support to be secured? What role was to be played by the kinds of interest representation characteristic of political parties in liberal democracies as contrasted with the declared desire to build an organic coalition or historical bloc around a societal project? On a more exalted theoretical level, how were reformist, catch-all politics to be linked to a transformative hegemonic design for the working class?

These strategic themes with all their ambiguities proved advantageous in the situation of basic political stability and oppositional status of the 1950s and 1960s. They allowed the party to maintain its core identity while exercising a degree of political opportunism in a situation in which the chances for breakthroughs were miniscule and the dangers of isolation considerable. In the context of change and crisis of the 1970s, however, new opportunities and new perils, both related to the party's increasing power, made some hard choices and clarifications necessary. The evolution of party strategy and action in the '70s falls into three relatively distinct phases.

II. PHASE ONE: SEEKING TO CATCH THE WAVE

1968–1969 can only be seen as a turning point in postwar Italian history, a period when stability and predictability were replaced by uncertainty and the possibility of historical breakthrough as the underlying themes of Italian political life. One should not exaggerate the degree of change. There was, of course, much governmental instability in the preceding years and there had also been great economic and social transformation, yet the fundamental political alignments and the social bases on which they had been built remained stable. These bases continued to weigh heavily on what followed. Nonetheless, before the rise of the student movement and, more importantly, before the "hot autumn" and collapse of hopes attached to the Centre-Left, the limits of change were rather clearly defined, the principal actors and their interests understood, the political agenda under the control of the party elites. None of this was true after. Economic, social and political conflict within well-defined parameters and rules become a struggle about the limits and regularities which should govern economic, social and political life.

It is unnecessary to recapitulate the events which so dramatically mark this period; they are covered in other essays in this volume. The aspects of particular significance for the PCI need, however, to be underlined. First, for the first time since the immediate postwar period there was a breakdown of the close linkage, control resting at the top, of the relationship between mass society and the political and social elites. The wave of social mobilisation represented a "withdrawal of delegation from those holding power and indirectly from the political institutions."[3] The PCI and its relationship with the trade unions and working class was not exempt from this questioning of authority delegation. Second, the social mobilisation and the demands it posed dealt a death blow to the Centre-Left formula. The parties continued to form coalitions, but these became way-stations, as each of the coalition partners, and particularly the Socialists, began to orient themselves to differing visions of what might come after. Taken together, these developments constituted a crisis of governance for Italy. In the face of new demands, backed by mass mobilisation coming from society government's willingness, and ability to respond other than through accession to the loudest, most insistent, best organised voices disappeared.[4]

The new situation was quickly perceived by the PCI to offer dramatic opportunities. The wave of social mobilisation, promoting demands generally consistent with the PCI's reformist programme, the increasing unity among the union confederations and the crisis of the Centre-Left seemed to mark the exhaustion of the social and political relations which had provided the bases for Communist exclusion. It appeared that what came after would have to involve an expanded, and eventually governing, role for the Communists. Rather than being condemned to permanent opposition, the PCI suddenly found the possibility of movement along both the political and social alliance dimensions of its strategy.[6]

Yet the party did not fail to identify possible dangers and pitfalls in the emerging situation. Social alliances might be expanded, but they could also be narrowed. The intensity of the social mobilisation might prompt anti-labour and anti-Communist calls for a return to order, especially on the part of the northern urban middle classes. If the demands of the mobilised sectors did not incorporate and adjust to the interests of unmobilised sectors of the population, these sectors might become alienated by the process of radicalisation. This danger was particularly acute with regard to a wide range of social strata in the South which, as in the past, were only marginally caught up in the mobilisation in the North. The weakness of the government only increased these dangers, for the absence of effective governmental action in response to the social mobilisation might add to the potential for societal fragmentation. Under such conditions, the DC might be tempted to move to the right, seeking to capture the support of groups left out of and alienated by the possibility of change, As early as March 1969, Longo and Berlinguer spoke of the dangers for the PCI's strategic prospects of "power vacuums" at the centre of the Italian State.[7]

What policy did the Communists develop in the face of this "dialectical" analysis? They sought to advance their interests by supporting the changing balance of power in society while, at the same time, attempting to lead the mobilisation toward ends compatible with their evolving alliance strategy. Ideally, this involved directing the social pressure away from primarily labour market action in pursuit of economic gains or narrowly defined reforms toward political goals with broader constituencies and requiring political mediation. In this, however, the party only partially succeeded. The picture which emerges from this period is of a PCI seeking to catch the wave of social mobilisation.

The party's XII Congress has generally been perceived as marking a "militant turn" in the PCI's strategic development and there are reasons for adopting such an interpretation.[8] Nonetheless, what is also striking are the efforts of Longo and Berlinguer to control and channel the enthusiasm of members for the new social mobilisation and to assure that the role of the political, and the party, retain its importance. Berlinguer, for instance, used his closing speech openly to chastise participants for their over-emphasis on social activism, insisting on the intimate link between social and political struggles.[9] Furthermore, he argued that precisely the character of the social mobilisation raised the political to a position of priority. 'We can say that there is no struggle, even the most immediate and elementary that ... does not objectively, and increasingly subjectively, give rise to problems of a political nature ...'[10]

The party leadership also focused its attention on the more immediate political situation created by the onset of the crisis. Here again Berlinguer's analysis, while fundamentally optimistic in tone, was cautious and measured. On the one hand, he emphasised that the prospect of PCI governmental participation was not on the agenda. On the other hand, he stressed that this did not preclude the pursuit of reform through political action, including the extension of political alliances and pressure on government. Arguing against those who wanted to concentrate on action in society and especially the workplace, Berlinguer maintained that the crisis opened the possibility of re-establishing firmer links with the Socialist Party and of encouraging more progressive policies on the part of the Christian Democrats and thus of the government.[11]

It is in this light that one must read the proposal which gave the XII

Congress its militant, radicalising air: that the crisis created the opportunity for the working class and the PCI to proceed with the construction of an "historic bloc" of social and political forces which could attain the political direction of the nation under the hegemony of the working class.[12] The themes of historic bloc and hegemony had been missing from party rhetoric during the dreary, defensive 1960s.[13] They are now returned to enthuse members and to give theoretical reference and rationale to the actions which the party was to pursue. What is to be noted, however, is that Berlinguer presented these themes in the context of a discussion of the PCI's strategy of reforms and of the specific State policies which were to be pursued to advance the building of alliances: "The strategy of reform is, therefore, essentially a strategy of alliances which, in the last analysis, has always been and remains the central problem in any revolutionary process."[14] Here, then, was a formulation which might, at one and the same time, provide a radical and transformative political thrust, thereby placing the PCI at the head of the social mobilisation, while maintaining a stress on the importance of social and political alliances and, therefore, on the need for political mediation and appropriate public policies.

The party leadership did not succeed in this balancing act. By early 1970, leaders were lamenting the insufficient leadership and direction which party activists were exercising among the socially mobilised sectors. At the same time, it was also clear that members were enthused by the new social movements and sceptical about the party's attempts to assume a moderating role. The wave of social mobilisation was sweeping away many of the barriers which had been blocking an advance of the left. Despite the misgivings and desire for control of party leaders, there seemed to many members little reason for the PCI to take the lead in channeling the protest.[15]

III.   PHASE TWO—1970–1973: RESISTING THE CURRENT OF REACTION

The tension between stategic analysis and day-to-day activity became acute in the years from 1970 to 1973. In the face of a series of social and political developments embodying some of the worst fears of the party leadership about possible reactions to the new power of the working class, there was an accentuation of some of the more defensive aspects of the party line, an increased willingness to criticise the social movements, including the trade unions, and a willingness to assume policy responsibility in Parliament. This phase culminated in the proposal of an historic compromise between the Catholic and marxist worlds, between the DC and the PCI. The most important features of that proposal as well as the logic underlying it, however, appeared earlier.

From 1970 onwards, the PCI was faced with a distinct and rapid shift to the right which directly threatened its strategic prospects.[16] At the social level, the long revolt in Reggio Calabria marked by increasing visibility and boldness on the part of rightist and neo-fascist groups, a similar uprising in Acquila culminating in the sacking of the PCI federation and a crisis of party organisation in the Mezzogiorno signalled a loss of "presence" among the poor of the South. At the same time, there was a conservative mobilisation of middle-class groups in the Northern cities, exemplified by the formation of the self-styled "silent majority" in Milan. These developments coincided with the rise of (primarily) rightist terrorism and almost continuous street demonstrations by extra-parliamentary groups of the left and right. At the political level, a succession of governments appeared unable and/or unwilling to respond effectively to continuing demands for reform or to the rise of terrorism and other illegal political activity. Some important reforms were passed (regions, the Workers' Statute) but they appeared wholly out of proportion with the rising discontent; police action seemed either ineffective or a stimulus to further violence. Finally, and most importantly, there were distinct signs that the electorate was moving to the right and that the DC was not only ready to follow but might even seek to take the lead.

For a party acutely concerned about the need for the working class to build social linkages to the South and to the middle classes of the North, and to maintain the Christian Democrats on a moderate, if not progressive, path these were ominous signs indeed. The fact that these developments were appearing without a general erosion of the new strength of the working class and the trade unions only made the situation more dramatic. A gap was opening between the working-class movement and other sectors of society, but it was a gap which could still be narrowed and closed. Thus, the party increasingly sought to promote those themes and policies specifically intended to prevent a societal breach, encourage more effective governmental action and discourage a rightward swing in the DC.[17] It was in developing this line that the Communists gradually introduced the specific proposals which, in the fall of 1973, were drawn together into the call for an "historic compromise."[18]

That proposal can be summarised in the following propositions:

1. The PCI had long committed itself to work for a socialist transformation within democratic institutions and must continue to do so.

2. Under the economic, social and political conditions peculiar in part to Italy, a programme of democratic renewal, the first step on the road to transformation, would require the consent of a large majority of the population (well over 51 per cent) and the development of social alliances extending far beyond the boundaries of the traditional working class. Few, if any, social strata should be abandoned, a priori, to the opposition.

3. This large majority and wide-ranging set of social alliances was a necessary condition to impede the development of a mass-based reactionary front around those sectors of the population which would be most damaged by the implementation of even a moderate programme of structural reforms.

4. The required electoral and social majority could not be attained, however, without the building of political alliances, not only among the parties of the left but also between those parties and the major party of the centre, the Christian Democrats. Failure to do so might well result in an organic and stable alliance of the centre and right and a reactionary victory. Success in building alliances extending to the DC, in contrast, could potentially shift the Italian political axis, and the balance of power within the DC,

to the left, creating the conditions for further advance along the road to socialist transformation.

5. The need for the broadest possible social alliances and for a political alliance with the DC was particularly acute in the light of the prevailing conditions of economic, social and political crisis which aggravated threats from the right, as they created opportunities for the left.

Here truly seemed to be a startling proposal from the leader of the Western world's largest Communist party. In the value assigned to democratic institutions as the *sine qua non* of the party's strategy, in the size of the electoral majority and breadth of social alliances sought, above all in the direct appeal made to the DC, Berlinguer was replacing sharp class analysis, the primacy of economic relations, struggle and militancy with compromise, accommodation and national unity as the central themes of party action. Mobilisation and activity outside the Parliamentary arena remained critical, but they were to be tailored to, and constrained by, the new priorities. To many observers it seemed that the PCI itself was undergoing a profound transformation.

Upon close examination, however, this clearly was not the case. The policy of the historic compromise did not represent a sharp break with the party's strategic traditions. Furthermore, the specific proposals, even in their most startling details, were anticipated in party documents of the immediately preceding years.[19] What was noteworthy was that Berlinguer and his colleagues appeared to be abandoning some of the ambiguities which had traditionally characterised the "Italian road to socialism." In addition, the rather dramatic presentation of a political proposal consolidating the several strands of the party's strategy created links between arenas of party action which had in the past been allowed to develop with some autonomy. In doing so, coherence and clarity of purpose were increased, and the "Communist question" became the central issue of Italian political life. The party's image of reliability and credibility with potential social and political allies was also augmented. At the same time, however, precisely these characteristics reduced tactical flexibility and increased the probability of internal party dissent. Strategic consolidation created new opportunities to ward off reaction and perhaps even to make major gains, but it also narrowed the possible lines of retreat. Ironically, the seemingly very moderate proposal of an historic compromise represented a major risk for the Communists.

Why the PCI embarked on this risky course and how it subsequently evolved can only be understood if we examine briefly the strands of party policy which from 1970 to 1973, represented the party's response to the unfolding domestic crisis. The first and most general strand is an ever more insistent attempt to direct the militancy of the working class and of the social movements generally toward public policy goals requiring the mediation of the political parties. We have seen that in an earlier phase the PCI was seeking to promote a balance between working class demands in the labour market and factory demands in the political arena; it now sought to channel action toward the political institutions. Denouncing "workerist" ideological tendencies, the leadership insisted that it was through action within the democratic State that workers could best promote their interests. Social mobilisation should be used as an instrument in the struggle for reforms more than as a means for advancing the immediate interests of workers in the factory. Such arguments obviously promoted the party to a leading role.[20]

It would be incorrect, however, to view the PCI's desire to channel social mobilisation toward centralised, political goals as solely an expression of Leninist instincts for control (*i.e.,* the party) over spontaneity (*i.e.,* the social movements) or of conflicts for power between competing institutions. At least as important were more substantive concerns, rooted in the party's strategic perspective, which expressed themselves in the strands of party policy concerned with social alliances, the institutions of the State and the DC.

Throughout this phase, the PCI steadily broadened the array of social alliances to be pursued. Prior to 1970 the emphasis was still on links between the working class and "productive sectors" of other social strata. As the crisis deepened and there were perceptible shifts to the right, this kind of differentiation not only disappears but is explicitly eschewed:

> Naturally, a policy of alliances is not to be understood and undertaken is a schematic or static manner. We do not limit ourselves, for example, to the search for convergence with well-defined social entities, but tend to include in an array of alliances entire strata of the population, like the mass of youth and women, the Southern populations (with the exception of the most reactionary), the forces of culture, etc. . . .[21]

Not surprisingly, this stress on very broad alliances was accompanied by a willingness to subordinate specific programmatic goals to the search for allies: " . . . in the relationship between reforms and alliances, the priority criterion by which to measure the validity of a [political] line must remain that of alliances."[22] The leadership was promoting an ever broader and more defensive interpretation of the party's traditional social alliance policy in order to counteract what was perceived as a crisis of the social and political order which was threatening to the prospects of the left.

A similar orientation appears in the party's approach to government and to the bureaucratic and coercive arms of the State. Beginning in the summer of 1970, PCI cooperation enabled the weak Centre-Left governments to pass measures (which otherwise might have failed) to deal with the emerging economic difficulties and at least partially to respond to the demands for reform. Despite sometimes intense internal criticism of this co-operation, the leadership argued strongly for it: failure to achieve some results at the political level would promote precisely the kind of societal fragmentation and sectoral selfishness and militancy which would only aggravate the crisis and damage the interests of the working class (and the party).[23]

The second major innovation in party policy toward the State in this period was the attempt to break down traditional party hostility toward the bureaucracy, the army and the police and to encourage instead attempts to increase Communist influence in these institutions.[24] This reorientation of

PCI policy fits clearly with those already described. The party had adopted a posture of institutional defense in the face of the crisis. The bureaucratic and coercive corps of the State were critical to the defense of the institutions. Once having determined that a deepening of the crisis, especially a decay of public order, could only work to the detriment of its strategy, the Communists had little choice but, through compromise and accommodation, to seek to influence all those social and political forces with considerable influence on how the crisis would proceed.

These considerations bring us back to that strand of party policy in this period which is perhaps most perplexing: its approach to the DC. By the autumn of 1973, the party chose to seek compromise directly with the whole DC, to consolidate its long-standing strategic orientation toward the Catholic world in a decidedly institutional form. Whatever the continuing ambiguity about how much change had to occur within the Catholic party before stable agreements could be attained, discussion of splitting the DC or of directing most party action toward "progressive" social forces within the Catholic world was abandoned. Furthermore, the critical role of the DC in the system was recognised, for the historic compromise meant a rejection of "the alternative" of a government of the left and of a purely majoritarian principle of government formation.[25]

This approach to the DC emerges gradually from 1970 to 1973. At the beginning of this phase, Berlinguer stressed that the path to alliances with the Catholics lay through an electoral weakening of the Christian Democrats; they had to be shown that an abandonment of their democratic and "popular" commitments was electorally costly.[26] However, once elections in 1971 and especially 1972 had shown that the DC could shift to the right without suffering a significant erosion of its more progressive electorate, the PCI increasingly shifted its policy towards attempting to influence directly the balance of power within the DC leadership. The party made it ever clearer that it was willing to deal with the DC as a whole, and to use the offer of direct compromise as an instrument in seeking to affect the Catholic party's internal equilibria. Well before the events in Chile, the ground for the historic compromise had been laid.[27]

What explains the shift in party policy toward the DC? The answer seems to be that, from the PCI's strategic vantage point, almost everything which had occurred since 1970 had affirmed the central structural role of the DC in the Italian system. This was the case in several senses. Electorally, the DC had demonstrated its ability to maintain its interclass electorate in spite of both the mass mobilisation of the working class and the rightward tilt of the Catholic party's leadership. Furthermore, it was also evident that the DC was central in the sense of being "in the middle" of the party system —between the parties of the centre-left and a party on the right, the MSI, which almost thirty years after fascism remained a potential reactionary coagulant of social discontent.

The electoral and party system centrality of the DC meant that it was also central to the problem of system legitimacy. Events since 1970 suggested that the long-standing Communist concern about the possibility of a reactionary turn in Italian politics had become not a theoretical but a practical issue. The electoral stability of the DC, however, meant that mass mobilisation of progressive sectors of the DC's base and fear of electoral losses would not represent a sufficient check on a rightward movement of the Catholic party; other forms of pressure would be necessary. This goes a long way toward explaining why the Communists became increasingly less interested in promoting a left split in the DC: it was of far greater importance to have, and to encourage, a progressive counterweight within the DC than to split off what would certainly be a small minority, risking that the remainder would be even freer to shift to the right. The game had to be played within the DC.

DC centrality was also institutional, and increasingly in this phase the PCI saw in the outputs of the State the crux of possible solutions to the evolving crisis. Reform, public order, greater social cohesion all depended on how government, the bureaucracy and the police performed, and all these institutions were deeply penetrated by the DC. The Christian Democrats might not be relied upon to use these institutions in ways desired by the PCI. Nonetheless, DC participation in a compromise was more likely to provide access to, and leverage over, these institutions than would its opposition to a government of the left.

Finally, these various forms of centrality meant that the DC would be pivotal to overcoming perhaps the major obstacle to an effective Communist governmental role: legitimation of the PCI itself. For some time to come, the mediation of the Christian Democrats would be necessary if important social strata and institutions (and the United States)[28] were to accept the Communists as a potential partner in national power. Without at least the implicit *imprimatur* of the DC, more likely to be won through accommodation than through confrontation, the PCI could only expect a virulent reaction to its accession to government. In this sense, as in the others, fifty-one per cent would not be sufficient.

There was, of course, a dark irony for the Communists in all this. It meant that compromise would have to be sought with a party which was deemed responsible for the crisis, which had been moving to the right and whose structure represented a heavy weight against reform. Although the DC had been identified as so much a part of the problem, it would also have to be part of the solution. This was the most graphic sign of the DC's centrality,[29] the most fundamental reason for the search for an historic compromise.

But what kind of compromise? Some of the old strategic ambiguities remained, albeit in new guises. The historic compromise would not be a capitulation to the DC but instead the policy best adapted to translating the continuing strength of the working class and the left into effective pressure on the DC to move in a progressive direction. How to move the DC and how far it had to move before compromise could be struck remained open to question. There is nothing in the documents of this phase to indicate that the PCI leadership had answers. The policy which subsequently emerged, therefore, was probably more a function of responses to evolving economic, social and political conditions than a calculated pursuit of specific, pre-established ends.

IV.   PHASE THREE—THE TIDE TURNS: 1974–1978

The proposal of an historic compromise was primarily defensive. Yet just as it was enunciated, the tide of the preceding years was turning. The electoral, social and political alliances of the left, rather than receding, came into flood. Nonetheless, the PCI neither abandoned its new policy nor altered its basic logic. In fact, the years from 1974 to 1978 were marked by an accentuation of those features of the policy more oriented toward elite compromise, alliance with the DC and State centralisation of policy making. At the same time, however, the irony of pursuing a seemingly conservative policy during a period of political advance was expressed in a growing tension and debate within the PCI itself. First, sporadically and then ever more forcefully, leaders and activists argued for a more sceptical and even hostile attitude toward the DC, more social mobilisation relative to elite manoeuvre, more willingness to think about the *alternativa* along with compromise. As this third phase of the crisis proceeds, there is growing internal debate between those committed to the strategic consolidation of 1973 and those wishing to return to the more traditional ambiguities of the *via italiana*.

Three basic developments of special interest to the PCI characterise this phase. At the economic level, there is the onset of what can be considered a crisis of accumulation in the Italian economy, exposing in dramatic form the structural weaknesses of the economic order and, in the party's view, threatening to create severe divisions within the bloc of social alliances which lay at the heart of the party's strategy. The issue for the PCI became how the economic developments might be used to enhance the party's strategy rather than becoming a source of weakness and strategic decay.

The second major feature of the period was the rise of terrorism and other forms of extra-legal political protest on the left. The activities of the Red Brigades, the Autonomists, the Metropolitan Indians and other self-styled and publicly perceived leftist groups created an air of social tension and uncertainty which the Communists did not hesitate to compare with that after World War I. A party as sensitive as the PCI to its links with the middle classes could not help seeing the leftist disorder as a major threat.

The two preceding developments could be expected to reinforce the cautious, defensive stance inherent in the search for compromise with the DC. Electoral and political developments, however, pushed in quite another direction. The divorce referendum, the elections of 1975 and even the elections of 1976 suggested that the Christian Democrats could no longer hold together their traditional electorate and were finally paying a significant electoral cost for the conservative (and corrupt) policies which they had been pursuing. While the 1976 elections made clear that the DC would not crumble easily, they also indicated that the DC's ability to maintain its strength would be increasingly dependent on the absorption of ever more rightist voters, thus seemingly casting further doubt on the Catholic party's availability for progressive programmatic compromise. The country seemed to many to be moving toward a bi-polar situation: the DC representing the conservative pole and the PCI and PSI the progressive one. There also seemed good reason to believe that the balance of electoral and political strength would continue to shift to the left.[30] Thus, the historic compromise, with its image of moderation and openness to progressive Catholicism, looked like an enormously effective electoral tactic but an unnecessarily cautious political strategy.

The PCI in this phase rejected any such conclusion, whether raised by critics outside the party or by opposition within its ranks. Instead, the party doggedly pursued the principles which underlay the historic compromise proposal and the search for alliances with the DC.

We have seen that in the first two phases of the crisis the PCI sought to channel social mobilisation toward broadly based reforms, even at the expense of incisiveness and credibility with the party's traditional constituency. Nonetheless, the reforms sought were extensive, and sharply redistributive. In this phase a significant shift occurs. Welfare reforms increasingly become absorbed into the larger themes of austerity and reform of the country's economic structure.

> The Italian Communist Party battles for . . . a severe austerity policy which, however, must be socially fair and must serve at the same time . . . to initiate a grand policy of social transformation.
>
> The problem which we pose is that, while one must act in the first place to introduce into the restrictions the greatest possible degree of equity—which for us is obvious—it is also necessary at the same time democratically to create a public will which uses austerity as the opportunity to introduce the necessary qualitative changes in the overall Italian economic and social structure.[31]

Here was the theme of hegemony of the working class in a new guise. Rather than just asking the working class to use its strength to promote social policy reforms with a broader constituency, the party was asking for sacrifices in the face of what was deemed a deep crisis of accumulation which could threaten not just the isolation of the working class but a historical defeat.

Understood only in these terms, the austerity theme might seem just an extension of the previous defensive posture. There was, however, another side to the coin. Economic sacrifice, the party made clear, could not be expected unless the economic margins created were channeled into investment directed toward a restructuring of the economy. How might this occur? Only through a process of planning which would assure the unions and the left a considerable degree of direct and indirect control over the investment process. Austerity had to be matched by gains in power for the unions and the working class parties, a reduction in the prerogatives of capital, structural reform of the entire way in which economic, and therefore distributive, decisions were reached. Austerity, had to be linked to fundamental changes in basic class relations of power.[32] Thus, the new policy, even more than the old, sought to combine the defensive and offensive aspects of the party's strategy. This policy was difficult to "sell" to constituents. If political gains were clear, in terms of government policy and/or of growing political legitimacy and power of the PCI, success might be possible. Should it prove difficult to win significant political advances, disillusionment might easily set in.

PCI policy toward public order in this phase also continued to reflect the principles developed earlier. We have seen that after 1970 the party accepted the critical role of the State in dealing with political violence and sought to have it act more effectively. This posture had been an easy one to adopt toward terrorism of the right. Political violence of the left, however, was more problematic, for it could be argued to be simply the expression of extreme discontent with many of the same injustices which the party was itself denouncing. Such reactions appear to have been rather more widespread in the party base and the industrial working class than the PCI would have preferred. Nonetheless, the Communists became ever more vehement about the necessity of working-class vigilance and in denouncing terrorism and other extra-legal activity. Defense of the democratic institutions was an inherent component of the historic compromise policy and of the party's strategy more generally. Without it, the party's efforts to increase its legitimacy could not hope for success. Again, however, the party encountered diffidence on the part of its own constituents.[33]

The third and most important area in which Communist policy continued to follow already established lines despite the changes in electoral balances was relations with the Christian Democrats. The decline of DC electoral strength was not accompanied by an increased interest in the alternative but rather by intensified efforts to cement direct alliances with the Catholic party. At the national level this was not, superficially, surprising. The outcome of the 1976 elections created a stalemated Parliament requiring some form of DC–PCI co-operation if a government was to be formed, much less function effectively. Communist behaviour, however, represented something more than simple accommodation to necessity. On the one hand, the party justified co-operation as not just the only, but the best, way the country could hope to deal with the 'emergency."[34] On the other hand, the PCI showed itself unexpectedly willing to accept only very gradual, small and sometimes symbolic gains in power in exchange for co-operation. The sequence of governments after the 1976 elections is indicative. They show a PCI pursuing incremental gains in legitimacy and influence on the internal balance of power in the DC, even at the expense of direct control over governmental policy making. As this phase progressed, such a trade-off became increasingly difficult to defend or sustain.

Communist behaviour at the sub-national level displayed even more clearly the dogged pursuit of the tenets of the historic compromise. Despite the fact that after the 1975 elections, the party could control a vast number of sub-national governments in alliance with the Socialists, it chose instead to seek coalitions which would, in some form, enlist the co-operation of the DC. The policy elicited protests from the PSI and sometimes strong resistance from local Communist officials and grass-roots members. Nonetheless, the party persisted in its policy, linking sub-national policy to national strategic goals.[35]

We have suggested at several points that the policies pursued in this phase by the PCI's national leadership found increasingly less favour among the party's constituents. This discontent began to be reflected in national party policy in the winter of 1977–1978 when, following a mass demonstration of metalworkers in Rome, the party withdrew from the "programmatic majority" and demanded seats in the government. The crisis was resolved, after tortuous negotiations, with the PCI accepting much less—participation in the parliamentary majority supporting another all Christian Democratic government. Incrementalism and the search for accommodation still won out.[36]

The following winter a more serious rupture developed. After an extended period of increasingly bitter complaints about the DC's arrogant disregard of the parliamentary majority, the Communists again withdrew from the arrangement to co-operate, demanding direct governmental participation. This time, their resolve was firm. A lengthy series of negotiations demonstrated that the PCI was willing to accept little short of full cabinet participation and that relations between the two major parties were worse than they had been in years; Parliament was then dissolved and national elections called. It appeared, despite Communist protestations, that the strategy of the historic compromise or even of the pursuit of accommodation with the DC had come to an end.[37]

Before reaching such a conclusion, however, it is worthwhile considering the underlying logic of action explaining PCI behaviour in this third phase of the crisis, seeking to understand why the party pursued alliance with the DC with such tenacity despite the change in electoral strengths and why it then decided, at least temporarily, to abandon this stance. This may allow us better to speculate about the conditions under which co-operation might be resumed after the elections.

Our basic argument is that from about the middle of 1977 the costs of the strategic consolidation embodied in the historic compromise came, first slowly and then more rapidly, to outweigh its benefits. By winter 1978, a return to a more flexible posture, including the possibility of a period of opposition, became a more desirable, if not enviable, option than continued accommodation with the Christian Democrats.

The rising costs of the PCI's policies were to be measured primarily in terms of a marked degeneration of the party's relations with its members and electorate. The historic compromise had never set entirely well within the PCI. As early as the fall of 1973, party President Luigi Longo questioned the notion; numerous Central Committee meetings and articles by party leaders in the party press sought (sometimes in contradictory terms) to clarify the concept, suggesting that there was considerable confusion and disagreement at the grass roots. Subsequent polling and other data, furthermore, indicates that the membership remained sceptical and often unfavourable towards the policy.[38] Until the first results of national collaboration became evident, however, protest was relatively muted. After all, the policies associated with the historic compromise were paying off: the party electorate was growing, vast numbers of local councils had been captured, the PCI had become perceived as crucial to the resolution of the crisis and was on the threshold of a governmental role. And all of this was at the expense of the power of the DC. The pursuit of compromise appeared reconcilable with the traditional hostility toward the DC.

After the period of national collaboration began and the party had to shoulder some of the responsibilities which were the natural outgrowth of its success—requiring sacrifices from some of its traditional constituencies and sometimes failing to meet the inflated expectations built up in previous years —protest became more concrete. Complaints by party leaders about specific policies became more and more frequent and intense. It seemed to some that the party was being too moderate, failing to press for sufficient change and thus disappointing and demobilizing social groups on whose strength and enthusiasm the party's gains and eventual success depended.[39]

Numerous signs appeared to bear this out. Debate at grass roots meetings was heated. Furthermore, members appeared to be withdrawing from the kinds of commitments to party and union activity which are the backbone of the PCI's character as a mass party. The slogan, launched in December 1976, of the "PCI, Partito di lotta e di governo" (PCI: Party of Struggle and of Government) expressed the tensions, and numerous articles in *Rinascita* in 1977 indicated that it had failed to convince and motivate the base. At the same time, after almost a decade of membership growth, stagnation set in: no gain in 1977, a small but significant loss in 1978.[40] Finally, the party also began to suffer electorally. Elections in May, 1978, the referenda in June and further elections in the autumn indicated that the PCI had lost its electoral momentum especially among some critical electorates: Southern voters, northern middle-class voters in major cities, the young and even certain industrial working-class voters.[41] Thus, members seemed increasingly to be translating their long-standing scepticism into both more intense "voice" and into "exit"; electoral supporters were also losing faith. The costs of party policy were clearly on the rise. The only time when the tide appeared to have been turned was in the winter of 1977–1978 when the party withdrew temporarily from collaboration.

Nonetheless, we have seen that at that time and until the following winter the party persisted in seeking accommodation with the DC. The benefits of its policy must have been seen as sufficient to warrant going ahead despite internal discontent and the threat of electoral erosion. What benefits, from the standpoint of the PCI's strategic perspective, derived from accommodation and what changed to make these no longer sufficient?

Nothing about the evolution of the crisis after 1973 altered the basic calculation which had originally led the PCI to press for a direct alliance with the DC. Nor did political developments—the electoral difficulties and leadership changes in the DC and the growth of the Communist electorate —significantly affect that reasoning. On the one hand, the economic crisis and the rise of left terrorism only augmented the centrality of the DC. The economic situation increased the importance, in the PCI's view, of effective government action. The struggle against inflation and an equitable and strongly reformist policy of austerity, if they were to win the support of the working class, required a political *quid pro quo* dependent on political leadership and bureaucratic intervention. Implementation of the necessary policies could not await a victory of the left or the creation of a more politically neutral bureaucracy. Furthermore, both the crisis of the economy and the policies the PCI sought to promote to deal with it further increased the need to maintain and extend ties with the middle classes. The mediating role which the PCI assigned to the DC with regard to all these issues remained crucial and thus so too did the necessity to seek to influence the balance of power in the DC and to co-operate with the Christian Democrats in government. Only a national unity coalition, the Communist leadership argued, could expect to gain broad consent from diverse strata of the population necessary to undertake the economic and social policies the crisis required.

Similar arguments applied to the spread and intensification of terrorism. Since the violence now came predominantly from the left, the PCI had to show it fully supported effective police action. This would require the full co-operation of the DC in the context of agreements among the major parties. Finally, nothing about the changing character of the crisis made the Christian Democrats any less important as a source of legitimacy for the Communists. If anything, the deepening economic and social crisis and growing PCI strength increased the need for some counter-weight if traditionally anti-Communist sectors of the population were to accept as a legitimate potential governmental partner.

There was, of course, a critical assumption in the PCI's reasoning: that the DC appear willing to play the game. The Christian Democrats had to be shown willing to accept the PCI as a legitimate, if junior, partner and to allow the Communists sufficient influence over government to make austerity credible to the working class, to restructure government policy more generally and thereby to seem available for eventual full Communist governmental participation. Communist policy goals and power remained linked, and both depended on the availability of the DC for compromise, The crisis of the DC after 1973, the decay of the left of the Christian Democratic electorate and the assumption of leadership by the Moro group all appeared to make this more likely. This judgment was borne out after the 1976 elections when the new DC leadership showed itself willing to reach agreements with the PCI and to grant the possibility that the PCI might be a legitimate governmental partner. The programmes and policy implementation of the first two Andreotti governments also suggested that PCI influence was on the rise. Nonetheless, with the internal costs of the policy rising, it is not surprising that the PCI sought to raise the stakes of collaboration.[42] Thus, in the first two years after the 1976 elections there was a cycle of greater PCI pressure, DC resistance, inter-party compromise and then, after a period of relative calm during which some Communist expectations were disappointed and internal pressure once again rose, renewed Communist pressure for greater influence and symbolic status. Up to the summer of 1978, however, the process of accommodation—of two steps forward, one step back—continued to pay (and to offer the prospect of further paying) which made the internal costs acceptable for the Communists.

In the second half of 1978, this no longer proved the case. Changes in the internal balance of power in the DC after the death of Moro brought to the fore personalities known for, and willing to state, their inalterable opposition to Communist governmental participation. The DC seemed increasingly ready to risk confrontation rather than make any more concessions to the PCI. This new situation was reflected in the performance of the government. A series of decisions suggested clearly that the opinions of the PCI and of the trade unions were being given short shrift and that the Parliamentary majority was unable to exercise control of effective influence over even the most important governmental decisions. Finally, the Socialist Party, which the PCI had tended to ignore, launched a doubly dangerous attack: on the one hand, from the right, suggesting that the PCI still was not a legitimate democratic party and that the Socialist Party might itself once again become available for coalitions which would exclude the PCI; on the other hand, from the left, presenting the PCI as too moderate, both in its stances on political-economic policy and on public order. Rapidly the PCI found itself besieged and on the defensive, internal disaffection mounting, major electoral losses looming and ever less reason to expect, or to be able to convince others, that it could continue to convert the policy of accommodation with the DC into further gains. Withdrawal from the majority (with its probable enthusiastic reception by the membership) and even the danger of some electoral losses appeared under these conditions more than the fruitless pretense of co-operation and the likelihood of continued organisational and electoral erosion.

CONCLUSION

With the results of the June 1979 national elections in hand, it would appear that the minimally tolerable expectations of the PCI when it broke with the majority have been realised. The party suffered important electoral losses, perhaps slightly larger than anticipated, particularly in those areas of the country and among those social strata in which its organisational presence was weakest, but, significantly, also among both young voters and some northern workers in major industrial sectors. Its losses among the latter two groups, whatever the other causes, seem partially to have reflected disillusionment with the party's accommodationist policies and with its image of cultural rigidity and only very cautious ideological and political evolution. On the other hand, several aspects of the elections would lead one to surmise that the party will accept its losses without major upheaval. First, despite the erosion of its electorate, the PCI maintained a considerable portion of the dramatic gains made in 1976. Second, reports indicate that the party organisation was rivitalised by the return to opposition and by the election campaign. Third, and most important, an initial examination of the results suggests that the party was primarily punished by those voters who were profoundly dissatisfied with the three years of experience of PCI collaboration with the national government. If this proves upon further analysis to be correct, it would lend support to the party's decision that withdrawal from the majority was preferable to continued collaboration under conditions of increasing DC hostility and declining control of governmental behaviour. The fact that the DC did considerably worse than anticipated in the elections only confirms this judgment.

The question which naturally arises is whether the withdrawal from the majority and the outcome of the elections presage a major shift in PCI strategy from that pursued in the last decade. In part, the answer would appear to be, yes. The historic compromise, understood as a consolidated interpretation of the party's strategy, has become ever less prominent in party rhetoric in 1979 and was not a major point of discussion at the party's XV Congress in March.[45] The experience of the last three years, including the withdrawal from the majority and the June elections would only seem to encourage this trend. Return to some of the strategic ambiguities characteristic of the period before September, 1973 appears likely, as does a more combative attitude toward the DC.

Nonetheless, this should not suggest that the PCI will undertake a major strategic revision or abandon its basic commitment to constructive opposition, to the search for influence over national government policy or to the attempt to influence the internal balance of power in the DC. All the structural conditions which initially encouraged the evolution of the party's strategy in these directions remain. So, too, do most of the disadvantages of seeking to build *l'alternativa* which would exclude the DC. Finally, taking the broader view, the party's successes in the last decade have been considerable. Thus, basic continuity of strategy would seem probable. That the party will often appear less pliant, less available for compromises reached at the top, more critical of the DC and more willing to use mobilisation to advance its positions is also likely. Both the gains made and the costs paid since 1976 promote such a posture. This should not, however, obscure underlying continuities and their roots in the party's basic strategy and in the structure of the Italian system.

NOTES

1. For a discussion of changing public opinion about the PCI in the 1970s, see Giacomo Sani, 'Ricambio elettorale e identificazioni partitiche: verso una egemonia delle sinistre?' in *Rivista Italiana di Scienza Politica*, V (1975), pp. 516–544.
2. For some discussions of postwar PCI strategy, see Donald L. M. Blackmer, 'Introduction' and 'Continuity and Change in Postwar Italian Communism,' in Blackmer and Sidney Tarrow, eds., *Communism in Italy and France* (Princeton: Princeton University Press, 1975); Tarrow, *Peasant Communism in Southern Italy* (New Haven: Yale University Press, 1967), Chs. 5 and 6; Stephen Hellman, 'The PCI's Alliance Strategy and the Case of the Middle Classes,' in Blackmer and Tarrow, *op. cit.*; and Peter Lange, 'Il Pci e possibili esiti della crisi italiana,' in Luigi Graziano and Tarrow, eds., *La crisi italiana* (Turin, Einaudi, 1979), pp. 657–675.
3. Carlo Donolo, *Mutamento o transizione?* (Bologna: Il Mulino, 1977), p. 12.
4. For a synthetic discussion of this period, see Paolo Farneti, 'I partiti politici e il sistema di potere,' in Valerio Castronovo, ed., *L'Italia contemporanea* (Turin: Einaudi, 1976).
5. *Ibid.*, and Lange, *op. cit.*, pp. 667–669.
6. Donald L. M. Blackmer, 'Italian Communism: Strategy for the 1970s,' *Problems of Communism*, May–June, 1972, pp. 41–56.
7. See Berlinguer's and Longo's concluding remarks at the XII Party Congress in *XII Congresso del PCI: Atti e risoluzioni* (Rome: Editori Riuniti, 1969).
8. See Stephen Hellman, 'The Longest Campaign: Communist Party Strategy and the Elections of 1976,' in Howard Penniman, ed., *Italy at the Polls* (Washington, AEI, 1977), p. 161 and *passim*. There is no question that the Congress was perceived as a militant one. With hindsight, however, this impression needs to be tempered by the more moderate themes which were also present and which became prominent subsequently.

9. Enrico Berlinguer, 'Costruire una nuova unita internazionalista e compiere un passo avanti verso il socialismo,' (Conclusions to the XII Party Congress), now reprinted in Berlinguer, La 'questione communista' (Rome: Editori Riuniti, 1975), p. 35.
10. Ibid., p. 24 and passim.
11. Ibid., pp. 34–36.
12. Ibid., esp. pp. 30–32.
13. For an interesting discussion of the concept of hegemony in PCI strategic analysis, see Biagio De Giovanni, 'Gramsci e l'elaborazione successiva del partito comunista,' in Egemonia, stato, partito in Gramsci (Rome: Editori Riuniti, 1977). For a rather different view of the relationship between Gramsci and contemporary PCI strategy, see Massimo Salvadori, Eurocomunismo e socialismo sovietico (Turin: Einaudi, 1978).
14. Berlinguer, 'Costruire . . .,' p. 31.
15. See Ugo Pecchiolo, 'Un partito comunista rinnovato e raffozato per le esigenze nuove della società italiana,' and the interventions of Luigi Longo and Enrico Berlinguer collected in a pamphlet with the same title as Pecchioli's speech and distributed by the PCI. The speeches were made at a meeting of the Central Committee and Central Control Commission of the PCI in January, 1970. It is important to note that the problems which the leadership found in moderating and directing the enthusiasm of members may, in part, have been due to the fact that often in their own speeches party leaders gave unequivocal support to the trade union struggles and tended to present even the search for moderation as 'revolutionary.' See, for instance, Berlinguer, 'Le lotte operaie e popolari indicano i c-ntenuiti della svolta da compiere,' in La comunista, pp. 83–92.
16. For discussions of the events leading up to the 1972 national elections, see Mario Caciagli and Alberto Spreafico, 'Introduzione,' in Caciagli and Spreafico, eds., Un sistema alla prova (Bologna: Il Mulino, 1975), pp. 5–21, and other essays in the volume, especially for detailed analysis of electroal developments.
17. The PCI's analysis of the developments in this period and particularly of the dangers of a dramatic rightist backlash is found throughout the documents of this period and in numerous articles in Rinascita, the party analytical weekly. For the most important statements, see Berlinguer's opening speech and conclusions in XIII Congresso del PCI: Atti e risoluzioni (Rome: Editori Riuniti, 1972) and the following articles and speeches by Berlinguer, all now reprinted in whole or in part in La 'questione comunista': 'Un anno dall' 'autunno caldo',' 'Classe operaia e blocco sociale,' 'La nostra riposta agli attachi fascisti,' 'I pericoli di destra si respingono con una politica di sviluppo demo-cratico e di progresso sociale,' 'La nostra lotta per l'affermazione di una alternativa democratica,' and 'Per una effetiva inversione di tendenza e per avanzare verso una svolta democratica.' It is in these documents that one finds most of the specific proposals and analyses which are eventually consolidated into the call for an 'historic com-promise.'
18. See Berlinguer's three articles, published in Rinascita September 28 and October 5 and 12, 'Riflessioni sull' Italia dopo i fatti del Cile,' and reprinted in La 'questione com-unista,' pp. 609–639.
19. The unwillingness to govern with only 51 per cent, for instance, appeared in an article by Gerardo Chiaromonte, 'I conti con la DC,' Rinascita, 25 May 1973. In general, it would appear that the events in Chile simply provided a dramatic context for the consolidation and presentation of party positions which had been developing for more than two years. This, of course, suggests that the primary explanation for those positions, at least in the most direct causal sense, lies in domestic Italian developments rather than in international ones.
20. Berlinguer, 'A un anno dal' "autunno caldo",' (October, 1970) is an excellent example of this reorientation.
21. Berlinguer, 'I pericoli di destra . . .' (July, 1971), p. 332.
22. Berlinguer, 'La nostra lotta per . . .' (November, 1971), p. 383. See also 'I pericoli . . .,' pp. 331–332.
23. Berlinguer, 'Economia e democrazia,' (July, 1970), in La 'questione comunista', pp. 200-204. More generally, the party increasingly identified the poor performance of government as the 'major point of danger': Berlinguer, 'La nostra lotta . . .' (November, 1971), p. 372.

24. *Ibid.,* pp. 393–394.

25. Hellman, 'The Longest Campaign . . .,' p. 167, makes a similar point.

26. See, for instance, Berlinguer, 'La DC ha paura,' (May, 1970) in *La ·questione comunista',* pp. 195–199.

27. See note 19.

28. We have focused our attention in this article on the domestic sources of the PCI's strategic evolution because they appear to us of greatest importance. The role played by the U.S. position toward the PCI in encouraging the Communists to seek alliance with the DC as a source of international legitimation, however, cannot be ignored. Ironically, the U.S. traditionally a strong advocate of two-party alternation in government, has functioned as a stimulus to the historic compromise rather than the alternative in Italy.

29. Our analysis of centrality clearly shares some points with Giovanni Sartori's analysis of the role of the DC in his well-known 'European Political Parties: The Case of Polarized Pluralism,' in Joseph La Palombara and Myron Weiner, eds., *Political Parties and Political Development* (Princeton: Princeton University Press, 1966). We differ, however, in at least two major respects. Our interpretation of the DC's centrality is much broader than Sartori's, for he concentrates his attention on the party and electoral system. Our basic argument is that the DC's centrality has had a centripetal effect on Communist behaviour whereas Sartori suggests the effects on the party system will be centrifugal.

30. See Giacomo Sani, 'Ricambio elettorale . . .' and 'The Italian Electorate in the Mid-1970's: Beyond Tradition,' in *Italy at the Polls.* For a different and extremely stimulating analysis see Arturo Parisi and Gianfranco Pasquino, '20 giugno: struttura politica e comportamento elettorale,' in Parisi and Pasquino, eds., *Continuita e mutamento elettorale in Italia* (Bologna: Il Mulino, 1977).

31. Berlinguer, *Il Pci e la crisi italiana* (Rome: Editori Riuniti: 1976), p. 72, from an October, 1976 Central Committee address. On party economic and social policy in this period, see also Berlinguer's preparatory speech for the party's XIV Congress, 'Per uscire dalla crisi, per costruire un'Italia nuova, '(December, 1974) in *La 'questione comunista';* Berlinguer, 'Austeritá, occasione per transformare l'Italia,' (Rome: Editori Riuniti, 1977); PCI, *Prosposta di progetto a medio termine* (Rome: Editori Riuniti, 1977). For a critical analysis of the party's economic programme, see Alberto Martinelli, 'The Economic Policy of the Italian Communist Party,' *Challenge,* September-October, 1976.

32. Berlinguer, 'Austeritá, occasione . . .'.

33. This problem, hinted at in numerous articles in *Rinascita* in 1977 and 1978, was most clearly evident that it had been unable to promite the intensity of mobilisation it desired after the assassination in Turin of the vice-director of *La Stampa,* the newspaper owned by Fiat. On the party's reaction to the Moro kidnapping see Paolo Bufalini's report to the Central Committee printed in *L'Unita,* 15 April 1978.

34. See, for instance, Gerardo Chiaromonte's speech to the Central Committee explaining the party's position on the programmatic accord reached in the summer of 1977: *L'Accordo programmatico e l'azione dei comunisti* (Rome: Editori Riuniti, 1977). See also, Berlingeur, 'Why is the PCI Abstaining,' speech to the Chamber of Deputies, April 11, 1976, and 'The PCI's Proposals and the Goals of its Struggle,' October 18, 1976 speech to the Central Committee, both reprinted in *The Italian Communists,* n. 4–5, August-October, 1976.

35. See Armando Cossutta's speech to the Central Committee on the June, 1975 administrative elections, 'June 15: A Deep Change in the Italian Political Situation,' in *The Italian Communists,* no. 4, June-August, 1975.

36. On this crisis, see Berlinguer, 'An Emergency Government to Tackle a Crisis of Exceptional Gravity,' speech to the Central Committee in January, 1978 and 'Unity of All Democratic Forces in Defense of Republican Institutions and the State,' speech to the Chamber of Deputies on the confidence vote for the new government, 16 March 1978, both reprinted in *The Italian Communists,* n. 1, January-March, 1978.

37. For the party analyses of the degenerating relationships within the majority and the rightward movement of the DC, see *Rinascita* throughout the fall and winter of 1978.

38. Marzio Barbagli and Piergiorgio Corbetta, 'Una tattica e due strategie. Inchiesta sulla base del PCI,' *Il Mulino*, XXVII, November-December, 1978. See, also, their excellent and comprehensive article surveying PCI organisational development in the 1970s, 'Partito e movimento: aspetti e rinnovamento del Pci,' *Inchiesta*, VIII, January-February, 1978.
39. See especially the Central Committee meetings of October and December, 1976, the debates of which were reported in *L'Unità*, October 19–21 and December 14–16.
40. Barbagli and Corbetta, 'Partito . . .,' p. 11 and data announced at the XV Party Congress in March, 1979.
41. For a trenchant party analysis of the 1978 elections, see Paolo Franchi, 'Come ha votato l'Italia nel 1978?' *Rinascita*, 1 December 1978, pp. 5–6.
42. On the PCI's tendency to pursue a somewhat tougher policy in response to setbacks, see Berlinguer's speech following the party's sharp electoral losses in May 1978: 'The Innovating Force of the PCI's Policy of Unity and Rigor,' in *The Italian Communists*, n. 2, April-June, 1978.
43. See *L'Unità*, March 31–April 4, 1979. See also the theses for the congress, now printed in English in *The Italian Communists*, 1979 Special Issue.

The Italian Socialist Party Under Craxi: Surviving but not Reviving

David Hine*

I. THE STRATEGIC DILEMMA

The Italian Socialist Party (PSI) occupies an ambiguous position in Italian politics. It has managed to preserve its strategic importance in the party system despite an almost uninterrupted record of electoral decline. In thirty years its share of the electorate has been halved, and by the seventies it was dwarfed by the much larger Communist Party. Yet this decline has not destroyed the PSI's pivotal role. On the contrary, in at least some respects the Party's importance has increased. In the fifties the ruling Christian Democrat Party had the option of forming coalitions which did not include the Socialists, but in the sixties and seventies this option effectively disappeared. Thus, unless the Christian Democrat Party were to go over the heads of the Socialists to work with the Communists (which in the sixties was inconceivable, and still in the seventies remains improbable) any coalition has had to enjoy Socialist benevolence.[1]

This relationship has dominated the making and unmaking of Italian governments in the mid and late-seventies. It enabled the Socialists to play midwife to the Historic Compromise, by which in various stages after the 1976 election the PCI was gradually incorporated into the ruling majority. The same factor was the root cause of the long political crisis of 1979, for the decision of the Socialists to follow the Communists into opposition, at least temporarily, made the premature dissolution of parliament inevitable.

Nevertheless the Socialist Party's pivotal position has in the long run proved more a source of weakness than of strength. As a small party it can never hope to govern alone. It has to form alliances, and the existence of alternative alliances—leftwards to the Communists or rightwards to the Christian Democrats—has been a constant source of disagreement in the party. Moreover, in whatever relationship the party has established, it has proved to be the subordinate partner. In the forties and early fifties, when closely associated with the Communist Party, the Socialists came to be seen as little more than an appendage of the better organised and more powerful PCI. And when, in reaction to this, they asserted their much-vaunted 'autonomy' and joined the Centre-left coalition, they found themselves even more the prisoners of the Christian Democratic Party than ever they had been of the Communists. Fearful of withdrawing from the coalition in case Italy should become totally ungovernable and fall prey to right-wing extremism, and increasingly dependent upon the spoils of government

* Department of Politics, University of Newcastle.

patronage, the PSI was for many years trapped in a fruitless alliance with the Christian Democrats which brought none of the promised reforms and irreparably damaged the Party's image.

Finally, in the seventies, the Party did break away, and in so doing it inaugurated a new phase in Italian coalition politics characterised by the gradual insertion of the Communist Party into the ruling majority. The change was not solely due to the Socialist Party, but it played a crucial role in the process. Even so, the change did little for the PSI. Rather, it aided the Communist Party which posed as the moderate and responsible party of the democratic left, and hence appropriated some of the Socialists' former electoral territory.[2]

An equally serious difficulty for the PSI, especially in the seventies, has been that its search for independence from both Christian Democrats and Communists has left it with the image of a vaccillating and dilatory party, uncertain of its own identity and irresponsible in its use of power. Indeed when this uncertainty has provoked the collapse of a government, or worse the premature dissolution of parliament, it has been punished by the Italian electorate.

Never were these problems more apparent than in 1976. At its 40th Congress the PSI appeared finally to have rejected the Centre-left coalition. It declared that its long-term aim was a 'Socialist Alternative' to Christian Democrat rule: in other words an alliance of the left similar to that which Mitterrand had forged with the PCF in France. But the new strategy was presented with much ambiguity. Indeed, the only certainty to emerge from the 1976 Congress was that the strategy had provoked the collapse of the government and the premature dissolution of parliament. It was unclear how the Party hoped to square its long-term aim with the existing political reality, which was the absence of a parliamentary majority for a left-wing alternative to Christian Democrat rule. In any case, even if such a majority were achieved relatively rapidly it would be a majority dominated not by the Socialists but by the Communists.

In fact this last consideration ensured that the new approach was presented with much caution. At the 1976 Congress the then leader, Francesco De Martino, argued that it represented a long-term strategy, not to be pursued actively until the PSI had regained something like parity with the Communists. In the short term, to face the worsening economic crisis, and to fill the political gap left by the collapse of the Centre-left government, what was needed was an 'emergency' government of all 'democratic parties', including both Communists and Christian Democrats.[3]

Such an emergency government did eventually materialise, but not before the PSI had paid the price of its ambiguity in the 1976 election. The Party did not actually lose ground compared to 1972 (although it did compared to the 1975 regional elections) but its failure to progress in circumstances which were highly favourable to the left as a whole, and which generated a huge increase in the Communist vote represented a serious moral defeat. Voters had found much too persuasive the Socialist argument that real reform could only come with Communist entry into government, and had voted directly for the PCI itself.[4]

Naturally there were other reasons why the Socialists did badly. They were identified as the main cause of the premature dissolution of parliament, and they suffered through the rise of the Radical Party, which won the support of a segment of progressive and libertarian middle-class opinion. But the root cause undoubtedly lay in the failures of the past and the ambiguities of the present. A decade of immobile government, of bitter factional rivalry and not a little corruption could not easily be erased from the Party's record. If the PSI was to regain parity with the Communists, therefore, it had to acquire an entirely new image; one still differentiated from that of the Communists, but not so much as to make the alliance which was to form the basis of the Socialist Alternative totally impractical.

The Summer of 1976 therefore represented a watershed for the PSI. The election was a profound psychological trauma felt throughout the Party. Unless some drastic change occurred, the Communist expansion seemed destined to absorb all but a fraction of the Socialist electorate, and there was a widespread feeling that if the PSI was to regain a place as one of the three main Italian parties, and not to settle for a permanently minor role, then a renewal, every bit as radical as that which revolutionised the old SFIO in France after the Congress of Epinay, would be necessary.

On sentiments such as this was forged the so-called 'rivolta dei quarantenni'. This palace coup brought to the helm a new generation of Socialist leaders in their forties who for some time had been impatient to overturn the gerontocracy which had taken the party from the era of the Cold War to the setbacks of the Centre-left and which, in the ageing form of secretary De Martino, still controlled the party machine. The coup brought Bettino Craxi, a 42-year-old Milanese deputy to the post of party secretary, and forged a new and in some ways unexpected alliance between the right of the Party, led by Craxi, and the left, led by Claudio Signorile.

To be sure the change was only partly generational. It was also an extension of the bitter personal rivalries which had scored the Party since the sixties. Indeed the Craxi-Signorile axis had been in the making at the Party Congress before the election setback, and it represented the response of their respective groups to the dominant hold over the party machine exercised by the centre faction led by De Martino. After the election a rather disparate group of leaders, including some from the new generation, such as Enrico Manca, but also several of the old guard, defected from the De Martino camp, and with their help, and that of De Martino's longstanding rival Giacomo Mancini, the Craxi-Signorile axis was able to win a majority in the central committee.

Paradoxically, therefore, the installation of the new leadership was due in part to the methods of factional intrigue which had so discredited the Party in the past. Nevertheless Craxi's election did seem to represent a widespread desire to overcome this factional infighting (the factions were ceremoniously 'dissolved' at the July 1976 Central Committee meeting) and certainly it marked an attempt to launch a new phase in both the ideological development and the electoral strategy of the PSI. The changes which have been wrought by Craxi and the new generation of leaders in fact represent an attempt to find a new strategy which will enable the Party not merely to

survive, but indeed to reverse the respective strengths of the PCI and PSI
and thus bring the Italian left into line with the mainstream social-democratic
values of the rest of the West European left.

II.   THE IDEOLOGICAL PREMISE

A central element of the new image which has been given to the PSI since
1976 has been the modification of party ideology. However, it is necessary
to proceed with some caution in looking at the change since, as with all
official party ideologies, that of the Socialist Party is eclectic in style, and
gathers together a number of more or less imprecise ideas from a variety of
sources. In fact, the weighty document entitled 'Project for a Socialist
Alternative' which the PSI published shortly before its 1978 Congress is
remarkably similar in its prescriptions for economic policy and institutional
and social reforms to the plethora of proposals for 'structural reforms' put
forward by the Party in the early sixties on the eve of the Centre-left.[5]

What has changed, in fact, with only a few exceptions, has not been the
detailed policy prescriptions drawn from party ideology, nor even perhaps
the fundamental values upon which the ideology is based, but rather the
confidence and the combativeness with which the Party has been proclaiming
these values. For it is possible to argue that by the mid-sixties, the Socialists
had already abandoned their maximalist tendencies, and that the 1966
'Charter of Socialist Unification' represented, at the least, a compromise
with principles of social, political and even economic pluralism, and an
attachment to liberal democratic methods.[6] However, caught between the
marxism of the PCI and the fierce anti-communism of the PSDI, the Socialist
Party could not, unlike the German Social Democrats, proclaim the change
too loudly. As in the case of the Communist Party in the seventies, which
arguably has abandoned Leninism but cannot admit it, the PSI was forced
to equivocate. It condemned not just the authoritarian features of Soviet
society and PCI organisation, but also the pragmatism of social democratic
reformism, and as a result, during the sixties, was never part of the mainstream of West European social democracy.

The real change has therefore been that the PSI has become, for the first
time, an *evangelist* of basic social democratic values. It no longer conceals
them but rather, with considerable self-confidence, it proclaims them. At
first sight this may seem paradoxical, given that there has been a reversal
in the alliance strategy pursued by the party during the seventies. It might
be expected that to abandon the Centre-left alliance with the Christian
Democrats in favour—admittedly in the long term—of an alliance with the
PCI would have led to, perhaps even necessitated, a move away from social-
democratic values. On closer reflection, however, this is not so. The rejection
of the Centre-left formula was in a sense an ideological liberation for the
PSI. While it was so closely aligned with the Christian Democrats it was
constantly a prey for attacks from the Communists. Equally, it never had the
moral authority of a party which was unambiguously part of the left, which
would have enabled it to challenge the PCI's conception of a socialist society,
or to challenge the cultural dominance of Gramscian analysis upon left-wing

intellectual circles. Throughout the Centre-left the Socialists were on the defensive, and this, and the sagging morale of party activists who identified social democratic moderation with the strategic moderation of the alliance with the Christian Democrats, made any full-scale revision of party ideology very difficult.

In recent years, however, the PSI has abandoned the prejudicial anti-communism of the Centre-left period, and has been restored unambiguously to its place on the 'left' of the political spectrum. Indeed to the extent that the PSI has advocated a government of the left rather than a compromise with Christian Democracy, it has been more radical than the Communist Party. Protected, in this way, from attacks from its left and from accusations of ideological capitulation, the Socialist Party has more scope to assert its own distinctive ideological position. Thus paradoxically the return of the Party to the left-wing fold at the level of alliance strategies has enabled it to assert with much greater credibility than before the basic social-democratic values of social, economic, and political pluralism against 'monolithic' conceptions of a socialist society.

In exploiting this position, moreover, the PSI has been aided by the much closer scrutiny which, since the PCI has come so close to power, has fallen upon the Gramscian political strategy that the Communists claim to be following. The first to concentrate their attention on this question, in fact, were not party politicians at all, but a group of intellectuals who, like Bobbio, Coen, Pellican and Salvadori were mostly linked informally to the Socialist Party. Their arguments concentrated not on the Historic Compromise itself, but on its main source of ideological inspiration—the writings of Antonio Gramsci—but it was clear that at issue in the debate were also the democratic credentials of the Communist Party itself.[7]

They argued that, contrary to many popular illusions encouraged by the PCI Gramsci was a 'Leninist'. His 'war of position' and his prescription of the gradual establishment of a hegemonic class and culture were inherently authoritarian designs. They might involve a pragmatic rejection of violence as a path to socialism, but they were ultimately no more tolerant of social pluralism than was Leninism. The implication of this argument was of course that the Historic Compromise was the living embodiment of this 'new Leninism'. Based on the concept of a dominant block of forces (Communist, Socialist and Catholic 'masses') cemented together in a grand alliance and dominated by the three mass parties, it represented an attempt to control society, and to suppress the expression of its basic conflicts. The Gramscian concept of hegemony, in other words, was incompatible with the liberal concept of pluralism.

Many of the same intellectuals who were responsible for this critique of Gramscian strategy contributed to the *Project for a Socialist Alternative*. This document, drawn up by a group of Socialist intellectuals, appeared shortly before the March 1978 Party Congress, and was designed as the showcase of the new modern Socialist Party. Like all such documents from the Italian left it is, to Anglo-Saxon eyes at least, a rather grandiose tract, beginning with a wide-ranging review of the historical and international background to present day Italy, and surveying the existing alignment of political forces and the existing 'crisis' of Italian capitalism. The second part defines the values, the institutions and regulatory mechanisms of the PSI's vision of a Socialist society, and the grand finale lays out the Party's 'Democratic Working Blueprint for the Resolution of the Nation's Crisis and the Construction of a New Reforming Alliance' (sic).[8] The most significant elements of the *Project* are those which deal with the relationship between 'communist states' and 'European socialism', with the concepts of social pluralism and political decentralisation, and with what the Party defines as 'conflictual democracy'.

The chapter which reviews the 'historical experiences of the workers' movement' compares unfavourably the achievements of the Communist states ('dictatorship over the proletariat') and the neo-imperialist designs of the Soviet Union, with the operation of West European social democracy. The chapter acknowledges, however, that there are now new limits to traditional income redistribution and social welfare reformism posed by the economic crisis, and sees the solution in the emerging ideas of worker participation and self-management being developed in the Swedish and French parties.[9] The essence of this section is therefore to stress the PSI's 'European' vocation, and to underline that the Party's previous isolation from the mainstream of West European social democracy is now over.

From this premise the Project proceeds to the structures of a new Socialist society. Here the crucial question concerns the nature of the economy, and the document emphasises the important allocative role of the market, and the need for a plurality of types of ownership, since certain types of 'bureaucratic collectivism' are incompatible with democratic socialism.[10]

Finally, turning to the alliance of forces which is to carry this out, the Project once again carries an explicit challenge to the PCI. It stresses the need for a democracy based upon *conflict,* which latter is indeed 'an essential and undeniable feature of democracy' facilitating the fullest and freest play of social forces:

> In specific reference to the present Italian situation the choice of conflictual democracy is based upon the conviction that the present tensions are largely due not to an excess but to an insufficient articulation of democratic powers and responsibilities, which latter exaggerates expectations and suffocates any response to them. *Compared to conflictual democracy the choice of consociational formulae based not on the primacy but indeed on the exclusivity of party mediation may give rise to a further suppression of social reality and in the long run generate even more violent social degeneration than at present.* (emphasis added).[11]

The project therefore represented the response of the new leadership to the challenge of Eurocommunism. It provided a counter-challenge of its own, calling upon the PCI to show its full legitimacy by denouncing the communist states of Eastern Europe, working with the PSI towards an alternation in power in the framework of competitive pluralism, and renouncing the essentially 'anti-competitive' strategy of the Historic Compromise.

The project thus not only provided an ideological foundation for the new Socialist image, but also served to embarrass the Communist leadership. In this respect the document was well-timed. Already on the eve of publication of the project the Communist leadership was under fire on two fronts—from its own rank and file for too much moderation, and from other parties for the equivocal aspects of Eurocommunist ideology, and later in the year these difficulties became even greater. Following the assassination of Aldo Moro the Communists suffered a major defeat in the May local elections while the Socialists made a significant advance. In such circumstances, with morale in the PCI beginning to ebb, the Communist leadership had little option but to unite the rank and file around the traditional 'revolutionary' role of the Party and to evoke a number of the images and symbolism of the past, including, significantly, the 'historical value of Leninism'.[12]

This provided the Socialist leadership with the opportunity it sought. In a fierce article published in the weekly *L'Espresso,* Craxi attacked the Communist leaders, condemning—in perhaps rather disingenuous terms— the philosophical thread linking the Jacobin tradition of élitist, centralising authoritarianism with the Leninist route to power 'dominated, like all forms of communism by the ideal of an homogeneous, compact, organic and undifferentiated society'.[13] Breathing new life into the long-forgotten works of Pierre Proudhon, the spiritual father of *autogestion,* Craxi emphasised Proundhon's distinction between 'socialism with a human face' and 'communism': an 'antediluvian absurdity' which would 'Asianise' European civilisation.[14]

III.   THE ELECTORAL STRATEGY

The new elaboration of Socialist ideology served two purposes. Firstly, it was designed to sow dissension in the ranks of the Communists and, in particular, to encourage the Ellensteins and the Althussers of the PCI to come forward with their own critiques of Leninism. It did meet with some success; Salvatore Sechi, for example, a Communist historian from Bologna, provoked a stir by publishing in *Il Mulino* a searing indictment of Communist Party organisation and the principles of democratic centralism.[15] On the whole, however, while the response of different Communist leaders to Craxi's attack varied, it did not have as dramatic an effect as had been hoped.

The second purpose was to lay the foundation of the Party's 'European' electoral strategy. The essential features of this strategy were:

(a)   The consolidation of the hold of the new generation of leaders on the party.

(b)   The forging of a new and updated image for the Party to identify it in electors' minds with the more successful social democratic parties of Western Europe—especially the French Socialist Party.

(c)   A major advance for the PSI in the first direct elections to the European Parliament in June 1979, when the party leadership hoped that the socialist image would be shaped less by its chequered past than by its association with the success of figures like Mitterrand, Palme, Brandt and Soares.

(d)   Arising out of this gain, a similar substantial advance in the domestic elections (again à la Mitterrand).

(e)   And finally, the establishment of a position from which the PSI might hope realistically to have an equal, if not the major voice in a government of the left.

The essential precondition for the realisation of this sequence of events was of course that the PSI could hold itself apart from both major Italian parties. This is why the party leaders shed nothing more than crocodile tears over the Historic Compromise. They condemned it as a long-term strategy, but in the short-term it suited their purpose. For, perhaps surprisingly, the PSI, as a pivotal party, seems to do better when the two larger parties are converging than when they are polarised. In the former case, the Party can afford to stand aloof and hope to win support from a variety of different groups opposed to the collusion of the giants. In the latter case, however, when the two main parties are far apart, although it might be expected that there would be more potential electoral territory for the PSI to occupy, this rarely proves to be the case because it is constrained to choose sides and hence its distinctive identity is merged with that of its larger ally.

It was thus important for the Party that it was not forced to make this choice too quickly. It needed a longish period to establish its autonomy from both parties and avoid the responsibilities of government. This was also important for the Party leadership. The palace coup of July 1976, as we have seen above, brought Craxi to the leadership almost by accident. In order to consolidate his hold on the Central Committee he needed a period in which the main centre of power in the Party would remain the party organisation itself, and not the ministries and para-state agencies which offered a reservoir of patronage through which individual leaders could obtain party members and preference votes independently of the apparatus. In this way the power of the older generation of *ministeriali* who built up their followings in the provincial federations and the Central Committee during the Centre-Left would be destroyed, and the essential support of the notables who brought Craxi to power would no longer be necessary.

Between July 1976 and the 41st Congress in March 1978, Craxi and Signorile were able to make substantial progress in this direction. The new generation of leaders installed in the executive, who now controlled much of the party machine—men such as Rino Formica, Fabrizio Cicchitto and Gianni de Michelis—were extremely successful at winning over the middle-level leadership to the new axis. In this they were aided by a much needed change in the internal electoral procedures—actually introduced in the organisational reforms of 1974/5 before Craxi came to power—by which the number of delegates to the national Congress that a particular region could send was proportional to the size of the Socialist *electorate* in general elections and not simply to the size of party membership.[16] This change helped to end the inflation of membership (particularly in the southern federations) which had allowed faction leaders to maintain their control over the party machine. It much reduced the followings of the two dominant

Southern notables, De Martino and Mancini, and it was noticeable that the new leadership restored to the Party a decidedly 'northern' image. The Craxi-Signorile alliance, which won 63 per cent of the Congress votes and 140 out of 221 seats in the Central Committee, had its strongholds in the northern regions. Of the seven regions of Piedmont, Lombardy, Trentino, Veneto, Friuli, Emilia and Liguria, only in the last did the alliance win less than 75 per cent of the Congress delegates. In the south, on the other hand, the only region in which it polled an absolute majority was Puglia: the home base of Signorile himself.[17]

This change was of considerable importance to the Party's new image. It marked a break with the years of the Centre-Left, when the Party had undergone a process of 'southernisation' which left it tainted with the corruption of patronage politics. The substantial majority which the Craxi-Signorile axis won at the 1978 Congress underlined this change. Unlike the Congresses of 1968, 1972 and 1976, the Party finally seemed to be united around one leadership group, and the dissolution of the main opposition to this group, led by Enrico Manca, further emphasised this fact. For the first time since the fifties, the Party seemed to have overcome the rigid factional divisions which had so distorted and corrupted party life. Sterile debate on short-term tactics, which determined the distribution of power inside the Party, seemed destined to be replaced by debate on weightier matters of policy on which there were no pre-conceived majorities or minorities. This impression was strengthened by the inclusion in the new central committee of a number of the intellectuals who had helped to write the *Project for a Socialist Alternative*. Bobbio, Ruffolo, Amato, Forte and Portoghesi were all found places in a move which was aimed at countering the impression that while the Communists could make room in both their central committee and their parliamentary group for prestigious intellectuals, the Socialists, dominated by the professional politicians, either would not or could not attract such figures.

A final element in the facelift provided at the 41st Congress—largely symbolic, but none-the-less important for that—was the change in the official party insignia. The traditional book, hammer and sickle and rising sun were reduced to miniscule proportions underneath an enormous red carnation in a rather obvious emulation of the French Socialist Party's rose.

Of course, to those brought up on the tradition of mass party organisation and the rigid ideological sub-cultures of Italian politics, all this, from the Project for a Socialist Alternative to the red carnation, looked distastefully like cosmetics. And so indeed it was. But, rightly or wrongly, Craxi and many of his associates judged that cosmetics and image-building could be just as effective among Italian electors in the late seventies, as they had long been in Northern Europe or the United States. In fact, the concept of the 'opinion party' appealing on a pragmatic, catch-all basis to a variety of social groups —the model of a political party which the PSI had for so long spurned in favour of the mass, class-based model of Marxist prescription—seemed to be exactly what the Socialists were striving towards.

At the heart of this strategy lies the conviction (or the aspiration) that a

K

substantial part of the Italian electorate is ready to turn its back on what the PSI sees as the anachronistic politics of the two totalitariansims: the Church of God and the Church of Marx. The Socialists aim to exploit the widespread fear among Italians that their party system, like their economy, is gradually becoming marginal to Western Europe, and then offer themselves as the only truly modern, efficient 'European' alternative to the Historic Compromise.

This in turn presupposes that the Italian electorate, like that of some other industrial democracies, is becoming more volatile, and that the immobility which once characterised it is disappearing, as individuals change their vote from election to election. There are certainly plausible reasons why this may be happening. Rising educational levels, the secularisation of society and the tendency for expectations to outstrip the capacity of the economy to satisfy them are all working to undermine the subcultural blocks into which the electorate has for long been divided.

The PSI under Craxi has sought to accelerate these tendencies. It has tried to appeal to a wide range of groups which it identifies as potentially new electoral territory. Its debunking of rigid ideologies is designed to appeal especially to the professional and technical northern middle-classes who want an efficient and progressive government. Equally, the Party has launched a campaign to try to woo progressive Catholics—particularly the Jesuits of *Civilta Cattolica*—arguing that the concept of *autogestion* is a 'profoundly Christian' idea. The Party has worked hardest of all to pose as the only true defender of civil rights, and here it is anxious to put a stop to the threat from both the Radical Party and some of the far-left groups. Amongst other actions it has prevented a covert agreement between Communists and Christian Democrats to limit the scope of the new abortion law. And in the referendum held last June on the repeal of the public security law (the Legge Reale), while the PSI had little option in the wake of the Moro assassination but to campaign against repeal, it allowed several of its leaders to campaign on a strictly personal basis, in favour of repeal. Perhaps its greatest gamble in this sphere came with the Moro kidnapping itself. Donning the mantle of Socialism with a human face, and a compassionate concern for individual liberty, the PSI stood virtually alone amongst Italian parties in suggesting, albeit in cautious terms, that some symbolic concession might be made to the kidnappers' demands, to save Moro's life.

Much the most important potential for new support, however, comes from disgruntled trade unionists, unhappy about the austerity policies the Communists and their allies in the main union confederation, the CGIL, have been imposing on them. Posing as the champion of trade union independence from the parties, and of the right of unions to engage in free and unfettered collective bargaining, the PSI leadership has supported those like Marianetti and Zuccherini who, from within the CGIL, have been opposing the self-restraint of the Communist Secretary General Luciano Lama. Similarly, the smaller socialist union confederation, the UIL has, under the leadership of Giorgio Benvenuto, been the least well disposed of the three main confederations to support the austerity measures.

In wooing these rather disparate groups of voters, however, the PSI has not yet shown that it is capable of going beyond the level of 'image' politics, and it may be storing up trouble for itself in the future on this count. In the first place, many electors may well be suspicious of a party which champions the causes of a number of more or less disaffected groups without at the same time putting forward concrete and co-ordinated solutions to the many urgent policy problems facing those with the responsibility of governing a fragmented society and managing a structurally weak economy. The PSI claims to stand for 'conflictual' democracy, for more participation, and for the articulation of more and yet more political demands. But many of the electors may with reason think that Italy has quite enough conflict already, and that the Socialists are simply evading difficult choices.

It is, of course, perfectly true that the Italian electorate has not, in the past, shown itself to be policy-responsive. As other electorates it tends to punish the policy failures of governments, but not to reward the policy proposals of the opposition, and this is not surprising in a society where political debate is dominated by ideological issues and questions of coalition formulae. In this sense, to concentrate on image politics may be perfectly valid. But here a second difficulty arises, in that, at a certain point the Socialist Party, if it finds itself in power, will be constrained to aggregate demands, and select priorities. In such circumstances the Party will be severely handicapped by its continuing tendency to formulate policies applicable not in the world as it exists, but in the world as Socialists would like it to be.

The central questions of economic policy in the last two years—the control of wage-inflation and the restoration of internationally competitive levels of labour productivity on the one hand, and the issue of Italian participation in the new European Monetary System on the other—are two cases in point. It is most unclear how either the encouragement of free collective bargaining in the short-term, or the proposals, contained in the *Project*, for workers' self management in the longer-term, have any relevance if the first of these problems. The PSI expressed its opposition to the Pandolfi Plan's proposals to hold down the level of real wages over the three years from 1979–81. Yet without such constraint it is difficult to see how the twin objectives of restoring the competitive edge to the Italian economy and tackling the mounting problems of unemployment among the Southerners and the young, can be reconciled.

Similarly in relation to Italy's role in the EEC the Party's suspicions of the EMS derive from an unwillingness to face the world as it is. Its objections to the system, unlike those of the British Labour Party, derive not from a basic hostility to European integration, but from the conviction that this particular method of integration will offload all the costs and burdens of integration onto the Italian working-class (continued demand deflation to hold up the value of the lira) and will further subordinate the weak Italian economy to the stronger German and French economies. Yet the alternative it puts forward, a *European Project* for full monetary integration and a massive redistribution of resources in favour of the less developed areas of the Community,[18] is hardly realistic in a grouping dominated by the individual needs of a set of rationally self-interested nation states.

On these, and other issues which have arisen recently, the PSI has done little to reassure the electorate that it has policies which are tailored to the reality of Italy's fundamental economic problems.

IV. SURVIVAL AND BEYOND

In any case, in 1979 the Socialists have faced new problems of an exclusively political variety which have undermined the carefully worked-out timetable of Craxi's European strategy. The collapse of the ruling majority at the beginning of the year, and the return of the Communist Party to opposition, have thwarted an approach which for a time, in 1978, looked as if it might enable the PSI not merely to survive, but indeed to regain some of the initiative from the PCI.

For to begin with things went well for Craxi. The gamble of the appeal for flexibility in negotiating for Moro's release appeared to have paid off, or at least not to have damaged the Party. Indeed, in the local elections of 16 May last year, and again in those of 20 November, there were real signs that the very electoral volatility upon which the PSI's strategy depended was developing. The May elections, involving over two million voters, registered huge losses for the PCI. Its vote fell from 35·6 per cent in the relevant areas in 1976 to 26·7 per cent. Again, in November, the PCI lost one-third of its vote. Equally important was the fact that in May the Socialist vote increased substantially—up from 9 per cent in 1976 to 13 per cent in 1978.[19]

However, these gains were made under particular circumstances and it was perhaps to be expected that immediately after a trauma such as Moro's assassination, when democracy itself seemed to be on trial, there should be a shift to the parties of the centre such as the PSI and DC. And in fact in November 1978 neither the PSI nor the DC made significant gains. Indeed the PSI actually lost ground both to local parties and to a new and rather unlikely alliance of the Radicals and the extreme left. The only crumb of comfort the PSI could derive from the elections was that once again there seemed to be some evidence of electoral volatility in the success of these smaller parties.

More serious for the PSI's electoral strategy than the November election result, however, was the deterioration in the political situation which set in in the Autumn of 1978.

The defeat in the May elections, and the subsequent ideological broadside from the Socialists began to have their effect on the Communist leadership, and on the cohesion of the parliamentary majority supporting Andreotti's government. With the prospect of a potentially difficult Congress the following Spring, a rank and file growing daily more restive about the lack of any apparent results from the Historic Compromise, and a mounting challenge to Communist control over the unions, the PCI leadership decided to take its distance from the government, and to undertake a tactical retreat on the ideological front, which led, as we have seen, to a resurrection of some of the old symbolism, and to a warming of relations between the Party and Moscow.

While at one level this gave weight to Craxi's ideological attack, it also threatened to upset the carefully planned timetable for the PSI revival. As the Communist Party became more critical of the actions of the Andreotti government attention was focused not, as the Socialists hoped, on the oppressive collusion between the two giants, but on the growing polarisation. In the Autumn there were serious arguments over economic policy and housing; at Christmas a furious row developed over Andreotti's decision to take Italy into the new European Monetary System despite Communist opposition; and by late January the Communists had withdrawn their support and Andreotti's government had collapsed. The comfortable position which the Socialists had enjoyed—part of the majority, covered on the left, and dissenting from much of what the government actually did—was rudely upset. Once again they were forced to choose, and their distinctive identity was under attack.

Their major objective was to avoid the premature dissolution of parliament, for that would mean that the general election would overshadow, if not indeed precede, the European elections. But this could only be done if the Communists could be prevailed upon to return to the majority. Berlinguer proved adamant, however, and would only do so if his party were given full cabinet status—a concession the Christian Democrats were in no mood to grant. Once again, as in 1976, responsibility for saving the legislature from collapse fell upon the Socialists. And once again, whatever the Socialist Party did, its precious independence was going to be damaged. If it saved the parliament, by supporting Andreotti or even joining his cabinet, while the PCI remained in opposition, then this amounted to a return to the Centre-Left and the Communists would once again be able to monopolise the opposition. If, on the other hand, it joined the PCI in opposition, this was a clear acknowledgement that it was tied to the Communists, and dared not act without their approval. It also had the disadvantage that the general election and the European election would be held almost simultaneously, and hence that national issues would predominate.

Whichever course of action the Party adopted, its electoral timetable would be upset. The new polarisation between the two major parties once again exposed the weakness of the Socialist position. Craxi fought desperately to keep the parliament alive, but eventually in late March it became clear that there was no conceivable formula acceptable to both the PCI and the DC. The only way of avoiding an election would have been to construct some form of Centre-Left coalition, and confronted with this reality the Socialists opted to join the Communists in opposition and face an election.

Worse was to come, however, when it became clear that for technical reasons it was not even possible to hold a general election simultaneously with the elections for the European Parliament. It thus took place one week earlier than the European elections, and despite Craxi's best efforts to elevate the debate to the European level and hence obtain in one operation all the advantages previously designed to come in two stages, the election was dominated by domestic issues. Indeed it was dominated by the single issue of the Communist Party's demand for a place in government, and was marked by a sharp deterioration in relations between the two major parties, with the Christian Democrats fighting a vigorous anti-Communist crusade, and the Communists pledging themselves to unequivocal opposition to any government of which they were not members. It soon emerged, therefore, that if the PCI were to return to opposition, responsibility for saving the next parliament from deadlock would fall upon the shoulders of the Socialists, and attention naturally focussed upon the choice the Socialists would make under such circumstances, and upon the possibility of a return to some form of Centre-Left coalition. This seemed all the more likely as the Christian Democrats waged an increasingly explicit campaign to entice the Socialists into such an alliance—some of them even going as far as to suggest the nomination of a Socialist Prime Minister to head the coalition.

These developments were deeply embarrassing for Craxi. His tirade against the PCI's 'leninism' had effectively ruled out any possibility of a left-wing alternative government in the short term, and given the impossibility of a grand coalition including both DC and PCI, he could not flatly reject an alliance with the Christian Democrats. As a result his campaign was inevitably rather unconvincing. Although studiously avoiding the use of the term 'Centre-Left'—officially consigned to the dustbin of 'unrepeatable experiences of the past'—he was careful not to rule out some form of alliance with the DC, as long as it was one which forced the latter to make substantial changes of personnel and policy. A relationship of 'parity' between the DC and PSI which would undermine the perennial Christian Democrat hegemony and give the Socialists an equal voice in government might be acceptable to the PSI, Craxi argued, especially if it was preceded by a purge of the old generation of Christian Democrat leaders, beginning with Andreotti himself. To make all this possible, the Socialists' campaign theme concluded, a major increase in the Socialist vote was essential, and was indeed the only means of bringing stability to the next parliament.

Judging this campaign on the PSI's previous parliamentary record, the electors could have been forgiven for looking upon it with some scepticism, and so they seem to have done. The election result proved a great disappointment for the PSI. The expected Communist losses did indeed materialise (although they were not as great as in the previous year's local elections) and the PCI ended up with 30.4 per cent of the vote in the election for the lower house: 4 per cent less than in 1976. These votes were dispersed in a variety of directions. Some went to the extreme left, others went to the Radical Party, and others still were accounted for by the 3 per cent drop in turnout and by the large number of blank and spoiled ballots. Very few, however, seem to have gone to the PSI, whose share of the vote rose only from 9·6 per cent to 9·8 per cent.

On the morrow of the election, therefore, the PSI leadership was confronted by an electorate that had shown itself largely indifferent to its efforts at renewal over the previous three years, and by a parliamentary situation which made the strategy it had been pursuing extremely difficult in the future. For although, at the time of going to press, it is too early to say exactly what form of government will emerge from the new parliament, the most likely probability is one based upon some type of relationship between the DC and the Socialists: a Centre-Left in all but name.

While the election was a rebuff for Craxi's strategy, however, it was not a defeat for the new generation of Socialist leaders within the Party. In fact, unlike the 1976 election, that of 1979 brought a radical renewal of Socialist deputies, and almost half of the PSI's complement of 62 were new members.[20] The hold of the older generation has finally been broken, therefore, but whether the new generation will prove substantially better, or, in another version of the Centre-Left, whether it will go the way of its predecessor remains to be seen. For in the present situation many of the same factors which so damaged the Party in the early sixties are re-emerging. The struggle over whether or not the Party should actually work with the DC at all, which contains the basis of a split between the Craxi and Signorile wings of the ruling majority, will intensify over the Summer. And if the Party does indeed enter the coalition the potential for a return to clientele politics offered by the availability of government patronage may prove irresistible to many party leaders.[21]

Considerations such as these, coupled with the knowledge that while the PSI is battling against Christian Democrat dominance inside the coalition the Communists will be monopolising the opposition and rebuilding their damaged links with the unions, may actually lead the Socialists to refuse to return to government unless the Communists are allowed to join them. If so, however, Italy may begin to look truely ungovernable, and the Socialists' prospects may look even poorer. What the three years since 1976 have shown, in fact, is that the divisions in the Italian left remain as substantial as ever, and that the Italian Socialist Party remains as far as ever from resolving its strategic dilemma. The PSI under Craxi is surviving, but as yet it is showing little sign of reviving.

NOTES

1. This article assumes a knowledge of the basic workings of the Italian party system and of the recent history of the Italian Socialist Party. Readers not familiar with these matters are referred to two publications by the author on the PSI: 'Social Democracy in Italy', in W. E. Paterson and A. H. Thomas, (editors), *Social Democratic Parties in Western Europe*, (Croom Helm, London, 1977) pp. 67–85 and 'Socialists and Communists in Italy—Reversing roles?', *West European Politics*, Vol. I, No. 2, May 1978, pp. 144–160.
2. On the success of the Communist Party in the 1976 election see Stephen Hellman, 'The Longest Campaign: Communist Party Strategy and the Elections of 1976', in H. Penniman, (ed.), *Italy at the Polls*, (American Enterprise Institute, Washington, D.C., 1977) pp. 155–182.
3. De Martino's speeches at the 1978 Congress are reported in the PSI daily newspaper, *Avanti!*, March 4 and March 9, 1978.
4. On the PSI's difficulties in the 1976 election see Gianfranco Pasquino, 'The Italian Socialist Party: An Irreversible Decline?', in Penniman, *Italy at the Polls*, op. cit., pp. 183–228.
5. The Project was published in full in *Avanti!*, 29 January 1978, pp. 7–20. It is particularly interesting to compare the 1978 Project with the 1962 economic planning document produced by the PSI's economic committee 'Il Contenuto Economico della Svolta di Sinistra', reprinted in the *Annuario Politico Italiano, 1963*, (Comunità, Milan, 1963) pp. 1194–1201.
6. Partito Socialista Italiano, *La Carta dell'Unificazione Socialista*, (PSI, Rome, 1966).
7. See, inter alia, F. Coen, (ed.), *Egemonia e Democrazia: Gramsci e la Questione Comunista*. (Quaderni di Mondo Operaio, Rome, 1977) and L. Pellicani, *Gramsci e la Questione Comunista*, (Vallecchi, Florence, 1976).
8. *Avanti!*, 29 January 1978, p. 14.

9. *Ibid.*, p. 10.
10. *Ibid.*, p. 13.
11. *Ibid.*, p. 19.
12. Berlinguer, Interview, *La Repubblica,* 2 August 1978.
13. 'Il Vangelo Socialista', *L'Espresso,* 27 August 1978.
14. 'Communism cannot coexist with the critical spirit, the questioning method the plurality of philosophies; in short with everything which the cultural patrimony of lay, Western and liberal civilisation represents'. Ibid., p. 98.
15. Salvatore Sechi, 'L'austero fascino del centralismo democratico', *Il Mulino,* XXVII, no. 257, May–June 1978,, pp. 426–438.
16. As a result of this new regulation, in any area where total party membership exceeded one fifth of the total party electorate in the previous general election it was deemed, for Congress purposes, to be limited to this ceiling. The wild fluctuations of party membership during Congress years appear to have been overcome by these changes, and membership is being held reasonably constant at around 430–450,000. For the Party's new internal election rules see *Avanti!* 29 January 1978.
17. Data drawn from *L'Espresso,* 26 March 1978, pp. 26–27.
18. See, for example, Giorgio Ruffolo, 'Sistema monetario e integrazione europea', *Mond operaio,* Anno 32, no. 4, 1979, pp. 27–32.
19. For an excellent analysis of local election results in 1978 see Giuliano Urbani, (ed.), *1978: Elezioni con Sorpresa,* (Milan, Biblioteca della Libertà, 1979).
20. In fact the PSI even managed to elect one or two intellectuals to parliament. In Lombardy the eminent economist Francesco Forte was returned, and in Pisa the able young Florentine economist Valdo Spini was elected. Nevertheless these isolated examples were no match for the large numbers of intellectuals elected as 'independenti di sinistra' in the PCI's lists.
21. Even while it has been out of government the taint of patronage has in any case never been entirely absent from the PSI. During the Winter of 1978–9 the Party appeared to be working hand in glove with the DC to fill senior management appointments on a party basis, and a Socialist senator, Augusto Talamona, was alleged to have been involved in two separate financial scandals. On these issues see "Come difficile essere Socialista!', *L'Espresso,* February 1979, p. 6–9.

The Available State: Problems of Reform

Giuseppe Di Palma*

It is said of the French state under the *Ancien Régime* that it was large and pervasive but neither strong nor cohesive. Common wisdom and reputable scholars say the same about the postwar Italian state. Because in turn the postwar state has been run by the Christian Democratic Party (DC), it seems apparent that the party and its grand electors, just like the French kings and magnates, carry the main responsibility for its predicament. On one side, the pre-fascist and fascist state, formally centralised and hierarchical, in fact cumbersome, incoherent, dispersed, and feudalised by corporate interests and privileged groups, largely survived the war. On the other side, the main reason why the state, though cleansed of the most visible authoritarian layers, remains otherwise unreformed seems to be the boundless greed of the governing DC, which saw in the pervasive but open structures of the inherited state a target for partisan appropriation. The inter-class social-Christian ideology of the DC, the pressures of postwar reconstruction, and the threat of a strong communist-socialist opposition set the DC on that course. The DC in power did the rest.[1]

The purpose of this article is to place some order in these accounts of the postwar state. The tendency to attribute the responsibility for the unreformed state increasingly to the governing party, and less to the presence of a strong opposition, to the point of reversing assessments of a few years ago, is interesting as sociology of knowledge, given the features of the present crisis: the loss of political credibility by the DC and the gains of the Communist Party (PCI). But even the fact that the state might well have remained unreformed in the absence of a strong left is beside the point, since the presence of the left has been inescapable. This alone is a concretely decisive, perhaps sufficient factor in arresting state reform. Recent communist evolution should not substantially alter this assessment.

First, without belittling it, we should not exaggerate the continuity in the 'Eurocommunist' strategies of the Communist Party, the party that hegemonised leftist opposition from the start of the postwar period. Backward projections from today's perspective ahistorically gloss over the fact that from the perspective of the Forties and Fifties at least, the PCI appeared, rightly or wrongly, as a delegitimising and seriously threatening force. Second and consequently, the two types of state reform that were broadly conceivable were variously impossible or risky. One type, inspired by criteria of rational effectiveness, would have meant a majoritarian plan of neo-capitalist inspiration, with a strong executive, a coherent technocratically-oriented

*Professor of Political Science, University of California, Berkeley. Research leading to this paper was conducted while the author was holding a German Marshall Fund Fellowship.

bureaucracy, and an industrial-labour system attuned to capital-intensive productivity. But besides the obstacle represented by traditional interests and structures, which made reform premature, there was leftist and labour opposition to anything smacking of modernisation from the top; an opposition which, to say the least, the DC did not have the stomach to overlook. Thus there was no ready majority for a 'neoconservative' plan. The other type of state reform, emphasising redistribution, participation, and deconcentration had no initial majority either, since such a 'progressive' plan, falling on a dispersed state, would have in reality opened major avenues to state appropriation by the extreme left.

In the first years it was the DC that carried the main responsibility for filling this reform void with its own partisan presence. Its electoral composition, its social Catholic matrix and the inchoate structure of the inherited state were of great importance in this regard. But, to begin with, the prime factor in arresting state reform was the early stalemate in the Italian political game. Moreover, the appropriation of the state has not been as exclusively partisan as it may at first appear. Ironically, in a democratic context and with a dispersed state, the strategy of the DC ended up by leaving doors open to the opposition itself, and eventually, under the crisis of the late sixties and seventies, to the 'progressive' plan outlined above. The present consequences for the operation of a coherent state are at least dubious.

In the first part of the article I will examine the constitutional and partisan stalemate; in the second the DC's state policies in response to the stalemate and the place of the opposition in the state. In the third part I will discuss the effects of the crisis of the seventies on state structures. I will conclude by raising the final question: are there majorities to reform the state?

THE CONSTITUTIONAL STALEMATE

Constitution-Making

Even when they governed together and joined in the Constituent Assembly of 1946 to write a mutually acceptable constitution, DC, PCI and its Socialist Party (PSI) allies had quite different ideas about the functional and territorial structures of the new state.[2] Christian Democracy originally favoured a constitutional plan of checks and balances inspired by the party's interclass organic pluralism: a stable executive with significant legislative powers, but balanced by ample regional autonomy, a genuine bicameralism with a Senate representing corporate-territorial interests, popular referendum, an activist Constitutional Court, an independent and self-ruling judiciary, and a President of the Republic with significant voice in the formation of the government and the dissolution of parliament. The constitutional philosophy of the PCI (and of most PSI leaders) was, on the contrary, firmly Jacobin and centralising, with little or no room for corporatist autonomies, be they functional or territorial, and with powers concentrated in a proportionally-elected national assembly.

With a singular shift of positions, the substantial constitutional disagreement between DC and PCI became even more evident after March 1947, when the cold war permanently broke the tripartite coalition. Now the PCI's unreconstructed support for parliamentary supremacy no longer served the party's rosy expectations in regard to power, but served just as well to protect it in its role as opposition. In fact, and for the same reason, the PCI came to embrace wholeheartedly some of the constitutional 'impediments' to assembly democracy originally advocated by the Catholics, realising that territorial arrangements, such as regionalism, or regulatory bodies, such as the Constitutional Court or the Council of the Judiciary (if selected by parliament), could weaken the Catholic hold upon power. By the same token, the DC showed increased unease with the system of checks and balances it originally masterminded and growing concern with executive stability. But by the time the coalition split, the constitutional framework had been largely fixed, and the almost even balance of power between left and DC advised restraint.

The charter approved at the end of 1947 was long on checks and balances (regional autonomies, Constitutional Court, Council of the Judiciary, National Council for Economy and Labour, popular repeal referendum, and popular legislative initiative), and might have been longer had it not been for initial leftist resistance. It was also generous on parliamentary prerogatives (no constitutional restrictions on the right of single parliamentarians to initiate and amend legislation), yet open and ambiguous on government leadership (no government prerogatives over the direction of legislative activities, limited use of executive decrees, right to dissolve parliament entrusted to the President of the Republic). To an observer oblivious of the different constitutional ideologies of its drafters and of the weight of the 1947 events, the constitution may look like a rationalised compact for mutual co-existence. Yet the fact that majority and opposition immediately began to squabble over its meaning and implementation reveals the compact's unsettled and instrumental nature. The question of who legitimately rules, with whom and how—the question of majority and opposition, their role and their mutual guarantees—became and remained central.

Constitutional Dissent

After 1948 the PCI seized upon such features as regional autonomy or the right of parliament to choose members of the Constitutional Court and the Council of the Judiciary to argue for a 'synchronic' or 'consociational' interpretation of the charter. According to it, the charter calls for the participation of all significant political forces in decisions at different levels and in different alliances, and corrects straight majority rule in a centralised state by giving the opposition an opportunity to share in the task of government and in the running of the territorial and functional system of checks and balances. Coming from a delegitimised PCI, the purpose of this interpretation is clear. Having abandoned constitutional Jacobinism under the constraints of the national and international situation, the party was progressively seeking recognition through a new rooting strategy of social presence, institutional penetration and political exchange designed at the same time to open and infiltrate the majority.

Although it was to take almost 30 years for the crowning achievement of this strategy—the proposal for a historic compromise—to win compelling attention, keeping the Communists at bay was not an easy job for the DC and its government allies. Orienting the constitutional order in a majoritarian direction, as the DC tried to do after 1948, was not sufficient. Such moves as postponing the establishment of the Constitutional Court and regional governments were greeted by the left as betrayals of the anti-fascist constitution and allowed the PCI to present itself as the conscience of the collectively reconstructed democratic order.[3] The same opportunity was offered to the left by a 1953 electoral law (quickly dubbed by the opposition as the 'swindle law' and quickly repealed) amending proportionality so as to give 65 per cent of the seats in the lower house to any party or coalition winning the absolute majority of the national vote.

But the majoritarian plan had other defects. In the hands of extended centrist coalitions such as the ones formed after 1947, the plan was reactive and defensive. Because these were, so to speak, negative and heterogeneous coalitions, thrown together to keep the extremes out, they did not necessarily agree on a politico-economic content to the plan.[4] Given this fact, and given that in the years straddling the forties and fifties the DC had still to rely organisationally and financially on a confessional Church, on business and agrarian interests, and on conservative and traditional constituencies, the drive for a majoritarian plan was threatening to propel the DC by inertia alone into the arms of the extreme right and away from that dead centre which it needed to occupy in order to fix its moderate-reformist image competitively. The drive in fact was threatening to propel the whole party system toward a left-right confrontation which it could ill afford in a context of extreme ideological polarisation. Last, majority rule or British-style party government would have found and did find an obstacle in parliament and in the central ministerial bureaucracy: the former stalemated by the presence of a strong delegitimising opposition, the latter historically and organisationally incapable of pursuing a majority plan, yet now politically crucial for the governing party.

THE 'AVAILABLE' STATE

With a civil and political society somewhat impervious to DC leadership—owing to divergent leftist strategies, an uncohesive centre, and a coalitionally unacceptable nostalgic right—and with a majoritarian reorientation of the constitutional order alone incapable of securing leadership, Christian Democracy moved toward other solutions. The inherited state, with its old practices of spoils and *sottogoverno*, proved an important asset in this regard. It provided the DC with innumerable opportunities to tie itself to important sectors of society through interest policies reaching beyond mere ideological anti-communism. Central to this strategy was the expansion of party penetration of the state sector of the economy (parastate).

The Parastate

Expansion and party penetration were facilitated by the size achieved by the public sector under fascism. For example, the Institute for Industrial Reconstruction (IRI), one of the largest holdings in Europe today and a corner-stone in the DC's strategy of state patronage, had been created in the Thirties to take bankrupt firms into receivership. They were also facilitated by the country's objective reconstruction needs, by the relative autonomy of the public sector from the more cumbersome ministerial bureaucracy, and by the administrative and budgetary compartmentalisation of the various public agencies making up the sector, each agency variously relying on self-financing, borrowing, and extra-budgetary lump endowments from the state. Milestones in the growth of the sector were the creation of ENI (National Agency for Natural Gas) (in 1953), of the Ministry for State Participation (1956), and of *Intersind* (1956–57)—an association of state-controlled firms independent of the private *Confindustria*. By 1963 the public sector's share of sales and service revenues by the 200 largest firms in the country reached 17·4 per cent.[5]

The partisan management of the parastate sector did offer Christian Democracy an opportunity to make itself independent of the financial support of business and to open channels of party leadership recruitment other than those of organised Catholicism. Because partisan management made possible and relied upon the operation of innumerable networks of public managers and institutional clienteles—each network being served and held together by a host of national and local structures trickling down and mediating business—it attracted towards the DC and the governing centre a wide array of constituencies. But the competitive edge thus gained over right and left would eventually have serious, though at the time possibly unforseeable, costs for state institutions and for the DC.

In the first place, because the public sector is autonomous and compart-mentalised, because it soon became a pawn in the competition for party control among DC factions, because in fact DC factionalism assumed traits of exasperated interest factionalism in the fight to obtain public resources,[6] because the DC was in no imminent danger of being voted out of office and yet was unable and eventually unwilling in the divided Italian context to pursue a majority plan, the partisan-factional management of the public sector tended to produce unco-ordinated and individualised public policies. Though public agencies individually had an unquestionable role in crucial aspects of reconstruction and development, their role had to come to terms with their mutual corporate autonomy, with the preservation of corporate interests, with the weight of partisan-factional-clientelistic ties. Thus the Ministry of State Participation became a captive of its own wards. Coupled with similar policy practices in other state institutions (to be illustrated below), this improvident way of distributing resources without redistributing them had a capacity to bankrupt state institutions under conditions of demand escalation and resource depletion.

In the second place, and concomitantly, the success of party control relied heavily on keeping state institutions as they were: permeable, large and incoherent.

In third place, communist and left opposition did little about this state of affairs, beyond moralising over the greed and corruption of Christian Democracy. In the 1950s the more visible isolation of the left had much to do with this. But as we move into the 1960s, it became more and more apparent that in a democratic system with a market economy infused with political entrepreneurship, the partisan appropriation of the state could not be exclusive and foolproof. In the short run, the Communist Party, in view of its new strategy of social presence and political exchange, stood to gain marginally from the inevitable spillovers of the DC game. In the medium term, and in the event of a DC loss of credibility, it could not be refused, by the game's very logic of parcelling, a formal share in the running of the state. In the long run, it could even replace the DC at the core of the coalitions controlling the state.

Illustrations of the three points above can be found in the structure and operation of state institutions other than the parastate.

Parliament

To say that because of the political stalemate the DC was unable to run parliament by strictly majority rule and diverted its attention to other state institutions is not to say that parliament was condemned to inaction. Rather, lacking executive and internal leadership, parliament made extensive use of those powers of initiative already incorporated in the constitution and distributed them more evenly among single parliamentarians and parliamentary groups. Further, given such dispersion of powers, parliament became an appropriate institutional locus for practicing that policy of patronage and individualised benefits on which the DC had come to rely for support. And as patronage encouraged organised interest factionalism in the party, control of dispersed parliamentary resources became another important ingredient in the factional fight for party and government leadership and in the party-factional uses of state bureaucracies. Thus, not only did government lack the capacity to curb and direct parliament, also, and more to the point, it had little interest in doing so.

The Communist Party in turn had no strong reason to resist such a parliament. Working from a defensive position, it stood to gain from the opportunities for legislative concurrence offered by an open patronage oriented parliament. As the activity of parliament has been deflected over the years toward the production of thousands of trivial bills rewarding special and often middling constituencies, Communists have been ready to offer their support. Over the years, approximately two-thirds of government legislation has been appoved with communist votes. In addition, private legislation, which in Italy is more abundant than in other parliamentary systems, has always included a fair share of communist bills, greater than the share of the opposition in other legislatures.[7]

Bureaucracy and Local Government

Needless to say, the fragmented legislative activism of parliament has placed parliamentary politicians and committees in a position of special political influence vis-à-vis the ministerial bureaucracy, which is called to implement legislation, and the local and functional interests it serves. For instance, because the ministerial bureaucracy has remained highly centralised and legalistic and because local governments have limited resources, relations between centre and periphery have been occasions for continuous exchanges between local and central administrators, with parliamentary politicians and committees acting as influential policy initiators and mediators.[8] This means that there has actually been an interest in the ruling party to leave the central bureaucracy unreformed and local government short of resources. There is a good deal of discretion in a bureaucracy that can hide red tape behind legality, and a good deal of influence that majority politicians can gather for themselves by stepping between the bureaucracy and local interests. But, as in parliament, these channels of political exchange are not easily closed to the opposition. Local communist administrators have made extensive use of them, thus engaging often and successfully in deals on behalf of their community with ministerial and parastate officials and government politicians.

The Available State

This is, in sum, the state with which Italy was governed during the fifties and sixties. It is formally centralised since, with the exceptions indicated, regional autonomy had not yet been implemented, but it is otherwise porous and progressively 'available.' We are used to thinking of this availability as referring to the partisan monopoly of the state by the dominant party. A number of factors explain this view: the fact that since 1945 every single prime minister has been a Christian Democrat; the fitting and visible example of the parastate; the initially equally tight monopoly over state radio and television; the outspoken and skilful denunciations of such state of affairs by the opposition;[9] the distaste of domestic and foreign intellectuals and scholars, distaste nurtured by the memories of fascism, for anything even generically shading into a one-party regime.

But I have tried to show that 'availability' referred also, even in those years, to other parties and social forces. Parliament was a convenient arena for political entrepreneurship, mediated but not monopolised by Christian Democracy and its factions. Local government, despite prefectoral control, the lack of more extensive regional autonomies and its dependence on state funds, by no means cut the opposition out of the game. There is, for example, no evidence that city governments controlled by the left were discriminated against in the often discretionary allocation of state funds and credit. Further, any inclination the DC showed towards monopolising the state was undermined in the Sixties by the entry of an ambitious and demanding Socialist party in the government coalition.

It is no surprise then to discover that an open parliament, a local government seeking preferment in Rome, and a porous bureaucracy were topped by a cabinet system itself less than cohesive. In point of law, a constitutional provision requiring an organic bill to regulate and presumably to strengthen the office of the prime minister, was never implemented. In fact, individual ministers jealously guarded their considerable independence from the cabinet and the prime minister, and cabinets fell once a year on average. With few exceptions (such as De Gasperi, Fanfani and Moro), prime ministers were rarely the recognised leaders of the party. More often, they were factional leaders or accommodating figures who attained office more by vying for the support of the other cabinet partners than by undisputed command of their own party.[10]

Finally, two aspects of the Italian state in the fifties and sixties deserve special mention to understand the crisis of the seventies and how the state responded to it. First, an 'available' state is a very expensive state. It is expensive to operate and it spends and distributes a lot of resources. But, despite a string of ministers for Bureaucratic Reform, not one of them was able to improve this or other aspects of the bureaucratic archipelago.

Second, the partisan-factional sharing in the positions and resources of the state for corporate-economic purposes possibly encouraged and ran parallel to a growing politicisation and even internal parcelling of many state bodies along corporate-ideological lines. Thus, for example, Italian judges divided their allegiance among competing professional associations vying for control of the Council of the Judiciary and covering the entire left-right party spectrum. Further, a split in the judiciary developed between usually younger judges favouring a socially interventionist and politically overt role and older judges favouring a more strict literal application of the written law. In the universities, the allocation of academic-administrative responsibilities came to reflect criteria of partisan and ideological balancing carefully negotiated among diverse constituencies. Public radio and television programming, once monopolised by the DC, came during the sixties to be progressively shared with other cabinet parties, expecially the new Socialist partner. In general, wherever an association or organisation bordered on the public realm, or wherever an advisory council, joint committee, or governing body came into existence, at the national or local level, the pressure to assign posts according to corporate-ideological criteria became inescapable. And the important point is that the DC and its friends were by no means always in the position to win the largest share.

This latter aspect of the Italian state often escapes foreign observers, yet its significance cannot be overemphasised. It may recall superficially the urbane politics of proportionalism practised by the consociational democracies of North-Western Europe. But that consociationalism is predicated upon the maintenance of the *status quo*, the reciprocal respect for acquired positions, and a state capable of keeping social ferment in check via the institutionalisation and freezing of overarching allocational agreements among corporate constituencies. And at least, even if the above features are not deemed necessary, consociationalism requires consensus on power sharing.[11]

The increasing politicisation of the Italian state apparatus, on the contrary, was another indication that the DC's original plan to harness a divided civil and political society to the state had been slowly reversing itself, and by the end of the sixties was exposing a state in crisis to the onslaught of increasingly demanding and dissonant constituencies.

Thus, three overlapping rhetorical questions may serve to set the tone for our analysis of the seventies. Can an expensive and available state be given streamlined coherence in times when state-fed expectations rise and explode? Can Christian Democracy, losing organised support and governing grip, preside over such a task—be in effect its own surgeon—without cutting vital connections in the short but decisive range? Would and indeed should the Communist Party surrogate the DC in the task, thus taking the risk (it is also a question of timing) of making the state less liable to seizure?

CRISIS AND REFORMS IN THE SEVENTIES

Much has naturally changed in the structure, operation, and services of the Italian state in the last ten years. In many ways, these changes, and indeed the changes in the larger society, are much more dramatic and pervasive than those associated with the economic miracle of the early sixties. A considerable degree of governmental and legislative activism, the more noticeable in view of previous immobility, also characterises the Seventies. And many factors conspired during the decade to propel Christian Democrats, Communists, and other parties willy-nilly towards convergence. But activism and convergence have produced two related types of changes in the state, neither exactly striking as designed to favour streamlining and co-ordination. One type emphasises deconcentration, overt proportionalism in government and in the *sottogoverno*, syndicalisation of neutral bureaucracies, and even forms of employees' collective participation in the management of their own bureaucracies. However disparate they may appear, these changes seem all to fall under a broad category of 'democratisation.' The other type points toward an extension of the services and the popular clientèles of the state.

One can understand why the PCI has openly favoured and in fact fought for exactly these types of change. For one thing, they are in keeping with the policies and mentality of the party, with its strategy of social presence and political exchange, with its populist image. For another, and more importantly, a state reformed along any other line—either technocratic or market-oriented—would be a more insurmountable obstacle to communist accession to full power than the thoroughly penetrated state of the Seventies.[12] And finally, why should the PCI have acted otherwise, seeing that the Socialists, and the whole trade union movement, including the Catholic unions, favoured and fought for exactly the same reforms?

In fact, Christian Democracy itself has gone along, at times stalling, at times remaining neutral, at times upholding the changes. The reasons can be found in the nature of the existing state. Everybody knows that the economic crisis of the Seventies was triggered by the trade unions' 'hot autumn' of 1969 and precipitated by the oil crisis of 1973. Briefly, the miraculous growth of the early sixties led to full-employment labour militancy and skyrocketing wages which an undercapitalised labour-intensive economy could not sustain. Cost-led inflation combined in turn with the increase in oil costs and the international slump of 1973 to produce a stagflation of unprecedented proportions in postwar Italy. But underlying these crisis triggers, which are shared to a lesser extent by other countries, the phenomenology of the Italian crisis points to a quite unique background: the crisis is not just of an improvidently undercapitalised export sector; it is a politico-economic crisis of the state, as it was shaped in the fifties and sixties. Any state confronted by the stagflation of the seventies had to step in to effect a rescue. The Italian state was no exception; on the contrary, its past practices made it a suitable and defenceless target of demands, to which it responded in the least painful and most familiar way—by unselectively extending the range of clienteles and claimants for accommodation.

Bankrupting the State

A decisive step in this direction had already been taken following the 1963 entry of the Socialist party in the so-called Centre-Left coalition. The presence of a new and ambitious governing partner—until recently allied with the PCI —the greater ideological and interest spread thus introduced into the coalition, and the initial success in the productive growth of the public and private sector, compelled the DC to accommodate the interests of new constituencies—the industrial working class, but also the spreading service sector and the very 'state bourgeoisie' created by the growth of the parastate. The momentum thus engendered could not possibly be arrested when the crisis hit. Because, however, the public structures were unchanged—cumbersome in the ministerial bureaucracy, fragmented and personalised its the parastate, costly in all cases—and because resources dwindled under the crisis, the added accommodations had a tremendous cost. The economy and the state began to go bankrupt. Governments were able to practice a policy of special benefits, without immediately visible costs as long as social change was contained and special constituencies were limited in number and demands. But in a context of rapid mobilisation followed by a recession, established government practices revealed their inflationary potential. Public expenditure grew from 30 per cent of the GNP in 1960, to 36 per cent in 1970, and 50 per cent in 1975.

The growth was hardly unique to Italy, to be sure. But it was the progressive imbalance between expenditure, revenue and productive capabilities that made the difference. For instance, belated efforts at tax reform in 1973–74, while contributing to a considerable and real increase in state revenue in the last few years, have been insufficient to remedy the expenditure spiral; hence the monetarisation of the public debt. It should also be stressed that this trend in state expenditures, though assisted and encouraged by the 'available state' put together by the DC, was driven during the crisis by the mounting pressures of the trade unions and of the left (a Socialist party in the coalition and a PCI in the opposition). There is in fact a close relation between the two factors—labour costs and state expenditure—chiefly responsible for the ominous imbalance between the monetary and productive bases of the system.

For instance, the very tight indexing of private and public wages won by the unions, coupled with adamant resistance to reallocation of labour resources and with a new labour charter (*Statuto dei Lavoratori*) greatly extending workers' and unions' plant rights, was an important factor in inducing the DC, often pressured by the left and labour, to use its own parastate and even to create new agencies (GEPI) for the purpose of rescuing uneconomic firms.[13] But the sector's new social investments of the sixties had already forced state enterprises to shift from self-financing (opposed, incidentally, by the left) toward state endowments and special public-bank loans extracted by politically influential managers. By 1971, reinvestments and the capital market, which had provided 43 per cent of all financing in 1962, were down to 19·5 per cent; endowment funds had gone from 7·6 per cent to 18·7 per cent, the rest coming from bank loans. Despite the fact that the state sector of the economy was achieving by the Seventies proportions comparable to the private one (see note 5), the above developments were already seriously undercutting its role in the expansion and steering of the industrial market. The added demands for rescue operations following the economic crisis thus became the proverbial straw on the camel's back.

The same allocation of partisan responsibilities applies to the crisis of the social services. A state geared toward a politics of individual preferment and long administered by a Christian Democracy with social-Catholic commitments could be easily swayed by an ideology of free social services, given new impetus and carried forward by the left. And, while elsewhere inflation advised containing social expenditures, in the never-never land of Italian politics it encouraged exactly such an ideology. The impossible feat of eating the cake and having it was noisily theorised and dignified as a 'new model of development', enshrining a higher level of social consciousness to be beheld by lesser Western countries. The damages done by this mentality have been as innumerable as the number of agencies that stud the social service landscape in Italy. I will limit myself to a few illustrations.

In the same way in which wage indexing has ironically fed inflation, so the universities, subject in the last decade to a string of unco-ordinated liberalising reforms, have burst at the seams under the influx of an open-enrollment of students second only to the United States. And if fees are minimal and 'student wages' amply expected and available, the quality of education has been degraded beyond recognition, while the opportunities for subsequent employment have been tragically curtailed by the economic crisis. Similarly, while urban demands have kept increasing, cities have been unable to provide their services at the minimal costs they were expected to keep. But indebtedness by local governments (and some of the most indebted have been left-wing cities running costly services) has been regularly redeemed or frozen by the central state—which explains why local government in recent years has taken the largest share of public deficit. Reforms of the pension, hospital, and health systems have had similar effects. Designed often to effect deconcentration and regionalisation, while increasing services and users without adjusting payments, they have overloaded underbudgeted local services with tasks they cannot perform and with discontented personnel which they can neither train, nor pay, nor fire. Thus the unmistakable increase in the number of people covered by various health plans (from 14 to 52 million, or almost every Italian, between 1951 and 1975) or, for example, the fact that most health plans include totally free (and compulsively consumed) medicines, have at most muted consequences for the health of the nation. But they have unmistakable consequences for the costs borne by the state.

'Democratising' the State

We have already variously stated one reason why Christian Democracy has accepted and gone along with the above developments, which couple state deflation with mounting discontent. By freely handing out benefits to larger constituencies, the DC hoped to stem discontent, continue to serve some of its favourite constituencies—especially those closely connected to the structures of the state and parastate—and to keep itself in power using the same methods as the past. A second and probably more important reason is that there was hardly any way out. In the mouth of a party that had supported analogous practices in the past, to denounce the inflation of demands as demagogic and the deflation of the state as ominous would have sounded self-serving and not exactly believable. More to the point, to make the denunciation stick would have required a confrontation with the left and labour exactly at a time when these forces were becoming most vocal; yet the DC's ministerial alliance with the increasingly restlesss and often obstreperous Socialist party was more important than ever. It had not been since the elections of 1948 and 1953 that the DC had sought such confrontation. But at that time, the DC was on the rise and the left on the defensive, while the reconstruction of an impoverished country did not favour revolutions of rising demands. Now economic growth-crisis, just like the rise and crisis of the Centre-Left coalition, had altered the balance. From this resulted the eventual and by no means foregone decision of the majority of the DC to settle for a strategy of corporate-economic largesse and of parliamentary and governmental accommodation.

That the balance between left and centre had been altered can be seen in the very structures of the state. True, the elections of 1968 and 1972 showed no significant tilting to the left. But the presence of the left and the unions, though hard to assess as a percentage value, was becoming more and more pervasive in the running and organisation of the state at the centre and in the periphery. We have, in sum, in the Seventies an unquestionable acceleration of that process of penetration of the state by competing corporate-economic and corporate-ideological constituencies already set in clear motion during the decade of the Centre-Left coalition. Though the left has not always replaced Catholic and moderate interests as the numerical majority, it is organisationally and culturally the most vigorous, placing other interests on the defensive, and now includes significant and even dominant components from the PCI and the new left. Thus Christian Democracy is no longer in the position to use the state apparatus as it wishes, and certainly no longer in the position to put it to different and cost-conscious uses.

Various factors have contributed to this 'democratisation,' or more appropriately, politicisation of the state, not least the student movement and contestation of 1968. But the decisive boost came from the militancy of the trade unions. Their ideology of expanding services and the social thrust of their 'new model of development' demanded that they have a recognised voice not only in narrowly conceived labour issues, but also in the broader political economy of the state—from housing to transport, health, education, social security, industrial and technological investments, regional autonomy and regional development, tax reform, monetary and credit policies, management of state-controlled radio and television, and so on. Further, having a voice did not mean the mere stipulation of élite social pacts held at the top by overarching multilateral committees and suspiciously adumbrating reformist co-optation within a neo-capitalist state. To be true to its social thrust, the 'new model of development' had to be participatory, continuously mobilising 'the masses' in the task of controlling and spurring the state and continuously expanding its own reach. In the context of the Italian state, already attuned to politicisation, this has meant more trivially and concretely that, as the unions have become a privileged party to government policies at the top, operative layers of the service state at the bottom have been shared amongst corporate and partisan interests, or have become arenas where union, functional, and ideological constituencies meet in permanent assembly. Thus the old politicisation by parties and factions has slipped into a newer and less controllable assemblearism.

I will limit myself to very brief illustrations. Radio-television, whose DC monopoly has been progressively diluted, after a DC-PSI duopolistic stage, by the cooptation in the audiovisual services of party-union appointees, including communist ones, is just one national example of partitioning. But more diffuse if less visible examples can also be found in peripheral agencies— for example in the staffing of various public co-operative banks and special credit institutes operating at the local level. State universities have become one macroscopic example of permanent assembly-government. The old mentality, by which merit and partisan criteria jointly presided over the allocation of academic-administrative responsibilities has proved receptive-impotent under the onslaught of often fulfilled demands for a more democratic and therefore 'meritorious' system of collective government, open to the various university constituencies and energised by the participation of corporate-popular community groups. But less macroscopic and not always as successful demands for assembly- or self-government are also found at other local and national sites: in high schools, city and neighbourhood governments as well as in neutral bureaucracies, including such unlikely ones as the judiciary and the national police. If not even the union confederations nor the parliamentary left, those most advantaged culturally and organisationally by such *potere assembleare*, can always control and direct it, Christian Democracy is condemned to even greater impotence.

In those few cases where the DC has effected a slowdown of processes potentially favouring a further partitioning and politicisation of the state, it has attracted leftist vituperation, of a nature to suggest not simply a defensive and unimaginative rearguard action but a momentous overturning of the tables. One such case is that of regional autonomy, an obviously ill-chosen one to make a stand, such as it was. Conceived by a broad political coalition in the second part of the sixties, and after much constitutional delay, as perhaps the most ambitious measure to refurbish the credibility of the Centre-Left, to effect a degree of democratic territorial planning, and even to break locally the dispersive stranglehold of traditional and party-related clienteles, region-alism unfortunately came to be implemented during the seventies.[14] Set against the background of a bankrupt state the devolution of generous financial and legislative powers has seemed to the DC too expensive a pro-position. Set against a politically partitioned state, it has seemed like another and perhaps momentous step toward the deflation of party and state power.

That is why, following the regional elections of 1975 and the boost in regional communist representation, the enabling laws on regional government narrowly contained regional powers and made regions almost exclusively dependent on state finances. Yet regional governments exist, include often the left—alone or in coalition—and ironically the very fact that they are kept short of power and money has added another layer to that network of centre-periphery political exchange which for years has worked to politicise state structures.[15]

An Antagonistic Partnership

It is a well-known fact that in the Seventies these structures are topped by a parliament and a government within which distinctions between majority and opposition have become progressively blurred. The decisive year in the development is 1976 when, following the parliamentary elections, the DC engaged for the first time since 1947 in various forms of official governmental co-operation with the PCI eventually leading to the entry of the latter in the parliamentary majority of March 1978. 1976 was also the year when, for the first time since the Constituent Assembly, a prominent communist leader became, thanks to DC support, president of the Chamber of Deputies, and seven out of 25 committee chairmanships in the Chamber and Senate were assigned to communists. But already in 1971, reforms of the standing rules of the two houses, designed to favour greater collective involvement by all parliamentary groups in the running of parliamentary affairs, had slowly set in motion new convergences between majority and opposition. And in 1973, the communist proposal for a historic compromise, coming on the eve of the Centre-Left's last throes, pushed in the same direction.

In view of what has been said in previous pages, however, it should not be difficult to grasp the meaning and limits of these convergences, and their implications for state performance. The widely acclaimed 'new centrality' of parliament and the undeniable legislative activism of the seventies, do not reflect a new-found agreement between government and opposition on a set of co-ordinated social and state policies. They reflect the collapse of all the political formulae employed by the DC since 1948 to keep itself in power and to control the state. They reflect a new and precarious balance of forces between the DC on one side, and PCI and the political and labour left on the other—a balance tilted toward the latter by the electoral growth of the PCI, the party's well-conducted battle for institutional presence and political exchange, the 'common-wisdom' appeal of the left's social demands, and the withering away of old majorities. They reflect an antagonistic partnership. It is in the interest of the DC's survival not to upset this balance by a costly showdown. It is in the interest of the PCI to avail itself of the institutional avenues laid open by the DC behaviour to expand its presence in the state and the left. Given an externally vulnerable legislature, lacking majority leadership and already geared to the day-by-day accommodation of the fifties and sixties, the 'new centrality' of parliament is thus understandable. In sum, the factors that account for the penetration of an expensive state by disparate corporate-economic and corporate-ideological interests, also account for the new parliamentary behaviour. But for all the accommodation, the game is played for ultimately different stakes, and the issue of who governs, with whom, how, and by what policies is still open.[16]

The last point is illustrated by various aspects of legislative behaviour in the seventies, suggesting that what appear superficially as planned legislative agreements are often hard-fought and shifting convergences—later arrested, distorted, renegotiated, reversed, or not enforced—on urgent and externally imposed demands.[17] One example of the difficulties of legislative planning is the fate of the most important of parliament's new standing rules, the one assigning a conference of parliamentary group chairmen the task of setting the legislative agenda. The conference has revealed itself largely unable to reach the unanimous agreement required by the new rules in order to organically plan legislative activities for spans of two to three months.Thus, when unanimity has been found, 'the plan' has been little more than a shopping list of reciprocal concessions. But more often than not, long range agendas have been replaced by shorter, fortnightly calendars of things to be done, for which unanimity is not required.

In either case, and with the impossibility of a concerted plan, the legislation more likely to succeed, either by occasional convergences between the DC and the left or by narrower majorities, has been largely of the type that in the Seventies has led to a further politicisation of an expensive state. In sum, the modes of parliamentary transformation of recent years illustrate and are instrumental in the crisis of the state.

WHAT MAJORITIES FOR WHAT REFORMS?

Are there majorities to reform the state? Coming at the end of the article, the question answers itself. In a way, the Italian state has already been reformed. With the tolerance shown by Christain Democracy, and driven by an expanding leftist culture, it has already turned itself into a huge social service apparatus open to root-and-branch control. But aside from differences of scale, does the state of the seventies represent a recognisable alternative to the DC state of the fifties and sixties? One purpose of this article has been to show the continuities between the two—in their distributive and partisan uses.

It is an unfortunate characteristic of political labels that they tend to misrepresent. If the DC and the centre may well be synonymous with policies of individualised patronage, we tend by reaction to associate the left with policies of collective reform, expecting from it a dismantling of the *ancien régime* state kept alive by DC rule. But the growth of a contentious leftist culture has proven of little use in achieving this goal. A sprawling and politically available state is ideal for a culture that, at least in Italy, emphasises expectations, immediate demand satisfaction and painless delivery, and has limited appreciation for delayed gratification and planned sacrifices—to the point of having degraded root-and-branch participation in the state into an assembly system for permanent agitation. Yet it is exactly a calculus of corporate-partisan sacrifices and long-range results that collective policies in regard to the state require.

Who then, can reform the state? Not the DC alone. Though it realises that the unreformed state has largely turned into a Trojan horse, it cannot change now—with a *potere assembleare* spreading through the operative layers of the state—what it could more easily have changed when this condition did not occur. The new middle classes themselves, in principle an important ally in any such change, may be insensitive to it in view of the 'common wisdom' appeal of the new leftist culture. The French *Ancien Régime* was overthrown by an objective convergence of reactionary and progressive interests, suspicious of the monarch's ambiguous efforts to rationalise the state and stay on top.

Christian Democracy would then need to be helped or supplanted, of all things, by the parties of the left, especially the PCI. One can take comfort in the PCI's belated calls for austerity and its increasing concern for the financial plight of the state. We should note, however, that what we have in Italy now is not consociational government but most likely an antagonistic partnership, within which the uneasy balance between the two partners is made unequal and expanding leftward because the left, besides sharing in the government and the *sottogoverno,* has an unmatched capacity to mobilise the *potere assembleare.*[18] This means that the moderation of the PCI, the few streamlining reforms it has advocated or supported, and its calls for austerity since the elections of 1976 can be parsimoniously and prudently understood as a conjunctural 'function of its proximity to state power'.[19] Who after all wants to inherit a totally deflated state? But the further and unanswered question is whether the PCI in power would repudiate the partisan use of the state—that partisan use which after all has been all along at the roots of the crisis of the Italian state. An 'economic compromise' would for one answer the question in the affirmative.[20] It would require among other things PCI and DC together dismantling, and/or reverting to criteria of cost-benefit effectiveness, the public sector of the economy. But a governing PCI, suffering very likely from lingering problems of legitimacy and authority, would find the sector a very convenient tool to help root itself. Christian Democracy has already shown the way.

Why then would anybody reform the State?

NOTES

1. A concise and incisive treatment of the points in the paragraph is in Sidney Tarrow, 'The Italian Party System between Crisis and Transition,' *American Journal of Political Science* 21 (May 1977), pp. 193–224.
2. A recent account of the constitutional ideology of the left is in Paolo Petta, *Ideologie costituzionali della sinistra italiana (1892–1974)* (Roma: Savelli, 1975), chapter 6.
3. The Constitutional Court was established in 1956. Though five special-status regions had already been in operation for years, the first elections for ordinary-status regions took place only in 1970.
4. Giovanni Sartori, 'European Political Parties: The Case of Polarized Pluralism,' in Joseph La Palombara and Myron Weiner, eds., *Political Parties and Political Development* (Princeton: Princeton University Press, 1966).
5. Romano Prodi, *Sistema industriale e sviluppo economico in Italia* (Bologna: Il Mulino, 1973). The figure went up to 37.8 in 1971.

6. Giovanni Sartori, 'Proporzionalismo, frazionismo e crisi dei partiti,' *Rivista Italiana di Scienza Politica* 1 (Fall 1971). pp. 629–655.
7. Giuseppe Di Palma, *Surviving without Governing: The Italian Parties in Parliament* (Berkeley: University of California Press, 1977), esp. chapters 2, 5.
8. Sidney Tarrow, *Partisanship and Political Exchange in French and Italian Local Politics* (Beverly Hills: Sage Publications, Professional Papers in Contemporary Political Sociology, Vol. 1, 1974).
9. If rhyming slogans have become a fixed and catchy feature of dissent in the seventies, some of the slogans with the greatest punch against the DC regime—even too short to rhyme—were coined in earlier decades by communist propaganda.
10. How the need of prospective DC prime ministers to rely above all on the support of the other coalition parties may explain DC factionalism is discussed in Antonio Lombardo, 'Sistema di correnti e deperimento dei partiti in Italia,' *Rivista Italiana di Scienza Politica* 6 (April 1976), pp. 139–161.
11. See on both points Luigi Graziano, 'Compromesso storico e democrazia consociativa: verso una "nuova democrazia"?' in Luigi Graziano and Sidney Tarrow, eds. *La crisi italiana* (Torino: Einaudi; 1979).
12. This does not mean that the PCI did not reflect and speak on the need to rationalise, streamline, and coordinate the state. See for an early example, AA. VV., *La riforma dello stato* (Roma: Editori Riuniti, 1968). However, incentives and deeds moved the PCI in another direction.
13. For an analysis of the respective responsibilities of the left and the DC for the economic crisis of the state in the Seventies, see most recently Giovanni Bognetti, 'Stato ed economia in Italia: "governo spartitorio" o crisi del "modello democratico-sociale"? *Il Politico* 43 (1, 1978), pp. 83–105. I am indebted to this article for many of the observations that follow in this section.
14. A discussion of these points is in Sidney Tarrow, 'Decentramento incompiuto o centralismo restaurato? L'esperienza regionalistica in Italia e Francia,' *Rivista Italiana di Scienza Politica* 9 (1979), forthcoming.
15. An interesting development favouring such political exchanges is the imminent devolution to local government, following the enabling decrees of 1977, of thousands of semi-public charitable organisations run locally by the Church since the last century. On one side, the spirit of the act is clearly secular-rational. On the other . . .
16. For a lengthier analysis of DC-PCI coalitional convergence and of its limits, see Giuseppe Di Palma, *Political Syncretism in Italy: Historical Coalition Strategies and the Present Crisis* (Berkeley: Institute of International Studies, Policy Papers in International Affairs, No. 7, 1978).
17. Giuseppe Di Palma, 'Parliamentary Responses to Regime Crisis: A Problem of Institutionalization,' in Luigi Graziano and Sidney Tarrow, eds., *La crisi italiana* (Torino: Einaudi, 1979).
18. Sartori speaks in this regard of polarised dyarchy. See Giovanni Sartori, 'Calculating the Risk,' in Austin Ranney and Giovanni Sartori, eds., *Eurocommunism: The Italian Case* (Washington, D.C.: American Enterprise Institute, 1978).
19. Sartori, *ibid.,* p. 171.
20. The proposal of an 'economic compromise' is advanced by Antonio Lombardo, 'Dal compromesso storico al compromesso economico?,' in Antonio Lombardo, ed., *Il Sistema disintegrato* (Milano: Sugar Co., 1978).

Italy: Crisis, Crises or Transition?

Sidney Tarrow*

'The Italian question' of the 1970s is like what one imagines the impact of the French Revolution to have been on people living in the 1790s: no one knew quite what it was, but everyone had an opinion. To some, Italy embodies the crisis of the West—an organic crisis for the Left, a crisis of 'governability' for the Right.[1] To others, the Italian crisis cannot be reduced to a single dimension, however profound, and consists precisely in the multiplicity of crises—economic, political, social and international—in which the country finds itself:[2] To others still, Italy is in a transition—confusing, contradictory, absurd or dangerous—but a transition nonetheless, toward a new synthesis of democracy, capitalism and social equality.[3]

Crisis, crises, transition, or all three? In order to make some sense out of this conundrum, let us first review a few salient features of Italy's postwar development, and particularly of its *political* development. I then propose to summarise various aspects of the Italian crisis of the 1970s, and to distinguish the elements that appear to be leading somewhere from those that go around in a circle. I want to return, finally, with a mixture of foolhardiness and trepidation, to the questions posed above. I will argue that central to the Italian crisis has been an expansion in the meaning and the scope of citizenship and that, whatever the political solution that results, Italy may be reaching a new plateau in the integration of the working class into the political community.[4]

I. ITALY'S POSTWAR DEVELOPMENT: 'LA DIVINA SORPRESA'

Italy has frequently been seen as the cripple of postwar European politics. Articles in the press and popular books seldom fail to make reference to rising inflation, intense labour strife, short-lived governments, and a high Communist vote. A typical example is from John Earle's *Italy in the 1970s*:

> The most cursory glance suggests that the motive forces in national life have lost momentum, or that their movement is downhill. Governments do not govern, but struggle to survive. The politicians, if we judge by their achievements, seldom rise above mediocrity and inefficiency. Men of stature are rare.

*Professor of Government, Cornell University. This is a revised version of the Introduction to Luigi Graziano and Sidney Tarrow (Eds.), *La Crisi italiana*, II Vols. (Turin: Giulio Einaudi, 1979), a collection of papers presented at a symposium organised by the Liugu Einaudi Foundation of Turin in March, 1977. For useful comments on earlier versions, I am extremely grateful to Luigi Graziano, Peter Lange and Gianfranco Pasquino.

'Is the country on the verge of revolution,' asks Earle, 'or of a complete breakdown in society?'[5]

A few facts may balance the stark picture drawn above:

1. Italy, as a republic, is 33 years old. It emerged from the ashes of a fascist regime that was heir to an illiberal constitutional monarchy itself only 61 years old at the time of its demise in 1922. During the generation and a half since the founding of the Italian republic, democracy has suffered virtually every ill that a democracy can endure, but it has endured, which is more than can be said of many of the young democracies founded amid such hope in the nineteenth or twentieth centuries. It would be amusing to apply the '33 year test' to Britain following the Glorious Revolution, to France after the Great Revolution or to the United States after the American Revolution, to place in better perspective the quality of democratic life in Italy today.

2. In addition to its maintenance, Italian democracy has shown elements of political stability as well, elements modifying the stark reality of governmental instability. For example, as Gianfranco Pasquino points out, cabinet stability has not been uniformly low, and, moreover, has been accompanied by a quite substantial stability of ministerial and prime ministerial personnel,[6] not to mention the thirty year occupancy of the State by the Christian Democrats and the remarkable partisan stability of the electorate during most of this period. (See Parisi and Pasquino's contribution to this volume.) On a scale established by David Cameron, we find that Italy ranks sixth out of 13 countries, ahead of Japan, Austria and Sweden, but behind Britain, France and, yes, the Netherlands for volatility of the electorate since 1967.[7]

3. The Italian multiparty system has often been blamed for the anarchic quality of Italian political life. Italy, it is said, trails behind northern Europe in the 'aggregation' of social and political conflicts on the part of parties that accept one another's legitimacy and succeed each other in power with hardly a change in policy. In 'civic cultures' like Britain or the United States, the argument continues, political cleavages are easily bridged and consensus is great, while in countries like Italy, cleavages are deep and consensus practically non-existent.[8]

There are three things that should be said about this contrast. First, however great the 'policy space' between the parties in Italian politics was once, it has been drastically reduced in the three decades since 1948.[9] Second, if numerous parties persist in Italian politics, this has at least the virtue of reflecting the spread of opinion in the electorate—in contrast to certain 'civic' political cultures in which opinion is forced into the narrow mould of a few quite similar parties. Third, while Italy shows little sign of the 'northern European' pattern of moderate multipartism, the same cannot be said of northern Europe, where the average number of parties increased over the past decade, along with the share of the vote going to sectarian or communal parties. Instead of Italy becoming more like northern Europe—the fond hope of liberals in the 1960s—some northern European party systems have been 'italianised' in the 1970s.[10]

4. All this has occurred during a period of dramatic social, economic and cultural change. For example, in 1945, Italy was an agrarian country with

industrial enclaves, but today it is an industrial country importing the bulk of its foodstuffs; in 1945, there were few cities with over a million inhabitants, but today the cities of the north are crowded with population from the South and the rural areas; in 1945, Italy had a conservative Catholic population and an established church that suppressed divorce, birth control and other forms of personal freedom, but today divorce is legalised, personal freedom has mushroomed and a large proportion of Italians consider themselves non-religious.[11] Educational levels have also improved; in an age-cohort analysis of the electorate carried out in 1976, Giacomo Sani found that 18 per cent of those under 30 had attended college, compared with 9 per cent of the 'intermediate' generation and 4 per cent of those who began voting during the 'Cold War' period.[12]

Against this background of social, economic, and cultural change it is not the instability of Italian politics that needs to be explained, but its continuity in much the same form since 1945.

5. Democracy has survived, one party has been at the helm for thirty years and the party system has resisted the recent European trend towards fragmentation—all during a period of rapid social and economic change. It would be odd if there had been no corresponding changes in the political orientations of the public. And indeed, the general public is now much more informed, more active politically and has a greater sense of political efficacy than was the case when Almond and Verba found little sign of a 'civic' political culture in Italy in the 1960s. Particularly younger voters—and among these many who vote for the Left—show a heightened awareness of political issues, a greater participatory orientation and a greater sense that ordinary people can effect the course of government policy than their elders.[13] Participation often takes extreme, and sometimes violent forms, but the important point is the involvement of the greater part of the younger generation in the existing political system.

II. THE GROWTH OF DEMOCRATIC CONSENSUS

What factors account for democratic continuity amid change and instability in Italy, and what do they augur for the future of the country? We can discuss only a few factors here about internal and external pressures, the party system and the political class, and political learning and legitimacy. These factors raise the question: is democracy in Italy the clear result of democracy's legitimacy or—as could be argued for the French Third Republic during its first decades—is it merely 'the republic that divides us least?'[14]

1. A number of these factors are negative: that is, factors 'in the absence of which' it was possible for an infant democracy to struggle to its feet. Among the most important has been the absence of any strong and determined right-wing extremist group like the ones that destroyed democracies in the interwar period. Related to this is the almost unique absence of a major foreign policy problem equivalent to the Algerian problem for the French Fourth Republic. A third factor has been the almost total absence of militant minority nationalism, during an era in which Europe's periphery has been revolting against the centre.[15] This relative absence of non-

negotiable internal or external conflicts has eased the burden on Italy's frail political institutions.

2. More positive factors are found in the economy and in the realm of civil society. It has become clear in recent years that the Italian economic 'miracle' of the 1950s and 1960s was a mixed blessing. But the fact remains that over the long run there has been a remarkable rise in living standards throughout the peninsula—even in the depressed South and on the islands. Among the causes was an astute, if one-sided 'liberal' economic policy identified with republican Italy's first President, Luigi Einaudi, and the flowering of State-aided, but basically private, entrepreneurship after two decades of suffocating State capitalism. However unbalanced was the Italian growth mechanism, it moved millions of people into roles in urban society in which they were released from the control of the landlord, the parish priest and the weight of inherited tradition.

We must be more cautious in interpreting changes in the relations of civil society, for these have undoubtedly preserved the imprint of an authoritarian past more deeply than either the economy or the political system. However, by the 1970s, attitudes towards work, consumption and social relations have become essentially 'modern', as expressed by the vitality of the women's movement and the trade unions in a country in which women did not acquire the right to vote until 1946 and unions were not fully 'accepted' even in the 1950s. Hierarchical social relations have certainly survived (for example in the universities) in uneasy mix with a mass consumption economy and a political system based on equality of rights. But this lack of 'congruence' has more often acted as a spur to substantive equality in social relations than as a brake on political democracy.[16] A long-range consequence seems to be a trend towards greater equality of relations in civil society.

3. More obvious causes for the survival of democracy are found at the level of the party system—the very home of the 'polarised pluralism,' the 'centrifugal democracy' and the 'imperfect bipartism' that have disturbed some observers.[17] While these scholars have understandably focused on the structure of the party system and on its dynamics, they have paid less attention to the social and ideological *content* of the parties, and to the consequences for democracy of the continuity in the political class.

As for the PCI, enough research has been done by now to state confidently, not yet that Communism is democratic, but that, given the existence of a large reservoir of radicalised lower class voters in Italy in 1945, the kind of a communist party that Italy possessed has helped to socialise them into democratic habits. The PCI's refusal of sectarian tactics, its broad political and social alliance strategy, its organisational innovations *vis-à-vis* the old Leninist model, and above all its acceptance and use of representative political institutions complemented the effects of economic growth and mobility in integrating the lower classes into the democratic system. A comparison with France may be useful: one imagines with a shudder the political integration of the more volatile Italian working class in 1945—after two decades of fascism—had it been under the guide of the sectarian and unimaginative French communists![18]

There is much disagreement—even among communists—about what Italy would become under the guide of the PCI, and some would argue—as Giuseppe Di Palma does in this volume—that in its policy stances over the past ten years the party has sought popular support demagogically at the cost of the system's efficiency. What one would like to know, I suppose, is how otherwise the PCI's leaders might have acted in the face of the popular protest of the last decade, and what results a more 'responsible' PCI strategy would have had for its potential—but by no means disciplined—supporters. In extreme form, PCI 'responsibility' might have had the result of the 're-sponsible' policy of German Social Democracy in the 1920s: delivering a large part of the party's support base into the hands of extra-parliamentary forces.

When we turn to the DC, there is a greater void in our knowledge, in large part due to the inability of most scholars to grasp the profoundly new character of this postwar party. A confessional party for some, an instrument of political anti-communism for others, the DC has been for most scholars profoundly influenced by its thirty year occupation of the State, an occupation which both eroded its ideological roots in social christianity and, to some extent, supplanted anti-communism as a weapon with the more subtle tools of clientelism and State patronage.[19]

But there are several things to be said about the DC's 'system' of power, sometimes mistaken for a kind of latter-day Namierism.[20] First, as Gianfranco Pasquino correctly points out in this volume, the DC is not only a patronage machine. It is part conservative party of business, part anti-communist bastion, part confessional party, part party of defence of the 'little man', and, most basically, the Italian version of the postwar phenomenon of the 'catch-all people's party.'[21] This 'syncratic' character of the DC helped to prevent a postwar polarisation between labour and business and forced the opposition parties to adopt competitive electoral strategies. As we shall see below, its major defects lay in the policy area, where it developed an inability to make hard choices and dispersed resources, rather than concentrating their impact on chosen policy targets. But even here, 'Namieriem' must be qualified, for the DC's largesse to small and medium industry, to backward regions and to its Catholic voting bloc constitute one of the main factors behind the remarkable economic performance of the 'third Italy'—the region of small-unit industry and commerce running from Northeast to Southwest between the industrial triangle and the South.[22]

Whatever else must be said of the DC, it served the historically critical function of acquiring a large part of the conservative Catholic middle class for democracy. By promising the preservation of Catholic values, the protection of the family, the small farm and the small business, defence against communism, and a solid American defence umbrella, the DC played a fundamental constituent role for democracy, as Italy made the difficult transition from an authoritarian Catholic society to something else. As to what that 'something else' is, we will offer some speculations below. The important point here is that the DC—corrupt, clientelistic, confessional and anti-communist—is an interclass party of fundamentally democratic persuasion, and this, along with other factors, has permitted Italy to survive as a democracy with not so bad a record of protection for individual rights and mobility for lower class groups.

4. Spanning the party system, Italy has a political class that has been variously described as corrupt, immobilist, élitist and subject to the whim of foreign powers. What shows through all the existing studies, however, is the tremendous continuity of the political elite, and the origins of even today's leaders in the crisis period of the 1940s.[23] This is frequently taken as evidence of immobilism, and it is certainly true that the experiences of the anti-fascist resistance and the early cold war did little to prepare today's leaders to deal with the problems of an advanced industrial democracy. But our concern is with the maintenance of democracy, and not with its efficiency of operation: where this is in question, the content of the Italian élite's formative experiences—anti-fascism, the establishment of democracy, national unity—seems more important than its age or lack of expertise. We may even suppose that a political class forged in crisis would possess more resources to deal with the crises of today than one that grew up amid the routine problems of administering the prosperity of the 1950s or 1960s.

In his monumental essay on the collapse of democracies, Juan Linz lingers on the many critical turning points as which the 'right' political decision could have prevented democracy's demise.[24] In reflecting on the short history of Italy as a Republic, one is struck by numerous mistakes too. However, at critical junctures—the attack on Togliatti's life in 1948, the reaction to the Scelba electoral law in 1953, the revolt against the right-leaning Tambroni government in 1960, the response to the 'hot autumn' of labour strife in 1969, organised labour's adoption of an austerity programme in 1977, the astonishing control revealed in the face of the Moro killing in 1978—Italy's political class appears to have learned how to manage the always frustrating, sometimes transcendent, never easy, political game called democracy. The current political situation has called into question Italy's devotion to complete protection for civil liberties, as the ordinary State machine has proven helpless before an onslaught of ever-bolder terrorist attacks. The next few years will show whether the country has reached the limits of tolerance for dissent—as did West Germany a few years earlier—or whether the recent crackdown on dissidents was caused by the political uncertainty of 1978–9.

5. Communist and Christian Democrat, business and labour, élite and masses: how do they relate to one another in the face of the deep cleavages and intense conflicts of Italian society? This is the key question in under-standing how democracy has been maintained in a country with weak political institutions and a low level of consensus. For some observers, Italy—like the Netherlands or Austria—is divided into airtight political subcultures that are isolated from one another by strong organisational networks. But unlike 'consociational democracies,'[25] Italy lacks a tradition of élite accommodation to compensate for closure at the base. For these observers, the presence of solid Catholic and Marxist subcultures, and the hostility between the political parties and mass organisations that control them, has been the primary constraint on its evolution as a stable parliamentary democracy.

But the 'fit' between Italy and a subcultural model of politics has never been perfect and has been decreasing in recent years. First, it is inaccurate to characterise Italy as bipolar in its subcultural system. After all, the 'marxist' subculture has two major branches and several minor ones; there is a small, but articulate 'secular' subculture that frequently mediates between the monoliths; as for the Catholic subculture, it is both internally diverse and extends in some ways as a general culture to most of the population.

Second, the social, economic, and cultural changes outlined above have reduced this 'fit' still further. Religion is less of a guide to political behaviour than it was in the 1950s and 1960s, and organisational membership—like union membership, for example—is far less linked to voting than it once was.[26] Among the electorate in general, there appears to be a far smaller incidence of the 'vote of *appartenenza*' that Parisi and Pasqunio discuss, and a growing body of 'opinion voters.' They are well-educated, favourable towards both electoral and non-electoral modes of participation, and prepared to change their vote in national elections and to vote independently of their parties in both local and regional elections and in referenda. This does not automatically mean that the traditional 'subcultural parties'—mainly the DC and the PCI—will lose their votes, but that only a more issue-responsive behaviour on their parts will retain the issue-oriented sectors of their electorates. The Communists' electoral losses in 1979 indicate the difficulty of responding rapidly to an active and volatile vote of opinion.

This raises the question of party activism. Is it possible for mass parties to change their programmes in response to mass opinion when they depend for their campaign organisation upon ideological party militants? Much depends on who the activists are and how directly they are linked to their parties' traditions and organisations. If they are old-line militants who see their roles as protecting their parties against the dangers of impurity, then party activists must inhibit adaptation and compromise. But younger activists coming from various walks of life and open to contacts with the opposition are more likely to operate as agents of political exchange—if not at the summit, then at the base of the political system.

Scattered evidence has begun to prove that today's reality lies closer to the second of these alternatives. For example, a recent study of 11,000 delegates to the 1979 provincial congresses of the PCI showed that the average delegate was in his early thirties. Research on the other Italian parties also shows a recent trend towards rapid generational replacement in the lower and intermediate levels of their organisations.[27] The PCI study also shows that a declining proportion of Communist activists come from PCI families or even from politicised ones. Recent research on local officials shows that the majority have contacts across the political system, read non-party as well as party newspapers, and no longer regard party activism as an identity that encompasses all other memberships.[28] The PCI study adds new evidence; when asked to list the qualities that are most important among a good communist cadre, only 26 per cent listed 'the rigorous application of the party line,' a response that was twice as common (40 per cent) among older delegates than among those who entered the party after 1970 (20 per cent).[29]

As these changes in the electorate and in political activism indicate, elements for political exchange have been growing up in the interstices between the ideological polemics on the surface of Italian politics. For example, the exchange relations within Parliament that result annually in hundreds of private member bills to service local constituencies, and which usually pass in committee with hardly a dissent;[30] the exchange relations between central and local authorities that guide the allocation of public resources to the grassroots, frequently through local governments controlled by the Left;[31] the exchange relations that led to a number of key policy decisions, such as the regional reform of 1970, exchange between business and labour, and—most recently—between the leaders of the DC and the PCI. As a result of this slow, incomplete and, in part, subterranean development of political exchange, the parties of the Left gained a stake in the existing system, the State was softened from an instrument of order and repression into an agency of distributive policies, and reconciliation of divergent interests could take place below the summit of the political system, hidden from the searing polemics of press and Parliament and closer to the spirit of the market-place than to that of the forum.

6. *A Coalition for Patronage.*[32] As these examples indicate, political exchange in Italy is neither high-minded nor global, but takes place through precisely the kinds of pragmatic bargaining arrangements whose absence was decried by earlier Anglo-American observers. At the centre of these arrangements has been the DC, a party which first colonised post-war Italian society through a coalition for patronage and then—as this coalition began to age and its elements to disperse—expanded it politically, first to the conservative Right (Liberals) and the moderate Left (Social Democrats and Republicans) and then, in the early 1960s, to the Socialist Party, without changing its essential nature. This expansion, while it kept the DC at the centre of power, created four new problems.

First, it left the bulk of the working class, represented by the PCI, excluded from direct representation. This extended to the factory, where the rights of the trade unions were extremely limited.

Second, as the coalition expanded, it became harder to manage and greater and greater effort had to be put into mediating its internal contradictions.[33]

Third, a coalition for patronage is inflationary in its use of State resources, to the extent that it substitutes the satisfaction of a congeries of special interests through the use of existing resources for programmatic changes that will create new ones.

Fourth, with the broadening of the DC's coalition for patronage, the original dispersed character of the Italian State was worsened, and the government's capacity to carry out structural reform or administer existing programmes effectively was weakened still further.

These rigidities and contradictions lie at the root of many of the aspects of today's Italian crisis. But what needs emphasising is that they are the problems of a dynamic and open system in which none of the major social or political actors was completely excluded from resources or threatened in its existence. The patterns of political exchange described above could not be expected to engender normative consensus of an Anglo-American variety; but they have engendered the conviction that, as in France in 1871, this was 'the Republic that divides us least.' To over simplify the problem, democracy has grown in Italy, not because of the legitimacy of democracy *per se*, but because it appears as the *modus vivendi* least likely to threaten the survival of any of the country's major social or ideological groupings. As we shall see below, this kind of democratic development is at the heart of many of the policy and political problems of the 1970s. But they are the problems of an expanding democracy; not those of a society in decline.

III. THE ITALIAN CRISIS

This leads us to the problems of the 1970s—for the main lines of the system described above were developing before then. Indeed, the major watershed between relative stability and permanent crisis was, in Italy, as in France, the combination of worker and student revolts between 1967 and 1970. Most of the major problems of today can be traced to that crucial watershed and to the government's political responses to it. In contrast with France, where the trend since then has been capitalist re-integration, resurgent State authority and growing support for social democracy, in Italy, the result has been a challenge to capitalism, democratisation, and increased support for the Communist Party.

In assessing Italy's problems, is it better to begin at the 'bottom,' with the cleavages in economy or society, or at the top, with the character of its institutions and public policies? What is striking is the extent to which the choice of a starting point correlates closely with the viewpoint of the observer, with Marxist and 'progressive' observers beginning from the economic or social roots of Italy's problems and conservative or 'liberal' ones starting from institutions or public policies. As in most cases in which intelligent observers study the same problem from different ideological standpoints, both perspectives have a great deal of force, as we shall see, in the crucial areas of economic management, the urban social crisis and the reform of the State.

A. *The Economy and the State*

As is well known by now, the Italian economic 'miracle' was based on a combination of cheap labour from the South and the rural areas of the North, an economy oriented towards export during a period of liberalised international trade, and a spurt of private entrepreneurship with a substantial input of State aid.[34] This growth model left considerable residues of backwardness in both industry and agriculture and a weak internal market that left the economy susceptible to recession at every downturn in the international business cycle. Public intervention took the form of subsidies to industry, a large nationalised sector and generous public assistance to a variety of social groups. What never developed was the capacity for concerted public activity to increase demand, to create or redirect employment, or to come to grips with the structural problems of an economy divided into modern and traditional sectors—in other words, economic planning.[35]

For some, the failure to plan was symbolic of what they took to be the hegemony of capital over the Italian political class, as if the latter were a mere henchman of the bourgeoisie and as if planning was equivalent to socialism. For conservatives, the main problem was the all-too-evident willingness of politicians to give into popular demands: for higher wages, for welfare programmes, and to salvage inefficient firms through national-isation. Insofar as public intervention is criticised, it is for the failure to use the techniques of macroeconomic management that are well known to central bankers throughout the world.

Three points deserve to be mentioned.

First, the Italian political class is both more or less than the henchman of capital: more, in the sense that governing coalitions have almost always represented a spectrum of social groups from poor peasants and Catholic workers, on the one hand, through small businessmen and white collar workers, and to big business on the other. As Alberto Martinelli's contribu-tion to this collection shows, the relations between Confindustria and the State have not always been cosy. And less than that, in the sense that the DC as a ruling party has lacked the coherence and unity to act as the political arm of the collective interest of capitalism.

Second, the technical instruments of economic policy have been used, and used successfully, to constrain demand in the mid-1960s and early 1970s. But once used in this negative way, they were set aside, and complementary tools—increasing productive employment, supporting domestic demand, solving the structural problems of traditional sectors like farming —were never developed. Michele Salvati's comparison of French and Italian economic policy shows that even a conservative regime like Pompidou's Fifth Republic—when energised by determined leadership and with a strong State—could successfully confront problems similar to those faced by Italy in the early 1970s in the face of similar political and social cleavages.[36]

Third, though there were substantial increases in public spending in the 1970s, these kept pace with the trend in other western democracies, according to data collected by David Cameron.[37] In fact, it was mainly because of the failure to increase government revenues proportionate to expenditures that public spending became so inflationary a factor in the 1970s, a factor that depends less on the raw increase in government spending than on an inade-quate fiscal system. It is in the collection of taxes from its 'middle con-stituency'—peasants, small business, artisans and professionals—that the failures of the fiscal system have been greatest, a failure that suggests that the 'technical' argument needs at least some admixture of political and social considerations.

All three observations above show that the conflict over government intervention in the economy cannot be approached by either technical or marxist determinism. The failure of planning, the absence of adequate demand management, the patternless subsidies to industry and the weakness of the fiscal system all point to the nature of the governing coalition and its internal contradictions as the funnelling cause of Italy's economic maladies. To put oversimply what must be amplified and demonstrated, the problem of Italian coalition government is that of 'syncretism': in Giuseppe Di Palma's phrase 'extended and inclusive coalitions that perpetuate themselves in power by the political cooptation of heterogeneous interests.'[38] As each additional element was co-opted—first from the small parties of the centre

and centre-right in the 1950s, then from the centre-left Socialists in 1963—
DC-led governments became more and more involved in trying to mediate
their internal problems and were thus less and less able to produce coherent
and effective public policies.

In a classically circular pattern, the answer to growing political weakness
was to increase the circle of participants in power and, thence, to increase
the quantity of resources distributed to the social groups constituting the
followings of these diverse and often factionalised parties. This can be seen
in cases like State aid to the South, social security in agriculture, the reform
of the tax system, and the survival of literally thousands of semi-autonomous
agencies of social insurance and public assistance to the present day. Though
the root causes of Italy's economic dislocations are not only political, the
pattern of political management of the economy has worsened and exacer-
bated them and left the path to their solution a minefield littered with vested
social interests and political sacred cows.

B. The Urban Social Crisis

There is an urban crisis today in all western democracies, particularly if we
look at the locus of the fiscal problems. However, in Italy the fiscal aspects
of the urban crisis are really aspects of the general crisis of the State's
finances, while the urban crisis goes much deeper into the fabric of Italian
society. In order to understand it, we must recall a few facts:

1. Italy traditionally was a country of cities, whose productive functions—
at least after the Renaissance—were dwarfed by their role as administrative
centres. The modern city, the industrial city, is a relatively recent product in
Italy, with only a few exceptions in the Industrial Triangle of the North.
Even there, the structure of the city was not prepared to absorb the immense
masses of people coming from the rural areas and from the South after 1945.
Urban infrastructure, a modern civic tradition, even the technical tools for
handling rapid real estate development without corruption were lacking, in
the face of the settlement of waves of people not prepared for the pressures
of modern urban life.

2. Italy is going through the second industrial revolution without having
fully completed the first. The country's industrial take-off at the turn of the
century was a relatively weak one, lacking a vigorous ideological stimulus
and failing significantly to transform agriculture, commerce or authority
relations in the factory. In the postwar period, strong ideological stimuli to
development have not been lacking, but with so long a road to be travelled
in so short a time, elements that resemble the earlier primitive accumulation
have not been absent, nor have forms of enterprise and authority that recall
the relations between 'master and servant' in the past of western Europe. As
Giuliano Amato writes, 'we Italians are in transit from the past to the future
of industrial capitalism without having lived through its present.'[39]

3. Connected with these two features, a new urban working class was
formed during the 1960s. A product of the recent rural to urban migration,
unaccustomed to urban life, and living in the squalid *baracche* and faceless
suburbs of the cities of the North, this new working class was partly employed

in a secondary labour market of unskilled or semi-skilled jobs, but also moved into skilled roles in the primary labour market alongside a northern working class that was organised, disciplined and politically conscious. These undisciplined and frequently militant 'mass workers,' and the politically sophisticated and well-organised workers of the 'industrial triangle' were a volatile combination in the dense concentrations of factories and working-class neighbourhoods of northern Italy, as would become clear in the labour struggles of 1968–72. As Marino Regini shows, the dynamism of grassroots labour militancy from 1968–72 caught union leaders by surprise, and helps to explain management and government willingness to accede to their demands, once they caught up with their volatile mass base.

4. But not all the new urban dwellers were working class; many had entered trade or commerce as independent tradespeople, others rook office jobs, and still others slipped into a shadow world of tertiary occupations that ranged from lumpenproletariat to lumpenbourgeoisie. In other words, they were outside the political reach of organised labour and the mass parties, but they were also outside the reach of the benefits of urban bourgeois society. Some of the leaders, but possibly many of the 'soldiers' in the fringe political movements of Left and Right in the 1970s appear to have come from these marginal groups in the cities. Equally important, their votes and their protest were far less easy to control than those of the organised working class.

5. A rapid pace of secularisation has accompanied these urban processes, as Italy changed from a predominantly rural, Catholic society to a predominantly urban, industrial one. In addition to creating a crisis in the Catholic movement, rapid secularisation has contributed to more spectacular changes like the end of church censorship, the sudden introduction of pornography, the spread of delinquency among young people, and the rapid spread of vulgarised anti-capitalist attitudes through the media and the schools. Here too, Italy is in transit from the past to the future, without having lived through the present.

6. The convergence in time between the urban and the secular trends outlined above is at the heart of the dynamism of the mass movements that arose in Italy after 1968: the 'hot autumn' of working-class revolt in 1969 and the years that followed; the volatile student movement and the extraparliamentary movements it eventually fed; probably the most militant women's movement in Europe; the organisation of the poor, of neighbourhood groups, of the unemployed; and eventually the increase in the PCI vote in the elections of 1975 and 1976, which was particularly great among young people.[40] It is ironic that the generation of the turn of the decade, anti-establishment and anti-communist at the time, became the major source for the growth in the electoral fortunes of the PCI in the mid-1970s. A movement which began, in large part, 'against politics', rejecting the mandate automatically allocated to the traditional parties of the left in the past, ended up, through one of those paradoxical transmutations that is common in history, nourishing the strength of one of these very parties at least until 1979.[41]

But the urban social crisis and the 'Italian May' also had some 'unwanted children'—the terrorist movement that haunts republican Italy today and that has begun to lead to a backlash against civil liberties and against the 'excesses' of democracy. Terrorism can best be regarded as the extreme wing of the urban social movement that emerged in the late 1960s, one which regards the Italian Left as having given up the dream of a new society in order to reconstruct the old. That the terrorists are at least partly correct does not justify terrorism, but it does underscore how thoroughly the Italian social crisis has been absorbed through politics. As Carlo Donolo writes, 'The Italian '68 found its ultimate outcome in the elections of June, 1976'.[42] As the Left—and particularly the Communist Party—gained in political influence under the umbrella of PCI leader Berlinguer's 'historic compromise' strategy, the split between the institutional, parliamentary Left and the spontaneous 'extra-parliamentary' one grew, and left-wing party and union leaders became the target—along with establishment figures and journalists—for the bombs and bullets of Italy's urban guerilla movement.

We thus return to the primary of politics, as in the case of the crisis of the economy, but for different reasons. If the failure of the Italian State to confront the problems of economic management result from the ways in which public intervention was used to organise the vote, the urban social crisis, which broke out in spontaneous mass movements in the late 1960s, has returned into the familiar world of party politics: leading first to an increase in the Communist vote; then to a left-wing takeover of virtually every major city in Italy; and finally to attacks on the very left-wing parties that are attempting to administer cities in crisis by movements of the poor, the unemployed and the generally alienated. The fruits of the mass mobilisation of the beginning of the decade are many; urban fiscal crisis caused, partly, by the State's attempt to placate discontent by expensive new programmes; an electoral trend to the left, and subsequent left-wing control of many of the cities that spawned the earlier movements; and the ultimate inability of the left to cope with the violent residues of those movements that lie at the origin of its electoral success.

C. The Institutional Crisis

'Governing without consensus', 'Republic without government', 'Crisis of the State': these are some of the characterisations of Italian political institutions that have grown common in the 1970s. While recognising their validity, it is important to keep in perspective what these problems are about, how they relate to democracy, and what counter-trends exist in the reform of Italian political institutions.

1. Since the publication of Samuel Huntington's *Political Order in Changing Societies*,[43] we have grown conscious of the fact that political institutions do not inevitably 'develop'—they sometimes decay as well. But can it be said that the problems of Italy's institutions are those of decay? That they work inefficiently, sporadically, bureaucratically is beyond a doubt; that they are riddled with corruption is also frequently the case; but that they are undergoing political decay—however that may be defined—is less than obvious.

Examples of the Italian institutional crisis are legion and are easily observed: a Parliament that is inundated with thousands of private member bills but becomes paralysed when faced with major programmatic legislation; local governments that are deeply in debt and lack the planning powers to control residential growth or the provision of services; a nationalised sector that has been used as a reservoir of patronage and has followed political criteria in the location of factories; a tax system that fails to capture an important part of the country's wealth and falls unfairly on the more visible portion of earned income; and, more recently, the utter inability of the police and security services to cope with increasingly open kidnapping and terrorism—all these are sure signs of institutional crisis.

But signs of institutional growth lie not very far beneath the surface; a Parliament that has preserved a great political role during decades in which the favourite old saw of many observers was the 'decline' of Parliament—both in Britain and on the continent; local governments—especially of the Left and Centre-Left—that have at times been extremely innovative in the provision of services and in avoiding the traps of national coalition politics; a nationalised sector whose 'political' location decisions often employ social criteria in industrial investment that have been lacking in some more 'rational' States—for example France; a tax system that has recently dramatically increased its yield through the adoption of a few technical changes. Finally, at least one of the inhibitions on the fight against terrorism has been positive for democracy —the memory on the part of political leaders and jurists of the not-so-distant-past when police and judicial repression were used to destroy political opposition.

2. If there is a 'crisis of instutitions' in Italy, part of it is inherited from the fascist-era and even from pre-fascist institutions that were taken over in 1945; part is the result of a latin culture that—for all the changes in Italian society— still survives today; and an important part is the reflex at the level of the state of the democratisation that has been occurring by fits and starts in Italian society. This takes the form, common to all western industrial democracies, of 'entitlements' replacing privileges in the State's social policies, as well as the form of the demand for direct representation within the State by citizens and public employees. Although the latter often takes egregious shapes like the *assemblearismo* that Di Palma condemns, or the breakdown of essential public services by public sector strikers, both seem to me to be part of the widespread democratisation of Italian society. Although this does not lessen the strain they cause on institutions, if I am correct it would be very difficult to classify them as evidence of institutional 'decay'.

3. Moreover, there are areas of true institutional reform in Italy today: in neighbourhood councils, at the local level, in the dramatic rejuvenation of the civil service, at the national level, and, in between, in the regional reforms that began in 1970, and have been continuing, amid reversals and contradictions, since then.

There was a time when regional reform seemed to be a panacea for Italy's many ills. For some, it raised the question of 'social and political renewal', for others, it would overcome regional inequalities, and for still others, it would lead to the reform of local government.[44] But regionalism meant too many things to too many people, and its translation from a noble idea into an institutional reality has been slow, tortuous and contradictory. For a start, the timid governments of the early 1970s—not to mention a diehard central bureaucracy—did all they could to delay it. Secondly, the economic crises from that period to the present have impaired the willingness of the government to give expenditure power to new, and possibly uncontrollable units of government. Third, despite its regional cultural and economic diversity, Italy has an extremely centralised political culture and party system. As a result, the regions have had a hard time developing autonomous political personalities that would not reflect the concerns and conflicts of national political elites.[45]

This has been most clearly the case for the Communists who began the post-war period as dedicated Jacobins, moving by fits and starts towards a de-centralised vocation as the DC consolidated its power nationally, and emerged as militant regionalists in the late 1960s and early 1970s. This vocation paled when faced by the economic crisis but, more important, when it had to compete with the Communists' even stronger 'governmental vocation', as they tried to fashion a coalition with the DC between 1975 and 1977. The dimming of these governmental hopes led to a renewed attack on the DC in the regions, along with increased peripheral militancy, as a prelude to the PCI's removal of its support for the national coalition in 1979.

But in the meantime, the regions exist, they function, they attract the interest—if not the loyalty—of the citizens, and they have begun to take on definite institutional personalities which differ from region to region and vary according to the political coloration of their majorities. In a recent unpublished analysis, Putnam, Leonardi and Nanetti have shown convincingly that regional governments are becoming meaningful institutions to their elites and constituents and also, alas—that they reflect the same differences in political culture and efficiency that are characteristic of the regions they represent —with a clear advantage to the North and Centre, which have the resources to take advantage of their new powers, while the southern regions appear to some extent to be lapsing into a new form of dependence on Rome.[46] But this reflection of the differing socio-cultural realities of Italy's regions means simply that the regions are taking hold, and appears far more promising for institutional innovation than a type of decentralisation—like that of France for example—that is both uniform and empty of content.

In conclusion, there are signs of both institutional growth and crisis in Italy today, with the most serious strains found in the areas of public order and public finance. In most of the areas discussed, the underlying problems are political, but this does not make them any more tractable or less complex. The Italian political genius has never been found to lie in sweeping changes or radical reforms, but in papering over differences, finding accommodations among apparently irreconcilable opponents and in putting off for tomorrow what could—at some risk—probably be solved today, for fear of upsetting delicate equilibria between social partners or political opponents. This genius is very much in evidence today, as are the risks it entails. One should not under-rate its risks for efficiency, for legitimacy, and for the ultimate survival of the regime. But the Italian political system—after over thirty years of such dangers —is undeniably still standing, and—by many criteria— more democratic than it was before. Like Michele Salvati (see above), I am reminded of Gilles Ceron's satirical parable of the 75th anniversary of the Italian Republic, which Salvati quotes at length in his contribution to this volume. (p. 46).

IV. CONCLUSIONS

In the observations made above, I have not tried to synthesise, or even to summarise the contributions to this volume. They appear to me, however, to have a common thread: amid the manifold social, economic, institutional and international roots of the Italian crisis, the crux of the country's problems is political. As we saw in the cases of the economy, of the urban social crisis, and of the State, the kind of political community that was established in Italy after World War Two—and which corresponded to a set of particular political needs—has largely succeeded in establishing democracy. But in so doing, the major preoccupation has been to buy time, to compose or paper over differences and to leave none of the major social or political actors with the conviction that more was to be gained by undermining the system than by working within it. Thus the bureaucracy retained its original dispersed quality; society remained politically divided, though the degree of cleavage and political space have been considerably reduced; and policy resources were squandered on a series of politically-inspired compromises, rather than being used productively to modernise the country's services or rationalise its institutions. Governments have been built around coalitions that expanded in scope to compensate for their lack of vigour and purpose, increasing the range of actors whose interests had to be taken into account in future policy-making and rendering still more difficult the solution of the country's problems.

Such a system was best at what it was established to achieve: to create a democracy in a country ridden with cleavages and with little experience of truly representative government, in the context of a capitalist society and of the Western Alliance. But can Italy maintain democracy without really fundamental change in the style of politics under the conditions of its fourth decade of existence? These new conditions include: an economy that must operate much closer to optimal efficiency in order to grow; a society that has gone through a period of urbanisation and secularisation that have produced an alert and demanding electorate; a working class that has made major inroads on profits, and a population that regards high levels of income and welfare as entitlements; a party system that no longer produces safe majorities for the centre, as it did in the 1950s, or for the centre-left, as in the 1960s; and a State that threatens to collapse under its own weight unless its reform is pushed forward.

Under these conditions, the 'system' of the past cannot survive: some would say it was already dead. For a while, between 1976 and 1979, it seemed that its replacement would be a semi-permanent cartel between a resurgent Communist Party and a DC that could not hold power alone but refused to go into opposition. The Italian form of this 'grand coalition' was peculiar, in that the DC governed alone, while it was supported in Parliament by first a six party, and then by a five party coalition, which provided policy directives through a near-permanent secretariat of party leaders meeting *in camera*. It was also inherently unsatisfactory, in that too many actors participated in policy making for satisfactory results to ensue, and because it gave the Communists—the major non-governing partner—responsibility for policies that they had no role in administering. At the same time, it increased the responsibilities of the trade unions and other professional associations in administration, thereby combining 'semi-corporatism' with the 'semi-consociation' of the party coalition.

These were the major reasons for the collapse of the Italian 'grand coalition' in March 1979 and for the elections that ensued the following June, although particular policy problems also played an important role. What needs to be assessed in the wake of those elections is the achievements of that formula and the alternatives to it for the future. A few points can be briefly stated:

1. Although the 'grand coalition' was neither grand nor a true coalition, it supervised important initiatives in the international economic field, in industrial reorganisation, rent reform, regional implementation, tax administration and the first halting steps towards an incomes policy. Given the political complexity of the coalition and the intractability of the problems it faced, these were not trifling accomplishments.

2. The 'grand coalition'—though it was seriously undermined by the terrorist events culminating in the kidnapping and murder of Aldo Moro in 1978—nevertheless took the country through that crisis with an extraordinary degree of national unity, given the macabre and terrifying quality of the crisis. In other words, though the coalition was not the result of true consensus—grand coalitions seldom are, almost by definition—it held the country together during the greatest period of strain in its history as a republic.

3. The 'grand coalition' at least temporarily solved the political problem of each of the country's two major parties—the Communists and the Christian Democrats. For the DC, it held at bay the wolves seeking its overthrow until its electoral following could be recomposed, and for the Communists, it was a sign that the 'historic compromise' with Catholicism was at least a possibility in the years to come, and justified the pressure to hold down wages that the PCI believed to be in the country's interest.

Rather than try to detail and justify each of these points, it will perhaps be most useful to conclude on the final one. Between 1969 and 1975, Italy appeared to be slipping into an organic crisis: one, that is, in which 'the knot of contradictions and different conflicts is so radical as to pose the problem of the historic bloc holding power'.[47] The shift to the left in national party politics from 1974 to 1976, and the involvement of the Communists in the majority in 1977–78, both extended the crisis in time and led it back from the social and economic into the political arena, where a political class skilled at bargaining, in dilatory tactics and in sectoral policies could defuse the crisis and deal with it sector by sector, in place of the general crisis that had seemed to be tightening its grip during 1974–75. To put crudely a hypothesis that ought to be clearly set out and demonstrated, the politicisation of the crisis prolonged it, but also allowed the elites to deal with it as a series of separate crises, enabling them to manage the transition to a new system with a minimum of threat to their own power. The 'grand coalition' was the instrument of this operation.

Though the 'grand coalition' was a casualty of the 1979 political struggles, some version of it may have to be revived, if only because no alternative may currently exist to take its place. My reasoning for this perhaps surprising conjecture is based on three considerations.

First, when we think of past coalition alternatives, the one that corresponds most closely to the mathematical balance emerging from the June 1979 elections is a four party coalition including the Christian Democrats, Republicans, Social Democrats and Socialists—in other words, a revival of the 1960s Centre-Left coalition. But although this is mathematically logical, it may be politically unstable, as it would wrench the Socialists away from the 'independent' course they have tried to chart for five years and lead to strains between them and the PCI in the trade unions and in the all-important local and regional governments that the two parties control together. This is not to say that the PSI will not ultimately allow itself to be enticed back into a revived *centrosinistra*, but only that the road there will be long and difficult, and the outcome uncertain.

The second alternative to a grand coalition is an alternation in power, with the DC going into opposition and an Italian equivalent of the Popular Front trying to govern instead. But although this was mathematically possible after 1976—when the Communists rejected it—the June 1979 election results make it seem most unlikely today, though some in the Communist Party and many Socialists look back longingly at the opportunity they threw away in 1976. In any case, as long as Enrico Berlinguer continues to lead the PCI, it will be very difficult for the party to jettison completely the idea that the road to power lies in some form of coalition with the DC—and not in a Popular Front that risks a Chilean outcome.

We are thus left with either a return to *centrismo*—a DC coalition like today's, with minor partners of the centre or the centre-right—or with a version of the grand coalition that takes account of the changes in party fortunes between 1976 and 1979. It goes without saying that the former would be the fond hope of conservatives in Rome, Milan and Washington—the former from the point of view of domestic economy policy and the latter from the standpoint of Italy's international posture. But it seems most unlikely that the DC could pull off such a return to the past for more than a short period in part because there is no Italian Thatcher (or even Giscard d'Estaing) but mainly because the balance of power in Italian society would not permit it.

This requires a brief excursion into social theory. The British sociologist, T. H. Marshall, posits that the nature, as well as the universality, of citizenship tends to expand as societies become democratised. This is no more than saying that democracy brings citizenship out from the realm of civil rights, where it began, first to the ballot box, where it affects the character of government, and ultimately into the realm of social policy, where it guarantees minimum conditions of life for the lower classes. Not only do the latter become full citizens in the political sense of the term; they expand citizenship from the right to speak out to exercise the franchise to a series of social entitlements—full employment, a national health service, automatic indexation of wages—that are far more relevant to their social position than the political and civil rights fought for and acquired in the last century by the upper and middle classes.

This achievement of full citizenship may be called the integration of the lower classes into the political community. For a variety of reasons, this process was blocked in Italy during several key historic junctures: the *Risorgimento* of 1861–71; the decade of industrial take-off at the turn of the century; and the two postwar settlements of 1918-22 and 1944-48. In the first of these postwar struggles, the working class was defeated and reaction ensued, while in the second—as we have seen—a DC-led coalition for patronage laid the groundwork for future democratic development, admitted the Communists and Socialists into the political community, but left the expansion of citizenship and the integration of the lower classes incomplete.

Since 1968, one barrier after another to the integration of the lower classes have been destroyed, largely by the newly-found force of organised labour, but also by the varied 'movements' that emerged after the student rebellion of the late 1960s and, eventually, by the parties of the Left which coopted many of their themes. These acquisitions may be quantitatively modified but they can never be rolled back qualitatively except by a regime prepared to roll back democracy itself. I do not see either the will or the inclination to do this in the current leadership of the Christian Democracy, despite its improved showing at the polls and the presence of 'Thatcherite' voices in its right wing.

To me this means that a return to 'centrism' would be untenable, and that the most likely subsequent solution to the Italian governing problem is some version of continued semi-collaboration among the DC, the intermediate parties and the Communists, even if the latter should be excluded—or exclude themselves—from the official parliamentary ruling coalition. The enactment and, even more, implementation of policies to complete the institutional integration of the lower classes into the political community will depend on the co-operation of either the PCI, the trade unions, or both in policy elaboration. Already, the unions participate in implementing a number of areas of social policy, and no one in Italy has suggested that this form of collaboration be reversed. As Italy moves inevitably towards some form of incomes policy— in which gains at the level of social legislation and economic planning are traded for union concessions in wage negotiations—the Communists will have to be included at every stage of the policy process, to guarantee trade union acquiescence.

Such relationships with the State, between business, the trade unions, and the parliamentary left constitute what Leo Panitch, in a brilliant essay refining a much abused concept, has called 'neo-corporatism'.[48] As Panitch shows, the historical vehicles of such collaboration in northern Europe have been strong social-democratic parties linked to unified labour movements in States with the institutional vision and flexibility to trade off gains in social policy for compromises in wages. Italy has neither a strong social democracy, a unified labour movement, nor political institutions of this sort. Does this mean that 'neo-corporatism' is impossible? Or does it mean that the imperatives of income management in the context of full citizenship will require—as they did in northern Europe in earlier decades—changes in this direction? It is hazardous to begin from historical imperatives and deduce from them 'requirements' for political or institutional change—especially in Italy! It would indeed be novel if Italy could be the first industrial country to arrive at a stable accommodation between labour and industry in the context of full democratisation, a strong Communist party, trade unions inclined to be independent, and a divided and demoralised business community. But Italy has surprised learned observers before—if only by maintaining itself as a democracy for as long as it has. Although the next decade will be extremely difficult, the transition has already begun.

NOTES

1. For an interpretation based on the idea of an 'organic' crisis, see Carlo Donolo, *Mutamento o transizione? Politica e società nella crisi italiana* (Bologna: Il Mulino, 1977), p. 10. For the crisis of 'governability', see Michel Crozier, Samuel P. Huntington, and Joji Watanuki, *The Crisis of Democracy* (NY: New York University Press, 1975).
2. For evidence of the multiplicity of Italy's crises, see the essays collected in Luigi Graziano and Sidney Tarrow (eds.) *La crisi italiana,* 2 vols. (Turin: Giulio Einaudi, 1979).
3. For a cautious view of Italy's transition, see Giuseppe Di Palma, 'Political Syncretism in Italy: Historical Coalition Strategies and the Present Crisis,' *Policy Papers in International Affairs,* No. 7, U. of California at Berkeley, Institute of International Studies. For a more optimistic view, see Luigi Graziano's 'Compremesso storico e democrazia consociativa,' in Graziano and Tarrow (eds.), *La crisi italiana,* Vol. 2.
4. The British reader will recognise here my debt to T. H. Marshall's ideas about citizenship and social class, as presented in his Cambridge lectures in 1946.
5. (London: David and Charles, 1975) p. 9.
6. Gianfranco Pasquino, CES Paper, March 1979.
7. David Cameron, 'Taxes, Deficits and Inflation,' Brookings Institution Project on Global Inflation and Recession, December, 1978, unpublished paper. Cameron's index is based on the sum of the absolute value of all changes in per cent of the vote going to all parties in all pairs of elections between 1968 and 1978 divided by two.
8. Gabriel Almond and Sidney Verba, *The Civic Culture,* (Boston, Little Brown, 1965), Chap. 12.
9. Representative samples are found in Franco Cazzola, 'Consenso e opposizione nel parlamento italiano,' *Rivista Italiana di Scienza Politica* (1972) and the articles by Donald Blackmer, Stephen Hellman, Peter Lange, Robert Putnam and Sidney Tarrow in Blackmer and Tarrow (eds.), *Communism in Italy and France* (Princeton, 1976).
10. A look at the *Political Handbook and Atlas of the World,* 1967 and 1977 allows us to establish that the numbers of parties actually represented in western parliaments has increased overall in western Europe, but remained stable in Italy.
11. I base this on the data in an unpublished paper presented by Giacomo Sani to the Seminar on the Italian Crisis, The Einaudi Foundation, Turin, March 24–27, 1977, called 'Generations and Politics in Italy,' Table 28. These data did not ultimately appear in the version of the paper published in *La crisi italiana* in precisely the same form.
12. *Ibid.,* Table 24. Sani's essay in *La crisi italiana* presents the data in a slightly different form.
13. See Table 11 in Sani's essay in *La crisi italiana,* vol. II, p. 311.
14. See Robert Mundt's essay on the Third Republic, in Gabriel Almond, et. al., *Crisis, Choice and Change* (Boston, Little Brown, 1972).
15. See Milton J. Esman, *Ethnic Conflict in the Western World* (Ithaca, New York, Cornell University Press, 1977).
16. For the idea that a lack of congruence in authority relations can be a correlate of political instability, see Harry Eckstein, *A Theory of Stable Democracy* (Princeton: Princeton University Press, 1962).
17. See Giorgio Galli and Alfonso Prandi, *Patterns of Political Participation in Italy* (New Haven: Yale University Press, 1972) and Giovanni Sartori, 'European Political Parties: The Case of Polarized Pluralism,' in J. La Palombara and M. Weiner (eds.) *Political Parties and Political Development* (Princeton: Princeton University Press, 1966).

18. For a comparison, see my conclusion to Blackmer and Tarrow (eds.) *Communism in Italy and France.*
19. For a view that perhaps exaggerates this transformation, see Alan Zuckerman, 'Political Clienteles in Power' Sage Publications *Professional Papers in Comparative Politics,* Vol. V, 1975.
20. P. A. Allum, *Italy: Republic without Government?* (New York: Norton and Co., 1973) chap. 4.
21. Otto Kirchheimer, 'The Transformation of the European Party Systems,' in La Palombara and Weiner, *op. cit.*
22. See A. Bagnasco, *Tre Italie* (Bologna: Il Mulino, 1977).
23. For a summary, see Galli and Prandi's data on the parliamentary elite in *Patterns of Political Participation,* op. cit.
24. Juan Linz, 'Crisis, Breakdown and Reequilibration of Democracy,' unpublished paper, New Haven, Connecticut.
25. See Arend Lijphart, *Democracy in Plural Societies* (New Haven, Yale University Press, 1977).
26. The version of Sani's analysis of political generations presented at the Seminar on the Italian Crisis makes this declining linkage between organisational networks and voting quite plain.
27. See *Rinascita,* April 6, 1979, pp. 16–17 for a complete presentation of these data.
28. Sidney Tarrow, *Between Center and Periphery* (New Haven: Yale University Press, 1977) chap. 6.
29. *Rinascita,* op. cit., p. 18.
30. These findings are from Giuseppe Di Palma's *Surviving without Governing: The Italian Parties in Parliament* (Berkeley and Los Angeles: U. of California Press, 1977).
31. Tarrow, *Between Center and Periphery,* op. cit., Chaps. 3 and 6.
32. The section that follows summarises my 'The Italian Party System Between Crisis and Transition,' *American Journal of Political Science* 21 (May, 1977) pp. 193–222.
33. Donolo, *Mutamento o trnasizione* op. cit., chap. 1.
34. Augusto Graziani, ed., *Lo sviluppo di un'economia aperta* (Naples: ESI, 1971).
35. Joseph LaPalombara, *Italy: The Politics of Planning* (Syracuse, NY: Syracuse University Press, 1966).
36. See Salvati's essay in the recent issue of *Daedalus* dedicated to the New 'Europe'.
37. Cf note no. 7.
38. 'Political Syncretism in Italy.'
39. See his essay 'Le istituzioni per il governo dell'economia.' in *La crisi italiana. op. cit.,* Vol. 1.
40. Sani, 'Ricambio elettorale' in *La crisi italiana,* vol. I.
41. Donolo, *Mutamento o transizione? op. cit.,* chap. 1.
42. *Ibid.*
43. (New Haven, Yale University Press, 1966).
44. P. Allum and G. Aymot, 'Regionalism in Italy: New Wine in Old Bottles,' in *Parliamentary Affairs* (Winter 1970–71).
45. See my 'Regionalismo incompiuto o centralizzazione restaurate? *Rivista Italiana di Scienza Politica* (Fall, 1979).
46. I am grateful to Professors Putnam, Leonardi and Nanetti for allowing me to summarise these unpublished results, which were presented at a panel on centre-periphery relations at the First Annual Conference of Europeanists, Council on European Studies, Washington, DC, April, 1979.
47. Donolo, *op. cit.,* chap. 1.
48. 'Recent theorizations of Corporatism: Reflections on a Growth Industry', presented to the Ninth World Congress of Sociology, Uppsala, Sweden, August 14–19, 1978.